Doing Public Ethnography

Ethnography and qualitative research methodology in general have witnessed a staggering proliferation of styles and genres over the last three decades. Modes and channels of communication have similarly expanded and diversified. Now ethnographers have the opportunity to disseminate their work not only through traditional writing but also through aural, visual, performative, hypertext, and many diverse and creative multimodal documentation strategies. Yet, many ethnographers still feel insufficiently proficient with these new literacies and opportunities for knowledge mobilization, and they therefore still limit themselves to traditional modes of communication in spite of their desire for innovation. As university-based, community-driven and politically mandated agendas for broader knowledge transfer keep increasing worldwide, the demand for public scholarship continues to grow. Arguing for the need to disseminate innovative ethnographic knowledge more widely and more effectively, this book outlines practical strategies and tools for sharing ethnographic and qualitative research through widely accessible media such as magazines, trade books, blogs, newspapers, video, radio, and social media. Drawing from practical experiences and hands-on lessons, *Doing Public Ethnography* provides social scientists across all disciplines with concrete tactics for mobilizing knowledge beyond the academic realm.

Phillip Vannini is Professor and Canada Research Chair in Innovative Learning and Public Ethnography at Royal Roads University, Canada.

Routledge Advances in Research Methods

Cross-Cultural Interviewing
Feminist Experiences and Reflections
Edited by Gabriele Griffin

Commons, Sustainability, Democratization
Action Research and the Basic Renewal of Society
Edited by Hans Peter Hansen, Birger Steen Nielsen, Nadarajah Sriskandarajah and Ewa Gunnarsson

Phenomenology as Qualitative Research
A Critical Analysis of Meaning Attribution
John Paley

Sharing Qualitative Research
Showing Lived Experience and Community Narratives
Edited by Susan Gair and Ariella Van Luyn

Walking Through Social Research
Charlotte Bates and Alex Rhys-Taylor

Social Research Methods in Dementia Studies
Inclusion and Innovation
Edited by John Keady, Lars-Christer Hydén, Ann Johnson, Caroline Swarbrick

Walking Methodologies in a More-than-human World
WalkingLab
Stephanie Springgay and Sarah E. Truman

Doing Research In and On the Digital
Research Methods across Fields of Enquiry
Edited by Cristina Costa and Jenna Condie

Qualitative Research as Stepwise-Deductive Induction
Aksel Tjora

Action Research in Policy Analysis
Critical and Relational Approaches to Sustainability Transitions
Edited by Koen P.R. Bartels and Julia M. Wittmayer

Doing Public Ethnography
How to Create and Disseminate Ethnographic and Qualitative Research to Wide Audiences
Phillip Vannini

Doing Public Ethnography

How to Create and Disseminate Ethnographic and Qualitative Research to Wide Audiences

Phillip Vannini

LONDON AND NEW YORK

First published 2019
by Routledge
2 Park Square, Milton Park, Abingdon, Oxon OX14 4RN

and by Routledge
711 Third Avenue, New York, NY 10017

Routledge is an imprint of the Taylor & Francis Group, an informa business

© 2019 Phillip Vannini

The right of Phillip Vannini to be identified as author of this work has been asserted by him in accordance with sections 77 and 78 of the Copyright, Designs and Patents Act 1988.

All rights reserved. No part of this book may be reprinted or reproduced or utilised in any form or by any electronic, mechanical, or other means, now known or hereafter invented, including photocopying and recording, or in any information storage or retrieval system, without permission in writing from the publishers.

Trademark notice: Product or corporate names may be trademarks or registered trademarks, and are used only for identification and explanation without intent to infringe.

British Library Cataloguing-in-Publication Data
A catalogue record for this book is available from the British Library

Library of Congress Cataloging-in-Publication Data
A catalog record has been requested for this book

ISBN: 978-1-138-08642-5 (hbk)
ISBN: 978-1-138-08643-2 (pbk)
ISBN: 978-1-315-11100-1 (ebk)

Typeset in Times New Roman
by Deanta Global Publishing Services, Chennai, India

Printed and bound in Great Britain by
TJ International Ltd, Padstow, Cornwall

Contents

Acknowledgments — vii

PART I — 1

1 The need for a public ethnography — 3
2 What is public ethnography and whom is it good for? — 14
3 Why and how more ethnographers are seeking broader audiences — 22
4 Beyond representation — 30

PART II — 39

5 Losing bad habits — 41
6 Sensuous scholarship — 47
7 Learning from documentary film — 59
8 Enlivening ethnography: In search of a more-than-representational style — 68
9 Writing in magazines and blogs — 82

PART III — 93

10 Multimodal ethnography — 95
11 Working with audio — 105
12 Working with images — 118

13	The basics of shooting and editing video	129
14	Sharing videos	139
	Filmography	149
	References	150
	Index	156

Acknowledgments

Doing Public Ethnography is the result of nearly 10 years of ongoing practice, experience, and reflection on the craft of public ethnographic research. Along the way, I have greatly benefited from the assistance and collaboration of many students and colleagues. Together we have dreamed, hoped, brainstormed, planned, experimented, tried, failed, tried again, failed again, and occasionally reached our goals. Often we have surprised ourselves with unexpected outcomes, regularly we have realized that failures lead to powerful lessons, and always we have striven to do better next time. This book collects all such lessons and realizations, and I am forever grateful to all those who learned about doing public ethnography with me along the way.

Chapter 1 was written together with Laura Milne and, in part, appeared in *The Public Sociology Debate*, edited by Ariane Hanemaayer and Christopher Schneider. It is partially reproduced here courtesy of UBC Press. Chapter 2 draws from the introduction to a special issue of *Qualitative Research* on the theme of public ethnography. It was co-written with Heather Mosher. Chapter 2 (and Chapter 9 as well, which also appeared in the same issue) are partly reproduced here courtesy of SAGE Publications. Chapter 3 consists of an original interview I conducted with Patricia Leavy, and to her I am indebted for taking the time to answer my questions. Chapter 4 was previously published in the journal *Cultural Geographies*, and it is reproduced here courtesy of SAGE.

Opening Part II, Chapter 5 expands on a previous writing I completed together with Sarah Abbott for the *Handbook of Methods for Public Scholarship*. My gratitude goes to Oxford University Press for the partial reproduction of the original material. Chapter 6 is an adaptation of a chapter originally published by Routledge in *The Senses in Self, Society, and Culture*. I am indebted to Dennis Waskul and Simon Gottschalk, my book's co-authors; and to Guppy Ahluwalia-Lopez and Jonathan Taggart for taking part in the research described therein with me. Chapter 7 is the revised version of an article that appeared in the *Journal of Contemporary Ethnography*, reproduced in part here courtesy of SAGE. Chapter 8, also reporting research conducted with Jonathan Taggart, is a revised version of a chapter that appeared in my edited collection titled *Non-Representational Methodologies*, published by Routledge.

Chapters 10, 11, 12, and 13 are entirely original and have never appeared elsewhere. The last chapter of Part III, Chapter 14, has benefited from the collaboration with Sarah Abbott for a chapter in *The Craft of Qualitative Research*. That book was edited by Carrie Sanders, Lisa-Jo Van den Scott, and Steve Kleinknecht, and it is published by Canadian Scholars Press—to whom my gratitude goes. Finally, I am deeply indebted to my editor at Routledge, Alice Salt, who has given her undivided attention, time, care, and patience throughout the production of this book.

Part I

1 The need for a public ethnography[1]

As part of a global popular advertising campaign plastered in more of the world's airports than I have been able to count, financial giant HSBC tells us that our planet is full of untapped resources and investment opportunities. In one particular ad, we are told that there are more people learning English in China today than there are native English speakers in the whole United Kingdom. I see a related opportunity of another kind: there are arguably more students learning the language of the social sciences today than there are journalists, documentarians, think-tank researchers, and policy pundits combined. That is not all. There are arguably more professional researchers writing scholarly monographs and articles on social issues today than there are non-academic authors penning trade books and paperbacks on the same subjects. Yet, neither social science students nor professional social scientists are particularly apt at speaking the language of the many publics they study or at speaking louder and more clearly than their better known "pop" counterparts. This, I find, is a missed opportunity for the social sciences. Without wanting to sound too much like a global bank, we should all treat this as a great "investment opportunity" for the new public scholarship of the future.

Public audiences have a great deal to gain from the critical messages contained in social scientific research, as eminent public sociologists such as Burawoy (2004) have articulated.[2] Indeed, a more public scholarship is the key to a more advanced democratic society. So, how can social scientists—students and scholars alike—make their voices heard? How can students and professional academics work together to popularize their work? What opportunities for the public to learn from social scientific research are made possible by different ways of communicating knowledge? This book argues that one of the ways in which social scientific research can play a greater role in public discourse and in shaping the popular imagination is by taking inspiration from some of the qualities of an important social scientific tradition: ethnography.

Ethnography is endowed with rhetorical and substantive characteristics that are of great appeal to the general public. When carried out with the information and entertainment needs and wants of the public in mind, ethnographic research can reach beyond the confines of academic discourse and can position social scientific knowledge at the nexus of public debate, current affairs, and popular culture. Through a fully public ethnography, social scientific research can better engage multiple stakeholders and play a key role in the critical pedagogy of the general public. But for that to happen, social scientists must first learn to understand the grammar of twenty-first-century public ethnography. They must recognize the importance of student and participant involvement and collaboration, the power of style, and the pedagogical affordances of multimodality.

Multimodality is of especially high importance. A multimodal message is one that depends on more than a single mode of communication (like writing by itself, for example). In our digital age, multimodality is not an option for ethnography but a necessity. To be sure, writing is an effective mode for communicating with specialists. Writing and its typical academic media, the journal article and the book, allow for technical information to be conveyed in great depth and with terminological sophistication. But writing journal articles and books alone is not an effective strategy for reaching a wider audience. Traditional mass media such as magazines, radio, newspapers, and television, as well as new media such as the internet and mobile communication devices, provide the general public with information that is richer, more aesthetically captivating, less time-consuming, cheaper, more accessible, and more user-friendly than typical academic media. The result is that it is much more convenient for Joe Citizen to watch a documentary on Netflix, iTunes, YouTube, Vimeo, or cable TV than it is to spend an hour poring over an article downloaded from JStor (provided they somehow had access to JStor or a similar database). If academics want their research to be relevant and to have an impact on society and culture, then they need to learn to be skilled at using other modes of information and to employ more effective communication strategies. Ethnography's impact and visibility can benefit greatly from a multimodal approach to knowledge generation and dissemination.

In this book, by *ethnography* I simply mean the in-depth study of people's ways of life, of cultures. There are many different kinds of ethnography, but in its most basic terms, ethnography is research focused on describing and understanding social life from the perspective of the people who take part in it. Regardless of the particular methodological approaches in which it is conducted, I believe that *all* ethnographic research has the potential to become public, but that potential is rarely exploited. That potential simply arises from the ways of knowing typical of ethnography, its tropes, and its typical contents—ways of knowing that are common to all ethnographers and most qualitative researchers. But this potential is seldom exploited in full for a variety of reasons. Public ethnography is thus ethnographic research that fully exploits this potential in a search for broader audiences. Public ethnography is part of a broader paradigmatic shift in ethnography and qualitative research toward reflexive, sensuous, interpretive, narrative, arts-informed, and more-than-representational qualitative research. But in addition, public ethnography is often deeply set in the technological currency of the times. That is, rather than taking place in an exclusively print-based world, public ethnography often thrives in a public domain inspired and informed by diverse popular media, genres, and communication modes (as we will see in Chapter 3, even when ethnographic research only makes use of writing, it can only become public thanks to an ethnographer's presence across a multimodal variety of media).

Public ethnography and public scholarship today

Public ethnography is not a new thing. Ethnographers like Margaret Mead played a highly visible public role in the twentieth century. More recently, throughout the first two decades of the twenty-first century, the social sciences have experienced various pulls and pushes for more publicly engaged forms of scholarship. Sociologists, for example, have debated at great lengths the merits and perils of a different social function for their discipline and have found numerous reasons to disagree with each other. Most of these differing viewpoints can be traced back to the competing differing epistemologies—such as positivist, humanistic, and critical—which for so long have fragmented that discipline. However, other social scientific fields and disciplines have responded to calls for public scholarship in different ways.

Human geography, for example, has been much less divided over its public role than sociology. As several commentators have noted, geographers have much to gain and very little to lose by playing a greater role in public discourse (Castree et al. 2008; Davis and Dwyer 2008; Fuller 2008; Fuller and Askins 2010; Murphy et al. 2008; Ward 2006, 2007, 2008). The cultural turn[3] in geography has influenced the subject matter of human geography's research agendas, research methodologies, and dissemination strategies—freeing human geography from many of the anxieties caused by traditional value-free research (for an example and broader formulation of these ideas, see Dear, Ketchum, Luria, and Richardson 2011). Also thanks in large part to the diffusion of more-than-representational theoretical ideas, human geographers are now at the forefront of methodological experimentation, collaboration with the arts and humanities, and theoretical innovation.

Cultural anthropology enjoys a similar state of affairs to geography. Due in large part to the historical acceptance and traditional relevance of general audiences-friendly approaches such as visual ethnography—with a foot firmly planted in the academic realm and a foot planted in the documentary film tradition, or the type of photographic documentary coverage made popular by wide-distribution magazines such as *National Geographic*—cultural anthropologists are potentially well equipped to play a visible public role (Borofsky n.d., 2000; Hedican 2016; Lamphere 2004; McClancy and McDonaugh 1994; Purcell 2000; Scheper-Hughes 2000). Indeed, pronouncements on the importance of an engaged and public anthropology have been met with little or no resistance, and wherever resistance has been manifested, it has centered more around the identity or historical trajectory of public anthropology or its relation to applied anthropology than around its inherent value.[4]

Ethnographers work differently from most other researchers in virtue of key qualities of their research, such as its ability to portray people, places, and times in vividly descriptive and intimate detail; and its emphasis on the researcher's immediate and direct involvement with, participation in, and experience of the lifeworld under study. These qualities are typical of all ethnographic research, but recent trends in interpretivist ethnographic forms of representation have further honed these qualities, emphasizing the narrative, sensuous, embodied, participatory, confessional, impressionistic, and non-representational value of some of the more arts-inspired ethnographic genres (e.g. see Knowles and Cole 2008; Leavy 2017). By *public ethnography*, therefore, I mean here a type of ethnographic research that—not unlike conceptual art—imaginatively enlivens and animates lifeworlds, evoking cultural dynamics that creatively render the strange familiar and the familiar strange for the purpose of better capturing the attention of wider audiences.

Ethnography is a simple and intuitive way of knowing that is well recognized by some members of the general public as a way of doing empirical social scientific work (Gans 2010). Joe Average and Jane Doe may not be able to define ethnography and may even never have heard the word "ethnography" before, but the idea of a researcher becoming immersed in a community to learn the ways of life of its members is a powerfully captivating and broadly understood idea. As Gans (2010) has outlined, all ethnographic research is potentially in a unique position to command the general public's attention. Ethnographic description and tropes resemble those of the novel. Ethnographic portraits of cultures, people, times, and places speak to the general public's predilection for intimate, personable, context-bound, curiosity-evoking renditions of life. Ethnography's anchoring in everyday life dialogues and interactions is also liable to make sense to a public that may otherwise be baffled by the abstruse conventions of laboratory experiments or, perhaps, the jargon of discourse analysis. Moreover, ethnography's tackling of contemporary topics speaks well to public needs for in-depth coverage of current affairs as they affect individuals and their local communities. In short, ethnography's treatment of culture and places can resonate well with audiences much broader than academic ones.

Ethnography has enjoyed good recognition in the social sciences. But at times, ethnography has suffered from a somewhat contested status. Positivism's dominant nomothetic and realist epistemologies have often translated into the underprivileging of the ethnographic tradition across some disciplines, and ethnography has therefore remained more or less relegated to a minority position in some contexts. From such a position, many ethnographers have had to fight hard to defend their legitimacy. These struggles have yielded various kinds of ethnographic techniques, procedures, and stratagems that have often lent certain currents of ethnography an aura of "scientificness," almost in an attempt to mimic the ways of positivist research. Triangulation, various kinds of member checks, grounded theorizations, anonymous and formal representations, the use of computer software for data analysis, and the like have often made ethnographic research more similar, rhetorically, to the hypothesis-testing flavor of its positivist and post-positivist counterpart than to more captivating travelogues and novels (see Adler and Adler 2008). As a result, despite its potential to attract the attention of the reading public, positivist and positivist-like ethnographies have not always fully realized their public promise and have had only mixed success at the bookstore (as any cursory look at the shelves of popular bookstores or bestseller lists will attest, ethnographies are not very likely to be "hot" items). Because of the broad influence of positivism on the social sciences, formal tendencies in ethnographic methodology have become relatively widespread. As a result, ethnography as a whole has often felt uncomfortable in its own skin and has often missed opportunities to play a greater public role.

Today, more and more advocates of a fully—that is, more self-secure—public ethnography, however, are coming forth (see Fassin 2017; Tedlock 2005). For example, within sociology, Herbert Gans (2010:98) has argued that public ethnography appeals to the public "more effectively than other ways of doing sociology at least when it reports on topics and sites of general interest." Not only does ethnography make for a better read than most research, according to Gans, but it also brings out some of the best virtues of social scientific research, as it is "about the lives and problems of ordinary people, and because it obtains much of its data directly from such people" (2010:99). For Gans, ethnography *has to* be relevant and accepted by the general public. Carefully chosen topics, timely coverage, accessible writing (which often translates into research that is less theory driven), and the ability to speak to issues that the public deeply cares about can make public ethnography more relevant and attention-demanding than what can be found in the news. Indeed, what Gans calls public ethnography can offer more depth than news and documentary journalism can. Its in-depth treatment of issues can aid in explanation and understanding—something that journalism often has neither the means nor the interest in providing. Similarly, Vaughan (2005) and Becker, Gans, Newman, and Vaughn (2004) have argued that public ethnography can capture the attention not only of the reading public but also of policy-makers.

The communication strategies of public ethnography have similarly been the subject of reflection within public anthropology. For example, in a notable collection by Waterston and Vesperi (2009), several ethnographers have reflected on the tactics they utilized to make their writing more engaging, thus broadening their audiences. For Scheper-Hughes (2009), making ethnographic work more accessible and accountable requires not only pleasant writing but also collaboration with journalists and the popular media. Thus, whereas for Gans, journalists and authors of trade books represent a form of competition to both learn and take distance from, for Scheper-Hughes (2009:1), the news world is potentially an ally characterized by "thoughtfulness, thoroughness, dedication to accuracy, and ... ethical and political sensibilities." While she recognizes some of the dangers at stake in playing a public role, she argues that rather than "contaminating" themselves by meddling with journalists and the masses, an ethnographer has much to gain from making one's research public.

In sum, ethnography has traditionally been—at least potentially—in a unique position to command the attention of the general public. Because of insecurities fueled by academic diatribes, however, not many ethnographers have taken advantage of the potential of their work to enter public discourse. But as calls for public scholarship writ large and public ethnography continue to mount, and as interpretivist trends continue to pull ethnographic research further away from some of its positivist tendencies, more ethnographers find themselves better actualizing the potential of their work by writing in more appealing styles and by engaging in public discourse together with journalists and popular media. The next step for the growth of this public ethnography as a form of public scholarship is to take advantage of the continuing changes in the acceptance of multimodality, as well as the expanding possibilities for producing and distributing appealing and wide-reaching multimodal research.

My experiments in public ethnography

My passion for public ethnography dates back to a very precise moment in 2008. It was early in the fall, a little past 8 o'clock in the morning. I was driving on the highway en route to the Royal Roads University campus in Victoria. The day before, I had spoken to CBC Radio about my research on ferry boats and their role in the regional economy and the coastal way of life in British Columbia.[5] Somehow, in the 24 hours in between my interview and the next day's commute, I had forgotten all about it, and it wasn't until I accidentally tuned to 90.5 on the FM dial that I remembered about my interview. Hearing my own voice on the radio while I was driving struck me as incredibly surreal. Even to this day, it is difficult to explain why that moment was so unique, and the best way I can make sense of it is by relating a profound sense of "realness" I felt. It was, in other words, as if my research had suddenly become real, tangible, visible, and audible—something other than a set of ideas existing within my head. Up until that day, my research was just part of my little world; it was mine and mine only. Hearing myself on the radio burst that bubble; what I was doing went beyond myself and my CV. Of course, I had, and still have, no illusion about the social impact of a 7-minute interview broadcast in the middle of a sleepy morning commute, but suddenly realizing that my work could have an audience of more than the usual thirty graduate students and colleagues who can access peer-reviewed periodicals changed my attitude toward my work.

Since that morning in 2008, I have experimented with public ethnography in a multitude of ways. At first, my public ethnographic research outputs concentrated on audio dissemination. Regional radio was always thirsty for content, and since the ferries were always in the news, I was called upon regularly to provide commentary based on the insights of my fieldwork. When that ethnography was over and my book was about to be published, I thought that short audio docs should accompany my writing. The result was a hypermedia book, which excited me about the possibilities of both multimodal communication and public outreach. In all honesty, the public component of my ethnography on ferry-boat travel had not been planned until the last phases of field research, and so the next project, I thought, should take a more comprehensive approach from the outset.

In 2012, I began my next multi-year ethnography: an investigation of the lifestyles of people who lived off the grid across Canada. Because public dissemination was by then a key aspect of my research agenda at the university, I was able to secure the funds to hire a Master's student to travel with me to each field location to film and photograph every interview. Jonathan Taggart and I, however, never quite imagined that our resulting film, *Life Off Grid*, would have the reception it did. Neither Jonathan nor I had ever made a documentary film, and back in 2012, most people were unaware of what "off-grid" actually meant. So we thought we'd reach a few niche audiences on Vimeo and at some film festivals, and little beyond that. A few years later, on one rainy morning, I found myself staring at a long line of people patiently waiting for the doors of one of Vancouver's largest movie theatres to open so they could watch our movie. The movie went on to have three consecutive sell-out shows in as many days. That, for me, was even more surreal than listening to my voice on the radio years before.

Now my next challenge is to write a book that actually ends up on a bookstore shelf. Though I am very happy with my favorite academic publisher, who is also publishing this volume, I ache every time I walk into a city's chain bookstore and find no trace of anything I've ever written. I get why: the general public does not necessarily care to read "research" while they sip a caramel macchiato, and most academic publishers face significant barriers in accessing that market, but I still ache. And not just for myself—my ego is not that fragile!—but for the hundreds of colleagues who write well (and much better than me!), who write passionately, who write about important topics, and who still get elbowed out from those shelves by Dr. Phil or by the latest, tired re-print of Marshall McLuhan's work. And I ache for the thousands of graduate students around the world who are reprimanded for writing well, in clear and plain English, because good prose won't get them hired. And most of all, I ache for "the general public" who do not get easy and affordable access to passionate and meaningful ethnographic work. And so this book is for their sake, and for our sake. It is an attempt to collect a few serviceable practices, a few techniques on how to craft publicly appealing research that can be enjoyed by many. It is an effort to reflect on what I have learned as a result of my experiments in public ethnography, from the mistakes I have made, and from the minor goals I have achieved. And in the end, it is an open call: an encouragement to all readers to give public ethnography, and public scholarship in general, the old college try.

Book organization

The book is divided into three parts. Part I focuses on the context of public ethnography. Following this introduction is Chapter 2, a reflection on the identity of public ethnography. I begin that chapter by establishing a clear but open-ended definition of public ethnography, and then I move on to elaborate on the value of this evolving tradition. I situate public ethnography in the broader context of public scholarship, I articulate its objectives, and I reflect on its limitations. I explain how knowledge mobilization is valuable to different stakeholders for various reasons, and I reflect in detail on how public ethnography is a very unique type of knowledge mobilization with particular advantages and disadvantages. I also reflect on ethical challenges as well as some of the more common difficulties inherent in doing public ethnographic work, ranging from costs, time consumption, and the need to be extremely sensitive to the information needs and wants of non-academic publics.

In Chapter 3, I offer some insights into why and how more ethnographers are entering the public sphere by turning to the experiences of Patricia Leavy, a scholar whose work has played an instrumental role in the growth of public ethnography. The chapter reports on an extended conversation Patricia and I had over the process of writing this book. Chapter 4 is an attempt to go beyond representation. In that chapter, I reflect on how public ethnographic research can draw inspiration from theoretical and methodological traditions pushing beyond representation. Briefly, non-representational theory (or, as it is sometimes referred to, "more-than-representational" theory) is one of the contemporary moment's most influential theoretical perspectives within social and cultural theory. Non-representational theory is, however, often poorly understood. This is in part because of its complexity but also in large part because of its limited application in research practice and because of its many unanswered methodological questions. How actually powerful and useful non-representational research is, in this sense, yet to be fully appreciated. This chapter tackles this subject by outlining a variety of ways in which non-representational ideas can influence the research process, the very value of empirical research, the nature of data, the political value of evidence, the methods and modes of research, the very notion of method, and the styles, genres, and media of research.

Part II of the book focuses on writing. I begin my reflection on writing styles with a cheeky chapter, Chapter 5. In it, I argue that if ethnographers truly want to reach a broader audience, they need to shake off some of the qualities that supposedly make academic research good. These are stylistic qualities that make our writing style generally unappealing to large audiences. By encouraging ethnographers to write differently for their target popular audiences, I urge them to avoid jargon, to write narratively, to abandon signposting and long sentences or paragraphs, to limit the fetishistic use of citations, to put their data in the foreground and theory in the background, and so on. I also invite them to organize their work differently, to speak from a personal and situated perspective, and to be vulnerable rather than all-knowing.

Chapter 6 focuses on precise ways in which ethnographers can experiment with more-than-representational styles. Whereas in Chapter 4 I reflect on non-representationalism in general, in this chapter I offer concrete suggestions on writing more-than-representationally by drawing examples from my own and others' work. I focus on six ways in which non-representational ideas have influenced ethnographic writing. These six qualities are vitality, performativity, corporeality, sensuality, mobility, and surreality. Whereas traditional and realist ethnography more or less posits the representation of research subject(s) as a faithful rendition of the word "as is," non-representational ethnographers consider their work to be impressionistic and inevitably creative. Although they are inspired by their lived experiences in the field, non-representational ethnographers do not claim to be able, or even interested, in reporting on those in an impersonal, neutral, or reliable manner. Thus, non-representational ethnographic styles can be said to be styles that strive to animate rather than simply mimic, to rupture rather than merely take account, and to evoke rather than just report. This style, I argue, is necessary for reaching new audiences for our ethnographic work.

Chapter 7 focuses on learning from the power of documentary film. The intent of this chapter is to learn lessons from the popular successes of documentary film and apply those lessons to ethnographic writing. More precisely, my intent is to reflect on the growing popularity of non-academic ethnographic films distributed through wide-dissemination media, such as hybrid TV channels, in order to assess what precisely characterizes these productions in terms of content and style and to reflect on what ethnographic writers can learn from ethnographic documentary filmmakers' representational practices. This chapter concentrates in particular on four qualities of participatory documentary film-making style from which, I argue, public ethnographers can learn a great deal: its intimacy, its detail-orientation, its narrativity, and its sensuousness. While these qualities are not unusual in ethnographic writing and qualitative research writ large, participatory-style ethnographic film has the potential to inspire us to write better, and perhaps somewhat differently, without losing sight of our interpretive and analytical responsibilities toward our academic audiences.

Chapter 8 takes on the argument of Chapter 7 further and develops the idea of writing *sensuously*. As of late, advances in the development of performative, narrative, reflexive, impressionist, embodied, and descriptive ethnography and related qualitative research strategies have paralleled an increased interest in the methodological potential of "sensuous scholarship" across disciplines. Sensuous scholarship has much in common with these research traditions, but it is also distinct from them. Sensuous scholarship generally refers to research, theory, and methodology that are *about the human senses, through the senses, and for the senses*. Sensuous scholarship builds upon many of the themes and ideas discussed in this book and pushes for the recognition of the meaningfulness of the sensory experience of the world, the performativity of the skillful activities through which we actively make and remake the world through our senses, and the evocativeness of our strategies of representation. Sensuous scholarship manifests itself in a writing style that is passionate, affective, emotional, and even carnal. In this chapter, I outline ways in which public ethnographers can draw inspiration from the tradition of sensuous scholarship in order to write sensuously.

Chapter 9 is a very practical chapter that explains the basics of how to publish in magazines, trade books, and hypermedia books. Many ethnographers enjoy writing and know how to write well. Yet so much of their writing ends up in journals that are inaccessible to audiences outside of the academy. Magazines, trade books, and blogs offer an opportunity to reach out to readers outside library paywalls. For example, many magazines publish good writing about human-interest issues, dedicate a great deal of attention to contemporary affair content, and can reach wide audiences. However, ethnographers have yet to learn how to take advantage of this medium's potential. My objective in this chapter is to examine the process of communicating ethnography through widely accessible media such as popular print magazines, web-based magazines, trade books, and blogs. In particular, I reflect on practical considerations that ethnographers might want to entertain whenever they attempt to popularize their work through these channels.

Part III of the book focuses on modes of communication other than writing. In Chapter 10, I reflect on what it means to compose ethnography multimodally. Multimodality refers to a communication message that employs various modes of communication such as writing, photography, audio, and video. For the last six years, I have employed multimodal strategies of dissemination as both a researcher and a series editor for the Routledge Series in Innovative Ethnographies. In this chapter, I outline some common ways in which ethnographers can communicate multimodally with the purpose of reaching readers, listeners, and viewers beyond the academy. This chapter also lays the foundations for the next chapters, which then focus in more specific depth on certain modes of communication other than writing alone.

Chapter 11 focuses on the subject of audio production. The chapter begins with a brief overview of when audio documentation is ideal, reflecting on the nature of research topics and the aesthetics of audio documentation. Subsequently, I move on to outlining practical considerations for sound recording, introducing ideal recording settings and format. I introduce the basic differences among various microphone types and their varying suitability for different tasks. I conclude with an overview of the editing process, focusing in particular on the production of short audio documentaries.

Chapter 12 is an introduction to image-making. The chapter encompasses both the creation of still and moving images by outlining practical ways in which ethnographers might make their images more appealing. Exposure and composition comprise the main foci of this chapter. While I realize that image production is a complex art that cannot be easily explained in a single chapter, I make a series of arguments about why ethnographers should develop their visual aesthetic sensibilities by honing their technical skills. The main point of this chapter is to encourage readers to abandon the automatic function of their cameras and gain full manual control over the image-making process in order to assert their full creative agency over the process.

Chapter 13 is an introduction to the production of editing of video. The chapter focuses on best practices for the creation of video documentaries destined for web-based dissemination (e.g. on YouTube, Vimeo, various VOD platforms) and for TV and even theatrical dissemination. I discuss ideal contents and forms, techniques, gear, and workflow. Particular attention is paid to the different demands of shooting action, interviews, and contextual b-roll. As part of my introduction to editing I discuss how to make cuts, and export video for a variety of screening purposes.

Following the previous chapter, in Chapter 14, I discuss strategies through which video ethnographers can reach broader audiences. Unfortunately, most research videos end up getting only a few hundred viewers on the web (if that many!). Drawing from experience and colleagues' best practices, I outline practical and achievable strategies for reaching larger audiences. These strategies include the engagement of social media, the utilization of new distribution channels (such as Tugg), dissemination through public TV, and the involvement of stakeholders in niche distribution.

Notes

1 This chapter is a revised version of Vannini and Milne (2014). Reprinted with permission of the Publisher from *The Public Sociology Debate* edited by Ariane Hanemaayer and Christopher Schneider © University of British Columbia Press 2014. All rights reserved by the Publisher.
2 The interested reader is invited to consult the myriad debates on this issue, conveniently inventoried on Michael Burawoy's webpage: http://burawoy.berkeley.edu/PS.htm.
3 Within the context of the social sciences, the "cultural turn" refers to a paradigmatic shift away from viewing culture as the bounded domain of society (tantamount to the arts and humanities-centered heritage of a group) and toward viewing it as an all-encompassing "way of life."
4 Gottlieb (1997), for instance, argues that public anthropology is valuable, but it is not significantly different from the well-established tradition of applied anthropology, and therefore the new "public anthropology" moniker risks glossing over that tradition.
5 The research project investigated the roles played by ferry boats in the lives of coastal British Columbia's ferry-dependent communities. As the research unfolded over the years, it became more and more clear that, besides interpretation and conceptualization, the topic also demanded committed public documentation of the social problems caused by escalating ferry fares. As the issue is of great regional relevance, it turned out to be rather easy for the author to influence public debate and policy-making through regular media appearances. In addition, even in its less political and controversial aspects, the research subject is of such obvious mundane relevance to islanders' and coasters' lives that it easily demands local publics' curiosity and attention. See ferrytales.innovativeethnographies.net.

2 What is public ethnography and whom is it good for?[1]

Within communication studies, a basic lesson is taught to every student in beginner courses: adapt your strategic message to your audience, to the situation, and to your goals. This is a simple principle of human relations that academics from all disciplines routinely practice in their work. For example, when explaining a complex concept or theory to an advanced graduate class, we utilize technical terminology and abstract ideas. But when we teach the same material to introductory undergraduate classes, we strategically employ a more basic vocabulary and simple examples in order to make the material relevant and useful to the students. In doing this, we instrumentally follow two different genres for our scholarly communication, genres that are defined by their different content, styles, and audiences. The purpose of this chapter is to introduce the idea of public ethnography as a strategic genre of scholarly communication.

As introduced in Chapter 1, simply put, public ethnography is ethnographic research strategically intended for a public audience, an audience that goes vastly beyond academia. It is nearly impossible to speak of a "public" audience as if it were an undifferentiated group of people. Multiple publics do exist, and strategic ethnographic communication must therefore be differentiated and strategically crafted to reach the intended segments of a specific audience. These strategies of differentiation may include a purposive selection of various modes of expression, engagement tactics, channels of communication, and dissemination techniques that are considered ideal for a target audience that is a subset of the "general public." But the point remains: a public ethnography—no matter how narrowly defined its intended audience might be—is not public unless it leaves the confines of the academic world and its typical genres and modes of expression as well as channels of dissemination.

It is important to clarify that a public ethnography must draw the attention of a non-academic public, but the doing of public ethnography does not exclude traditional dissemination through academic media. Because graduation, tenure, promotion, and funding still operate on the basis of publication in peer-reviewed outlets, it makes no practical sense to suggest that ethnographers avoid seeking traditional publications (see also Morse 2004). Therefore, public ethnographers who want to be employed in the modern university must be prepared to speak to both academic and non-academic audiences. Peer-review publication and broad knowledge mobilization are not mutually incongruent, but the content of these messages cannot be the same. Public ethnographers must be willing to regularly engage in code-switching, to make use of different media for their different audiences, and to adapt the content, styles, and mode of their research communication.

What public ethnography is (and is not)

The most basic definition of public ethnography hinges on the measure of its communicative success (Adler and Adler 2008; Gans 2010; Tedlock 2005; Vaughan 2005). Essentially, if ethnographic research is brought to the attention of a non-academic audience, then it can be said to be a public ethnography. The size of the audience does matter. After all, how truly public is an ethnography if it is read by only 250 readers or so? On the other hand, size is not everything. If an intended audience is supposed to be a small rural community, then a simple article published in a local newspaper, or copies of a book that are made fully accessible through a local library, might do the job.

Before going much farther with our definition of public ethnography, let us be crystal clear about something. Public ethnography is *not* a well-written essay penned for an academic journal or edited academic book. It is not a witty performance delivered at a conference. It is not a captivating classroom lecture. These traditional academic outputs are meant for the consumption of scholars and students, not members of the public at large. Similarly, ethnographers who rely on alternative modes of composition—such as ethnodrama, ethnopoetics, autoethnography, arts-based inquiry, performance, video, storytelling—but *who limit their research dissemination to scholarly outputs* (e.g. by publishing in academic periodicals or exhibiting their work in university classrooms) do *not* really engage in public ethnography either. These scholars' knowledge-transfer intentions may be genuine, but the social value of their research is restricted by their limited audience. And while we are at it, we might as well be clear about something else: in most cases, creating a website to share one's research findings is not enough to make research public, given the very limited traffic these sites generally get. In short: an ethnography that hardly anyone outside of the ivory tower reads, listens to, or views is not public enough.

Public ethnography is also not the same as performance ethnography (e.g. see Denzin 2003). Performance ethnographies may be scripted and enacted for a public audience, but until they are produced and actually take place in a theater frequented by a non-academic audience, there is nothing public about them. Public ethnography is not synonymous with critical ethnography either (e.g. see Madison 2011). Public ethnographies may be critical, but a keen interest in social justice and emancipation does not automatically mean public outreach. In this sense, my view of public ethnography differs from that of Bailey (2008), who treats critical and public ethnography as basically contiguous. An ethnographer can be as critical as she wishes, but to cry for better social policies in the pages of a journal read by no-one but liberal academics does not constitute a form of public communication. Furthermore, many public ethnographies are not driven by the need to ameliorate social conditions but perhaps more simply by cultural curiosity and a passion for documentation. Finally, public ethnography is not the same as postmodern ethnography. One may very well draw a wide public with a strategic translation of the most realistic and analytical version of grounded theory available. But enough with the misconceptions; let us now formulate a clear definition.

Public ethnography can be defined as *ethnographic research or in-depth interview-based qualitative research that makes conscious and strategic use of communication styles, modes, and media targeted at non-academic audiences*. Mine is not an original idea. Amongst the very first to articulate such an approach was sociologist Ken Plummer. Plummer advocated the need for ethnographic findings "to enter the common parlance of everyday folk ... not just in scientific tomes or great books like the past but everywhere—in films, photos, magazines, press, television, music, dance, videos, computers, and Web sites" (1999: 642). The "past" that Plummer refers to is the early days of classical anthropological and sociological ethnographic writing and thus the work of Ruth Benedict, Franz Boas, Margaret Mead, William Whyte, and other public intellectuals whose tales from the field captured the imagination of large lay audiences and formed the basis of public debate and policy for many years.

Adler and Adler (2008) implicitly agree with Plummer in suggesting that public ethnography has been around for a long time. Like Plummer (1999) and Gans (2010), they find that ethnography is in an advantageous position to capture the attention of lay publics because of its narrative and personally intimate characteristics. As opposed to classical and mainstream approaches, public ethnographies are stylized to fit the pages of "national newspapers and intellectual magazines" (Adler and Adler 2008: 19), as well as books destined for readers with perhaps less concern for methodological rigor or theory.

"Social criticism and public engagement" (Tedlock 2005: 152) as well as an open-access view of education are the core principles of public ethnography. Political transformation and cultural reflexivity on "the critical social issues of our time" (Tedlock 2005: 159)—by way of enhancing knowledge accessibility and public engagement—are the main products a public ethnography has to offer. Without sufficient exposure, these lessons become useless preachings to the choir. But by inscribing, translating, performing, and presenting their research to the general public, ethnographers can "emotionally engage, educate, and move the public to action" (Tedlock 2005: 159).

Public ethnography is an expression of public scholarship. Recent calls to public sociology and anthropology (e.g. Burawoy 2004; Borofsky 2011), for example, incite academics to transcend the limitations of peer-to-peer communication. Public scholarship calls for academics to continue to do what they do well, but to work harder at being relevant for a broader public, engaging citizens in contextualizing, interpreting, and actually using knowledge gained from ethnographic research. With Gans (2010), therefore, we should hold the view that public ethnography is not necessarily research that is done dramatically different than conventional ethnography (though it may be). Indeed, it "must meet the same research standards as the academic variety" (Gans 2010: 98). Regardless of how it is conducted in the field, public ethnography simply must be composed in a non-technical language so that it can be understood ..., relevant to and accepted by a significant part of the lay public" (Gans 2010: 98).

The benefits of going public

The ongoing debates for public or engaged anthropology (e.g. Borofsky n.d., 2000, 2011; Gottlieb 1997; Lamphere 2004; McClancy and McDonaugh 1996; Purcell 2000; Scheper-Hughes 2009; also see the essays in *Current Anthropology* 2010) and for public sociology (e.g. Burawoy 2004)—to name only two disciplines that have extensively batted around this issue—have framed the need for socially relevant research, research that is driven by the emancipatory power and transformative potential of knowledge. These arguments have been well received by ethnographers who believe that a critical (e.g. Madison 2011), decolonized (Denzin and Tuhiwai-Smith 2008), collaborative (Lassiter 2005), and policy-focused (Becker et al. 2004; Tedlock 2005; Vaughan 2004) orientation can allow ethnography to move from a simple do-no-harm ethic to a do-something-good ethic (see Borofsky 2011). But for whom, exactly, can public ethnography do good? I believe that four groups of people can benefit from public ethnography.

The first group consists of research participants. The people that take part in ethnographic projects can benefit from public ethnography in immediate and practical ways whenever a research study sheds light on a particular social problem or injustice they suffer from or a way of life in which they are invested. The exposure granted by an ethnography that reaches the public domain, and the more practical and hands-on solutions that collaborative and community-based research approaches can achieve, have clear and direct benefits for informants and collaborators. Even milder forms of impact such as improved understanding of a social issue, greater awareness of a problematic condition, or deeper and more insightful knowledge of a particular lifeworld can make an important difference. Of course, it is not easy to compose ethnographies when we know that "they" are reading/viewing/listening to our work (e.g. see Waterston and Vesperi 2009), but when research participants actually notice that their participation has been utilized concretely in one way or another, they will feel that their time and effort was not spent in vain. Participants who have the opportunity to see the "fruits" of their contribution to the research become more engaged in the topic and in future research efforts, and this makes the entire enterprise of scholarly research more feasible and sustainable in the long run.

The second group with an immediate stake in the development of public ethnography includes professional academics. Traditionally, for the purpose of tenure and promotion, research has been evaluated in ways that have marginalized publications in non-peer-reviewed channels. While peer-reviewed journal publications still matter greatly today, there are signs that new forms of research output are gaining respect. For example, more and more funding agencies are now explicit about the need for knowledge mobilization (or *knowledge exchange* or *knowledge transfer*, as it is sometimes known) as well as open-access publishing, and they strongly encourage funded researchers to make an impact outside academia. Public ethnographers are in a good position to achieve knowledge mobilization goals because of the form and content of their work (Becker et al. 2004; Gans 2010; Tedlock 2005), and this can greatly help their careers. Not only can knowledge mobilization improve ethnographers' chances of getting funded, but such efforts can also constitute a rewarding way of doing "service" for the university, and they can therefore substitute for other more mundane and less interesting administrative tasks. Furthermore, doing research in the public view can be a valuable learning experience: working with new genres and styles of writing and new forms of ethnographic representation and collaborating with members of new and lively teams that bring different skills to the table can teach new and valuable lessons to the most experienced ethnographers.

The third group is comprised of university students. University students have a strong stake in the development of public ethnography both as consumers and as producers. As consumers, students can learn a great deal from public ethnography because its lessons are unique in both form and content. Public ethnography's everyday-life orientation can teach volumes by shedding light on practical issues that are easy to relate to and be captivated by. Students can also greatly benefit from the development of public ethnographers as producers. Increasingly, ethnographers work in collaborative teams that comprise different members with different skills. Publishing in popular media, for example, may require that ethnographers collect photographs or video or that they work with web-based applications and software with which they are unfamiliar. Students with the necessary skills may then be hired to collaborate with professional ethnographers by helping with the development of social media–based messages, with the maintenance of blogs and websites, and with developing and maintaining rapport with news media and other organizations. Incidentally, these kinds of student jobs would also seem better suited to developing their future careers than traditional tasks like conducting literature reviews, transcribing interviews, and coding data.

The fourth and last group is made up of universities and colleges. In an increasingly competitive climate, higher-education institutions are under constant pressure to make themselves visible, accountable, and desirable places to study. Research has traditionally served as a commodity for universities keen on increasing their status. Research publications raise the profile of departments, schools, and a university writ large, but the limited diffusion of studies published in academic journals represents a crucial problem for the sake of visibility. The extremely limited visibility of academic articles and books contributes to raising the public's suspicion that academics are exclusive, elitist, and out of touch with the critical issues of the day. By explicitly composing for public media, or by otherwise reaching broader audiences through community-based interest groups and outreach programs, public ethnographers can make their universities more visible and more accountable to voters and politicians. And, by virtue of their public visibility, ethnographers can also help a university better market itself. Universities spend considerable sums of money in marketing and advertising campaigns (which, unfortunately, often tend to be rather corny and superficial), but public ethnographers' work is cost-free and better revealing of a university's character and mission than a typical advert.

Mediation and collaboration

Ethnographers interested in connecting with non-academic audiences have at least two ways of achieving their goals: by way of mediation and by way of collaboration (for a wide directory of the possibilities, see Vannini 2012). The first approach can be called *mediated public ethnography* and the second *engaged public ethnography*. The distinction is purely heuristic and refers to ideal types; in practice, the two categories cross over and blur lines of distinction, and in this book, I will not worry about making any further distinctions between the two after this chapter. Both types indeed rely on common orientations, purposes, and conditions. Public ethnographers of both kinds must be, for example, committed to serving the public interest, open to methodological innovations, ready to surrender at least some control over the research process, pragmatic about methodological procedures and decisions, and deeply invested in the reception and approval of their work by lay audiences. However, there are some differences between mediated and engaged public ethnography as well, as Heather Mosher and I described in a special issue of *Qualitative Research* (Vannini and Mosher 2013). Let us now describe briefly the two types.

A mediated public ethnography comes to life by way of research dissemination through non-academic media. Examples may include an article in a newspaper or magazine; a collection of photographs collected for an exhibit; a video or audio documentary shared through television, radio, theaters, or web channels; a widely distributed book; or a performance acted for a community theater stage—to mention only the most typical examples. These kinds of public ethnographies require that a researcher adapts the outcomes of scholarly ethnographic research for the particular medium of choice, the format conventions of that medium, and the expectations of a target audience. This may involve changing the style, tone, length, focus, or approach of one's typical scholarly ethnographic composition to meet the demands of a gatekeeper such as a curator; a newspaper, magazine, or book editor; or a TV or radio producer. These changes may feel like sacrifices to the novice public ethnographer accustomed to working with peer readers, but they are necessary for the sake of engaging public interest.

The advantages of doing a mediated public ethnography are not limited to the objective of connecting with a larger audience. The very need of popular media to compete for audiences' attention means that public ethnographers will often need to become more sensitive to these gatekeepers' prerogatives. Thus, successful public ethnographers may learn new practical skills. For example, they may learn to collaborate with artists (e.g. photographers, videographers, playwriting specialists, mixed-media artists, etc.) or public relations experts. Or they may learn to write how to develop shorter sentences, more captivating prose, more vivid descriptions, more intimate characters, and quicker and pithier arguments. Or they may learn to select topics that more easily lend themselves to media and public interest, topics that are not exclusively driven by theoretical agenda, and are more sensitive to the spirit of the times and their regional and national relevance.

In order to pull off a mediated public ethnography, researchers can engage in various practical strategies. For example, a research article published in an academic journal can be condensed in a short op-ed or invited contribution to a local or national newspaper. If photography is available to accompany writing, an ethnographer can submit a pitch to a magazine editor and, upon invitation, craft an appealing feature article. Working with the media relations department of one's university, a news tip can be sent to media organizations. Social media can also be engaged, especially when the ethnographer can rely on extensive personal networks or exposure on one's university's social media. A more sustained communication strategy can unfold over time and in various channels through differentiation of one's offer and constant strategic communication. The development of mediated ethnographies can eventually amount to a second job if one wants it, and at a time when tenured positions are scarcer and scarcer, a part-time academic ethnographer who is able to also write, produce, and edit works of popular interest can quickly and conveniently supplement personal income.

The second approach for conducting public ethnography, *engaged public ethnography*, is a form of community-based research and, more specifically, *participatory* community-based research. An engaged public ethnography transpires by way of *collaboration* between researcher and stakeholders within the lay public in the production, dissemination, and practical utilization of ethnographic texts. Examples of final outputs are similar to those of mediated public ethnography, but with an added dimension of participation by the lay public at some level in the ethnographic process. Public participation may involve researching an issue, testing new ideas, or implementing action for change, among others.

The main difference from mediated public ethnography has to do with *when* and *how* a researcher engages the public in ethnographic scholarship. The process of connecting with the lay public starts early in the research process and may include involving participants or communities in selecting the focus of the research, designing the research strategy and selecting specific methods to understand or document the issue, or participating at some level in analyzing data and interpreting the findings of the research, whether it be photographs, social maps, video, interviews—to name just a few of the many possible data forms.

The idea is that the ethnographic process engages the public in ways that shape the work, increasing its relevance, reach, and impact directly on the participating communities. This involves more than changing one's ethnographic composition to meet the demands of a gatekeeper (such as curator, newspaper editor, or TV producer). Instead, it requires a change in stance for the researcher from being an observer and an expert who takes away data to write their own interpretation and papers about the community, to being a participatory researcher who works with local people to understand and address issues *identified* by the people. This leads to results that are directly applicable and useful to the public for addressing the problems at hand. Ethnographers sacrifice some level of control in exchange for the advantages that come with this form of collaborative community-based method.

The advantages of doing engaged public ethnography go beyond new ways of knowledge dissemination. The engagement process not only increases the potential impact of our work but also adds valuable and often missing perspectives that contribute to a richer understanding of socio-cultural processes and issues. For researchers, using engaged public ethnography has an advantage in that they may gain new insights on the practical implications of their research and approach and learn new skills by translating the results of their research into action. They may learn how to use jargon-free language and meaningful visuals in ways that bring together and connect with a wide range of audiences.

A variety of strategies can be used to pull off an engaged public ethnography. For example, developing a research project advisory board of community stakeholders can lead to broader reach and more sustained impact through participants' and stakeholders' social networks. Training participants in self-reflective, arts-based, and collaborative methodologies can communicate authentic, lived experiences that resonate with the general public. Co-writing a screenplay made with research findings can translate the research into an easily understood format for greater impact. In whatever form it takes, the key to an engaged public ethnography is to develop deep roots in communities that may help build a broader base, building strong community allies for continuing our ethnographic work for social change.

I have listed the advantages of doing mediated and engaged public ethnography, but in concluding this chapter, it is important to keep in mind the drawbacks as well. First, public ethnography takes time. In addition to writing a journal article or preparing a conference presentation, the public ethnographer also has to, say, craft a magazine piece or plan for a radio-station interview. Second, the conduction of public ethnography may require additional expenditures. Of course, it is virtually free to write a newspaper op-ed or contribute to a blog, but the costs go up when you try and develop podcasts and even further up if you plan on producing a video. Third, doing public ethnography may result in establishing and maintaining interpersonal relations for the sake of collaboration. Whether you collaborate with research participants, students, or artists, you will need to invest time and emotional energy in cultivating these rapports. Fourth, public ethnography is rarely anonymous or faceless. To create an ethnographic film, you need to show the faces and voices of your research participants, and this may require jumping through a few institutional hoops if your university's human-subject review board is particularly pernickety. Lastly, to become a good public ethnographer, you will likely need to learn a few new skills. Luckily, for that, there is the remainder of this book.

Note

1 This chapter is a revised version of Vannini and Mosher (2013).

3 Why and how more ethnographers are seeking broader audiences

There are many good writers among academics. Academic writing as an institution, however, has traditionally discouraged good writing. Peer-reviewed scholarly publications—both journals and books—demand precise technical language and strict adherence to organizational formats that are more concerned with the appearance of rigor than with good style. As a result, academic writing is often dry, impersonal, dispassionate, and full of jargon. Thankfully, there are exceptions. More and more ethnographers are realizing that good writing can allow research to be broadly accessible and enjoyable, and more and more academic books are being published with public audiences as the main readership target.

In this chapter, I am going to engage in a conversation with Patricia Leavy, a scholar whose work has been of tremendous significance in inspiring, encouraging, and empowering students and academics to connect with broad public audiences. Few people around the world have done more, as of late, to promote the agenda of public scholarship, especially through the use of arts-based research. Leavy earned her Ph.D. in Sociology at Boston College in 2002. From 2002 to 2012, she was a tenured associate professor of Sociology at Stonehill College, where she also served as founding director of the Gender Studies Program and as the chairperson of the Sociology and Criminology Department. In 2012, she left academia to focus her full-time efforts on her work as an author, independent researcher, and public intellectual.

Patricia Leavy's published books include *Privilege Through the Looking-Glass* (Brill-Sense 2018); *Handbook of Arts-Based Research* (Guilford Press 2018); *Research Design: Quantitative, Qualitative, Mixed Methods, Arts-Based, and Community-Based Participatory Research Approaches* (Guilford Press 2017); *Low-Fat Love Stories* (Brill-Sense 2017); *Blue* (Sense Publishers 2016); *The Oxford Handbook of Qualitative Research* (Oxford University Press 2014); *American Circumstance* (Brill-Sense 2013, 2016); *Fiction as Research Practice: Novels, Novellas and Short Stories* (Routledge 2013); *Low-Fat Love* (Brill-Sense 2011, 2015); *Essentials of Transdisciplinary Research: Using Problem-Centered Methodologies* (Routledge 2011); *Method Meets Art: Arts-Based Research Practice* (Guilford Publications 2009, 2015); *Handbook of Emergent Research Methods* (Guilford Publications 2008); *Feminist Research Practice: A Primer* (Sage Publications 2007); and *Emergent Methods in Social Research* (Sage Publications 2006).

Published by Brill-Sense, Leavy's award-winning *Social Fictions* publishes novels, plays, and short-story collections that are informed by research and teaching experiences. A vocal advocate of public scholarship in the popular media, Leavy has appeared on national news and radio, and she is regularly quoted by the print and online news media (e.g. *The New York Times, The Los Angeles Times, USA Today*). She has regular blogs in *The Huffington Post, The Creativity Post,* and *We Are the Real Deal,* and she publishes freelance op-eds. In recognition of her significant contributions to the discipline of sociology, The New England Sociological Association named Dr Leavy the 2010 New England Sociologist of the Year. Dr Leavy received a 2014 Special Achievement Award from the American Creativity Association, which honors creativity and innovation in every field. The Special Achievement award recognizes her extraordinary work advancing arts-based research and the ground-breaking *Social Fictions* series. In 2015, Dr Leavy was announced as the youngest recipient of the Special Career Award given by the International Congress of Qualitative Inquiry. The award recognizes her entire body of work and particularly honors her advancement of qualitative and arts-based research. In that same year, Dr Leavy was also honored with the Egon Guba Memorial Lecture Award by the Qualitative Special Interest Group of the American Educational Research Association. In 2016, Mogul, a global women's empowerment platform, named Dr Leavy an "Influencer" alongside Chelsea Clinton, musician Melissa Etheridge, fashion editor Nina Garcia, and other notable women. In 2018, she received the Distinguished Contributions Outside of the Profession Award from the National Art Education Association and the Division D Significant Contribution to Educational Measurement and Research Methodology Award from the American Educational Research Association, and she was honored by the National Women's Hall of Fame.

I interviewed Patricia Leavy by email in the winter of 2018.

Q1. Why is public dissemination of scholarly work important to you?

Academics are among the most educated people in the world, and we use enormous resources conducting research, including our own time and expertise. Yet just about no-one will ever benefit from that research. I've read studies that have found that 90 percent of academic articles have an audience of three people (and they include the author and journal editor among the three). Other studies have shown that most academic articles have an audience of three to eight readers. I mean, seriously. It's like a bad joke. We spend years conducting research that ultimately is totally useless other than to create a line on our CVs and thereby allow us to hoop-jump in a tenure and promotion system that promulgates this archaic system. And it's not the fault of academics trapped in a dysfunctional system. They're just trying to survive. But most people don't like wasting their time, and most researchers find their work interesting or important. Beyond wasting resources, I believe there is an ethical or moral imperative for making our work accessible. Knowledge shouldn't belong to the few, but to the many. The current system is elitist. Stakeholders that have a vested interest in our research should have access to the findings.

Q2. In what ways do you think arts-based and arts-inspired research traditions can contribute to the popular success of public scholarship?

For starters, people generally enjoy art. Many elect to spend their leisure time consuming art. Consider how many people listen to music, watch television, or read fiction on a daily basis, or how many see a film, play, or dance performance on weekends, or the seemingly endless line of people on any given day at the MoMA in front of Van Gogh's *The Starry Night*. By using formats that people enjoy and find unintimidating, we have a real chance to reach them. Art is accessible in two key ways. It's jargon-free, so it's understandable and it circulates in spaces/platforms many people have access to. In the case of visual media, you even remove language and hearing barriers. There's also fascinating research on the neuroscience of art consumption that suggests the arts may engage our brains more deeply and contribute to longer lasting impressions than non-fiction prose. For example, research in literary neuroscience shows that reading fiction engages parts of the brain including those involved with touch. So when we're immersed in a novel and feel as if we're there, that's actually, in part, the result of a physiological process. Brain scans show that the impressions made reading a novel last longer than those from reading non-fiction prose. There are enormous possibilities for getting our work out in ways that are meaningful.

Q3. Can you share some of your experiences with doing public scholarship? In particular, what are the key writing strategies that you follow in order to make your work appealing to audiences outside academia?

When I'm writing fiction, I choose genres that appeal to the audiences I want to reach. For example, if I want to reach young women, I may use a chick-lit genre, which I then subvert from within. In the case of op-eds or blogs, I got great advice years ago I'll pass on. Try to use a catchy title; put something engaging, funny, or a hook in the first paragraph; teach one main point using up to three items of support (such as examples); and end with a clever last line that sums up the piece but leaves the reader lingering on your words. Also, op-ed editors may first read the opening and last paragraphs, to gauge if they're interested.

Q4. Have you ever encountered resistance to your work from traditional academic circles?

Yeah, sure, but less than you'd think. Anyone who does public scholarship encounters some measure of pushback from those entrenched in the academic establishment, who are frightened they will no longer retain their "expert" status if we make our work understandable to regular folks. And as an arts-based researcher, I've certainly experienced bias. I mean, come on, how is a novel research, or how is a play research? To some, it's not scholarship. So I've taken my knocks. There are some people who don't take my work seriously, and I've had unpleasantness including nasty remarks at conferences, journals refusing to publish me, not being awarded recognition for that paper I had earned, and never working in an elite research university. However, for the most part, I've found that when you try to do your best work and stay true to your values, others will support you. For every one person who has said something nasty, a hundred have said something affirming. When you do this work, you find your people. I spent ten years at a small liberal arts college where I was well supported, earning grant after grant that a more elite institution wouldn't have given me. I was able to carve my own path. The same is true in the larger research community. I've found organizations and conferences that support this kind of work, and as a result I'm a part of a true, global community of scholars. Life is short. It's best not to worry too much about resistance. Forge ahead. You won't be alone for long.

Q5. Do you believe that all research topics lend themselves well to the conduction of public scholarship?

Yes. Now that doesn't mean it's not more obvious in some cases than in others, but I believe if a researcher or research team is interested in sharing their work with relevant stakeholders outside of the academy, it's always possible.

Q6. Is it necessary for a public scholar to have access to large amounts of resources like money and time?

Money, no; time, well, that depends on your goals. One of the great things about doing public scholarship is that any researcher can do it from a financial perspective. There are many low or no-cost platforms online through which you can build your identity and audience. For example, social media is a great way to share your work. There's no cost to starting social media accounts. Even when you begin professional or community pages on Facebook, for example, there's no cost. It's true that there are strategies some people use to help build their audience that do come with a price-tag, such as sponsoring posts on Facebook, but you needn't do this to share your work on the platform, and if you are able to make some kind of financial investment, the size of that investment is up to you. There are also many tools available online to start your own blogs or contribute to established blogs. And contrary to most traditional academic writing, you may even get paid for your writing. Media outlets often pay freelance writers for op-eds and articles. Now there are some things that public scholars may try in order to boost their profile, such as hiring a publicist, but most do not do this, nor do I think it's necessary. Time is trickier. It really depends on the volume of public scholarship you want to produce and how much you do to promote it. For example, doing an interview for radio or a blog doesn't take that much time. But if you want your audience to hear/see it, you may need to spend some time sharing it in your network via social media or email. Things need a push to pick up steam online. Developing a presence on social media, for example, so that you have an interested audience with whom to share your efforts, requires time. Now whether that's minutes or hours a day depends entirely on you. Likewise, I've written novels grounded in my sociological research, intended for public audiences. Writing one of those novels takes more or less the same amount of time as writing a non-fiction academic book. The difference is in the promotion. With academic books, authors rarely do much to promote the work. There's a myth that academic books don't sell, so there's no point in trying. That's a whole different discussion. But when you're writing a book for a wider audience, you want to move copies, so you need to devote time and energy to promoting the book. That takes time, but you get so much more out of your work.

Q7. In your position as editor, you have come across many examples of public scholarship. Can you share a couple of examples of projects that have really left a mark on you?

Oh, there are so many. Years ago, a wonderful playwright, Mary E. Weems, sent me her short play titled *Meat*, which is about multiple Black women who were murdered. It was so powerful, it stayed with me for years. When I had the ability to do so, I published a collection of Weems's work titled *Blackeyed: Plays and Monologues*. *Meat* is the final piece in the book and has been widely acclaimed. You can see the pieces that have impacted me the most by the books I've chosen to publish in the *Social Fictions* series that I created and edit for Brill-Sense. We exclusively publish novels, plays, and collections of short stories and poetry grounded in scholarly research. I've also cited many examples in my book *Method Meets Art*. For example, I've always been drawn to film. *Rufus Stone*, a short film created and executive-produced by scholar Kip Jones and scripted by Josh Appignanesi, is one of my favorites. It's based on a three-year research study and explores life as a gay man in rural England. It follows Rufus, a young man who is outed and ultimately leaves his village, to return 50 years later to confront the past and present. Super powerful, and it really shows that with the right team and attention to detail, scholars can create great art. *The Hidden Face of Suicide*, by creative arts therapist Yehudit Silverman, is another standout film. It explores the experience of having a loved one who committed suicide. It's a tough watch, but also inspirational. It's not connected to my work as an editor, but I'm also a big fan of well-written blogs. You have to read popular writing in order to write it. One of my favorites is the Crunk Feminist Collective, which is a group of scholar-activists that identify as Hip-Hop Generation feminists. Their blogs contribute to many important dialogs. Robin Boylorn, one of my all-time favorite writers, is a member of the collective. Her blogs always teach me something new about power and privilege.

Q8. Of all your work, which project do you feel has connected more meaningfully with a broad non-academic audience? Can you describe the work, explain what made it successful, and share some of the more significant responses it has sparked outside the academy?

My first novel, *Low-Fat Love*. No one knew I was writing it except for my partner. I honestly didn't even plan to publish it. The whole thing was born out of frustration. For nearly a decade, I had collected interviews with young women about their identities, including their romantic relationships and body-image struggles. Over and over again I heard stories of loneliness, self-esteem struggles, and shame for not being empowered in the ways they thought they ought to be. At the same time, I was teaching college courses about gender, popular culture, and sexuality. Students constantly shared their stories with me both inside and outside of class. Over time I came to see a common thread of what I eventually called "low-fat love," which refers to settling for less than we want and trying to pretend it's better than it is. The problem was that I couldn't offer advice to interviewees or students because it wasn't appropriate. Nor did I have anywhere to put my cumulative insights because journal articles are based on specific studies, not the insights that develop from our cumulative teaching, research, and life experiences. So when I was on a sabbatical, I started creative writing as a means of getting my thoughts out. Soon I realized I was writing a novel.

Low-Fat Love is set in New York City and follows two editors at a publishing house as they struggle with how they've settled in life and love. Ultimately, each woman is pushed to confront her own image of herself, exploring her insecurities, the stagnation in her life, her attraction to men who withhold their support, and her reasons for having settled for low-fat love. The novel is underscored by a commentary about female identity building and self-acceptance and how, too often, women become trapped in limited visions of themselves. Women's media is used as a signpost throughout the book in order to make visible the context in which women come to think of themselves as well as the men and women in their lives. In this respect, I was trying to offer a critical commentary about popular culture and the social construction of femininity. *Low-Fat Love* suggests women seek new ways to see so that they are not dependent on male approval and will value themselves, confront their self-esteem issues, and reject degrading relationships.

Unlike anything I'd written before, the book has been widely read in college courses as a springboard for reflection *and* had a wide popular audience. But it's the nature of the response that's really moved and taught me. After the novel came out, I was flooded with emails and notes from readers. Everywhere I went professionally, people wanted to grab a minute with me to respond to the book. People stood in hallways at conferences or universities or waited in line at signings to whisper their most intimate stories to me. Readers have told me their own stories of low-fat love. They've shared their personal experiences with toxic relationships, alcoholism, domestic violence, sexual assault, loneliness, poor body image, and depression. Even friends have confided things to me after reading the book. The book brought me closer to people, both friends and strangers, which is interesting because the characters are all disconnected and suffer in isolation. What's hit me the hardest is that some readers or friends of readers have emailed me to tell me they were suicidal and the book pulled them off the ledge. There are no words to describe how humbling that is.

I also frequently hear people using the term "low-fat love." On social media I see people say things like, "don't settle for low-fat love." It's really remarkable how much the novel format enabled my research to develop wings. Due to demand from readers, we put out an anniversary edition a few years ago that includes an afterword and Q&A with me, answering the questions I'm most frequently asked. I still regularly receive emails about the book, and no matter what I'm talking about with the media, I'm usually asked about it. As for what made it successful, I think the characters' struggles resonated. It's pretty raw and I think that's why it struck a chord. My favorite line in the book is about the protagonist, and it reads, "Prilly lived in between who she was and who she wanted to be." I think a lot of people relate to that. I also think when I released the novel I was also releasing the idea of "social fiction" and that was new in the academy so it garnered some curiosity. To be perfectly honest, it's my least favorite of my novels. I've always said it's a mediocre novel and the weakest of my novels from a writing perspective. I hope that inspires others to try this kind of work. You don't have to be the best novelist or best whatever kind of writer. Honesty cuts through, and a mediocre novel, play, or blog is likely to be more enjoyable and memorable than any journal article.

Q9. What advice would you have for other scholars interested in reaching a broad audience through their writing?

Practice. Writing for or speaking to non-academic audiences requires a very different skill set than what many academics are accustomed to. If you want to write blogs or op-eds, start by reading a lot. Ask yourself some questions. What structures do writers use? What stylistically resonates with me? What do I enjoy reading? While you immerse yourself in different examples of public writing, start practicing. Develop a writing discipline. Devote X amount of time every day, or X number of days per week, to practicing. You don't need to publish these early works. The idea is to get used to the form and develop your voice. Like everything else, you get better the more you do. I've found that every form my public outreach has taken—op-eds, blogs, radio, fiction, media interviews—has improved my writing across genres, including traditional academic writing.

Beyond working on your craft, do a real gut-check with yourself. Think of this as emotional preparation. Most academics aren't used to having their work read or having to deal all that much with those who cite their work. Academic researchers are generally anonymous. Going public is a totally different experience. When you engage in public scholarship, you're likely to reach a larger audience, and there's likely to be a swift response. The feedback is immediate. When you put your work out there, you have no idea what you'll get back. Whether it's nasty comments on a blog or harsh reviews on Amazon, it can be hurtful, and it can feel quite personal. You need to make sure you're ready for it. You won't be low-profile anymore. Regardless of the size of your audience, you will have an audience, and you'll develop an identity or persona in their eyes. So make sure you're up for it. Remember, the point of going public is to make an impact, but you can't control exactly what that will be. Develop your own relationship with your work, one that's not dependent on external judgment, so that when you release it, you're at peace with it, come what may.

4 Beyond representation

I have always found ethnographies appealing because, among many other reasons, they are such a pleasure to read. Reading ethnographies (monographs much more so than articles) can be a little like reading novels or creative non-fiction. Ethnographies are not the product of fantasy, but just like creative non-fiction, they are often characterized by fully developed characters, interesting plots, a clear sense of place and time, and intimacy and emotion.

Many ethnographers deeply enjoy writing. As we saw in Chapter 3, public ethnographers in particular are very concerned with crafting writings that are sensitive to good prose—writings that bear the imprint of personal, embodied, and situated authorship. Not all ethnographies, however, are particularly nice to read. This is not always ethnographers' own fault. At times, ethnographers (students in particular) are openly discouraged from deviating from the neutral and impersonal voice typical of scientific writing and are dissuaded from writing narratively and passionately. Ethnographies that are too pretty to read, the old argument goes, are hard to take seriously because research loses its scientific value when it becomes concerned with form over content.

One of the many counterarguments that ethnographers can adopt in order to defend themselves from such criticism hinges on the more-than-representational value of ethnography as a way of knowing. Non-representational or more-than-representational theory (e.g. see Thrift 2008) is an influential contemporary social theory based on the idea that our understanding of the world need not be limited to realist principles of mimesis and correspondence. A more-than-representational view of the lifeworld does more than just "report." Whereas realist ethnography (Adler and Adler 2008) more-or-less posits the representation of research subjects as a faithful rendition of the world "as is," non-representational ethnographers consider their work to be impressionistic and inevitably creative, and even though they are inspired by their lived experiences in the field, they do not claim to be able, or even interested, in reporting on those in a naively faithful, impersonal, neutral, or reliable manner.

Non-representational ethnographic styles strive to animate rather than simply mimic, to rupture rather than merely take account, to evoke rather than just report, and to reverberate instead of more modestly resonating, in this sense offering a true "escape from the established academic habit of striving to uncover meanings and values that apparently await our discovery, interpretation, judgement and ultimate representation" (Lorimer 2005: 84). Now, I am not at all arguing that in order to be public, an ethnography needs to adopt a more-than-representational style. Much more modestly, I am simply proposing that by considering ways to go beyond traditional concerns with representation, ethnographers can be more aware of the narrative and affective dimensions of their material and thus can become more confident in rebuking realist critiques. More-than-representational ideas, in other words, can serve as useful practical tools to actualize the rhetorical potential of ethnographic work as well as useful epistemological tools to differentiate ethnography from foundationalist and realist research once and for all.

In this chapter, I focus on five ways in which non-representational theoretical ideas can inform ethnographic writing. These strategies correspond to five qualities of more-than-representational research in general: vitality, performativity, corporeality, sensuality, and mobility. This is not an exhaustive list; there are many other important qualities of more-than-representational research. These five qualities are non-mutually exclusive and clearly subject to varying definitional interpretations and applications subject to all the disagreements typical of a constantly evolving style (Anderson and Harrison 2010; Vannini 2015a). For better or for worse, these five qualities are simply the outcomes of my informed but highly subjective reading of the last ten years of non-representational ethnographic research studies. I will illustrate these qualities with a few examples from the writing of some authors I admire.

Doing research non-representationally

Before we get to the five qualities I mentioned, let us briefly review the key ideas behind non-representational epistemology, drawing from both recent theoretical and methodological writings. Given the limited space in this chapter, I will need to be concise, and so I invite the interested reader to consult a book on the subject that I edited recently (Vannini 2015b).

Non-representational or more-than-representational theory calls for "diverse work that seeks to better cope with our self-evidently more-than-human, more-than-textual, multisensual worlds" (Lorimer 2005: 83). Calling for resolutely experimental research that eclectically synthesizes the cultural sciences with philosophy, the arts, and humanities, non-representational theory (not unlike ethnography) aims to be an interpretive "supplement to the ordinary, a sacrament for the everyday, a hymn to the superfluous" (Thrift 2008: 2). Though it may focus on a variety of subjects, non-representational research is most ideal for the analysis of events, practices, assemblages, affective atmospheres, and the backgrounds of everyday life against which relations unfold in their myriad potentials.

Non-representational research emphasizes the fleeting, viscous, lively, embodied, material, more-than-human, pre-cognitive, non-discursive dimensions of spatially and temporally complex lifeworlds (Anderson and Harrison 2010; Vannini 2015b). Non-representational ethnography attempts to grapple with the challenge of sharing empirical narratives that make sense—or that, in other words, are inspired by and feel coherent with the world as encountered—while simultaneously underscoring the situatedness, partiality, contingency, and creativity of that sense-making. Arguably, one flippant way of putting it might be to quip that non-representational ethnography does not represent but instead "flirts" with reality (Crouch 2010: 17).

Even though there are no magic ingredients for an "authentic" non-representational ethnography recipe, several points of agreement amongst non-representational writers can be gleaned. For starters, as Allan Latham (2003) argues, the point of departure must be a fight against methodological *timidity*. Timidity is difficult to define but easy to recognize. Nigel Thrift (2003: 3), for example, finds the most prototypical expressions of timidity in the interview and ethnographic data "nicely packaged up in a few supposedly illustrative quotations" that are commonly displayed in qualitative research articles and more broadly in the "know and tell" (Thrift 2004: 81) mode typical of traditional qualitative research. To this effect, J. D. Dewsbury (2009: 324) calls for the disruption of research habits and for novel expressions of creativity. For him, the key to combating timidity lies in making research more performative. This does not necessarily mean staging research and acting out findings in a theater but in striving to find inspiration in the arts, in the poetics of embodied living, in enacting the expressive and impressive potentials of social-scientific knowledge, in taking dedicated risks, in exercising passion, and in finding ways to re-configure thinking, sensing, and presenting by emphasizing the singular powers of action, locution, and thought.

New styles can draw inspiration from the sensuous, embodied, "non-cognitive, preintentional, and commonsensical" (Latham 2003b: 2008) practices of everyday life, as these are laden with creativity and possibility. In the context of human geography, Latham (2003b: 2000) writes:

> I want to suggest that, rather than ditching the methodological skills that human geography has so painfully accumulated, we should work through how we can imbue traditional research methodologies with a sense of the creative, the practical, and being with practice-ness that Thrift is seeking. Pushed in the appropriate direction there is no reason why these methods cannot be made to dance a little.

To "dance a little" may entail a greater focus on events, affective states, the unsaid, and the incompleteness and openness of everyday performances. The key distinction of this approach is that—in the words of Dewsbury (2009)—it relishes the failures of knowledge. Erin Manning (2015), for example, incites researchers to embrace experimentation, to view the impossibility of empirical research as a creative opportunity (rather than a damming condition), to unsettle the systematicity of procedure, to reconfigure (rather than mimic) the lifeworld, and, in sum, to learn to fail—to fail better.

Non-representational ethnography engages in representation, yes, but rather than pretending to represent faithfully, it attempts to engage in a type of representation that can be called *animation*. By "animating" lifeworlds, non-representational ethnographic styles aim to enliven, render, rupture, and re-imagine, and to generate possibilities for fabulation. In so doing, non-representational styles become entangled in relations and objects as a way of reconfiguring our imagination of the lifeworld. So, let us now take a look at five ways in which this can be achieved.

Vitality

Everyday life is a mix of taken-for-granted realities, habit, and routine as well as impulse, novelty, and vivaciousness. Realist representational research typically downplays the latter characteristics and marginalizes them as exceptions to an ordered world—thus portraying social existence through the lenses of structure, rational behavior, politico-economic causation, cognitive planning, instrumental interaction, and mechanistic predictability. Instead, non-representational research renders the liveliness of everyday interaction through methodological strategies that animate, rather than deaden, the qualities of the relations among people, objects, organic matter, animals, and their natural and built environments. In other words, non-representational ethnographies aim to be as full of vitality as the lifeworlds they endeavor to animate.

Vitalist approaches argue that there is an exceptional quality to life: a certain impetuous ardor possessed by both inanimate and animate beings (Fraser et al. 2005) which makes life unexplainable by deterministic laws of prediction. As a result, non-representational ethnographies are restless, rich with verve and brio, constantly on the move, forever becoming something else—something originally unplanned. This is something that demands and fosters a new vitalist "material imagination," something that re-imagines both human and "non-human materialities as animated by dynamic and lively capacities to affect change and to participate in political life" (Richardson-Ngwenya 2004: 294). Non-representational ethnographers are therefore less interested in coding textual data to give rise to explanatory descriptive categories than they are in acknowledging the very limitations of their own understanding of the world and in the enchanting processes through which life constantly mystifies us.

The idea of vitality "makes a particular sort of demand on the researcher to attend to the complexity and indeterminacy of things in the world" (Greenhough 2010: 39), and non-representational ethnographers therefore view fieldwork encounters as exceeding representation and explanation: as events through which they and their informants make and remake their lifeworlds through their changing positions and relations (Greenhough 2010). This is the case, for example, with the "mysterious effect" (Saldanha 2005: 707) of so-called "inanimate" things like music. In Saldanha's analysis of the trance scene in Goa, music "changes people and circumstances, and it changes different people in different ways, according to differences in race, gender, and class" (Saldanha 2005: 707). Similarly, things like walls, stairways, and roof gaps—as depicted in Saville's (2008) study of parkour—"become real" when methods focus on how people can move with—not on or through, but "with"—material objects. A vitalist ethnography, in short, is an ethnography pulled and pushed by a sense of wonder and awe with a world that is forever escaping, and yet seductively demanding, our comprehension.

Performativity

Non-representational ethnography zeroes in on what actors *do*, as much as what they attempt to do and fail to do. This focus on action emphasizes the importance of ritualized performances, habitual and non-habitual behaviors, play, and the various scripted and unscripted, uncertain, and unsuccessful doings of which everyday life is made, no matter how seemingly mundane or unimportant. Performativity does not mean, exclusively, that life is a stage—in the dramaturgic, Goffmanian sense. Non-representational ethnographers are not necessarily interested in going behind the "masks" the subjects wear or in digging out authentic meanings hidden behind the stage. While interaction at times does have dramatic qualities, the idea of performativity underlines the broader relevance of concerted actions—or events—in our mundane existence and their fragility and, at times, inscrutability.

Take, for instance, Laurier and Philo's (2006) "undefined investigation" of a simple passing encounter in an urban café. By positing a passing encounter as a singular event situated at the faultline of representational language and the unspeakable impasses and silences of everyday unwriteable and unrepresentable interaction, Laurier and Philo find that the performative nature of ordinary speech challenges non-representational researchers to inhabit an aporetic space marked by doubt and possibility. Or consider how in Rose's (2010) ethnography of "New Age" pilgrims on a visit to Egypt, identity is not performed, or shown off, as something people have in order to display to others for validation. Identity, instead, is something *given*, something primordially and somehow mysteriously cast upon a subject by voices calling from the outside. Ethnography then, in this case, is not so much undertaken to explain but rather to make audible silences and invisible forces, to perform "a presence that presents itself as an absence, a nagging question, a distant calling whose contours remain wholly obscure" (Rose 2010: 196).

Being sensitive to the quality of performativity means tuning in to the eventness of the world (Latham 2003a), taking a witness stance to the unfolding of situated action (Dewsbury 2003), and being open to the unsettling co-presence of bodies affecting each other in time–space (Thrift 2003; Wood 2012). An ethnographic attention to performance, then, is an attention to identity performances, border-crossings, processes, contingencies, struggles, passions, improvisations, shifting subjectivities, and practices of all kinds. This is not the same as saying that non-representational ethnographies are performances. Performance ethnography is a distinct research strategy with unique modalities of expression that are not typically accommodated by the written page. Yet, non-representational ethnographies attempt to be performative in style by privileging "particular, participatory, dynamic, intimate, precarious, embodied experience grounded in historical processes, contingency, and ideology" and by "tak[ing] as both its subject matter and method the experiencing body situated in time, place, and history" (Conquergood 1990: 187).

Corporeality

Our presence in the world is embodied. Non-representational ethnographic research begins from the researcher's body as the key instrument for knowing, sensing, feeling, and relating to others and the self. Passions, orientations, moods, emotions, sentiments, sensations, dispositions, colors, sizes, shapes, and skills work as the vital fluids enlivening all relations in which ethnographic relations are entangled. From fatigue to enthusiasm, melancholia to keenness, pain to enchantment, non-representational ethnographic research is affected by bodies' capacity to affect the world and their capacity to be affected by it.

Affect, of course, is a central topic in non-representational scholarship (Thrift 2008). But to say that non-representational ethnography focuses on affect as a subject of research is not the same as to suggest that affect is a medium through which ethnographic research unfolds. Put in other words, it is not enough for non-representational ethnography to be about affect; it must also be affective. One of the most affective writers, I find, is anthropologist Kathleen Stewart. Stewart writes from the heart, from her embodied presence in the field, from being entangled in the very world she re-creates anew with her words. Her seemingly random sketches of everyday life in the United States "loosen the formal narratives ... and the heavy presumptions of a proper and automatic relationship between thinking subject, object, and world" (Stewart 2011: 445). Her ethnographic narratives weave theory and empirical material seamlessly, tying together strands of observation and interpretation. Affect, in her pages, comes to life through conceptual pauses as much as through descriptive interventions. Her stories affect us carnally, employing theory not as a cognitive weapon but as a touching composition of what is happening, what is hanging in the air. These are rare, beautiful rhetorical strategies also employed by other non-representational writers (see Lorimer and Wylie 2010; Wylie 2002) who are equally keen on using powerful storytelling to create emotional openings and move readers to feel something, rather than just think about it.

The corporeality of non-representational work most often comes through in ethnographies focused on body-centered activities that require the performance of skill, temporal sensitivity (e.g. rhythm), and kinesthetic awareness (e.g. choreographed movement). For example, Simpson's (2008) rhythmanalysis of street performance allows the reader to come to terms with bodies taking place through live, dramatically intense physical performances. Rhythmic considerations are also at the center of Reville's (2004) autoethnographic notes on the practice of French folk music. Reville's attention to the corporeality of music as a carnal experience unfolding through space—rather than, say, a genre or a text—reveals "the impact of rhythm, timbre, and melody on the body, highlighting the ways in which the physical practice of music shapes its aesthetic forms and social spaces" (Reville 2004: 202).

Sensuality

Lifeworlds are endowed with a fleeting qualitative immediacy that individuals encounter through embodied, practical, meaningful, sensory orientations

(Ingold 2011). These orientations are intentional but not always reflexive in a cognitive way. Non-representational ethnographies underline the not-necessarily-reflexive sensory dimensions of experience by paying attention to the perceptual dimensions of our actions and the habituated and routine nature of everyday existence. In doing so, they engage in sensuous scholarship: research about the senses, through the senses, and for the senses (Vannini, Waskul, and Gottschalk 2011). Sensuous scholarship invites us to appreciate the meaningfulness of our sensory experience of the world, the importance of the skilled practices through which we make sense of the lifeworld through our senses, and the value of the evocativeness of our strategies of animation (Stoller 1997).

The sensuality of non-representational ethnographies depends on a re-awakened scholarly body: a body "stiffened from long sleep in the background of scholarly life" that now "yearns to exercise its muscles" and "aches to restore its sensibilities" (Stoller 1997: xi–xii) by opposing the dullness of overly analytic, formal, anonymous, and unimaginative scholarship. In "Surfaces and Slopes," for example, Hayden Lorimer (2012) relies on a poetic essay memoir to describe the sensory work of running as an exploration of differently textured terrains and trails. In this beautiful essay, Lorimer speaks through the feet, as it were, allowing the thick carnal description to take precedence over any sort of theorizing, lengthy introductions, and detached conclusions. Lorimer's delightful approach is as exemplary in its more-than-representational richness as it is rare—for much too often, sensuous writing is still book-ended by the prescriptions of formal and traditional scholarship.

It seems as though sensuous geographers who aren't running are walking. The slow rhythms of walking, arguably, allow for ethnographies that are sensitive to spatial details and to the rhythmic pauses, stops, and re-starts of sensuous observation and reflection. In the case of Morris (2011), darkness goes a long way too. In her fieldwork on the Isle of Skye, Morris's own body, as well as the bodies of the participants in *The Storr* art installation, are forced to come to terms with their dark surroundings as they walk in the woods at night. Morris's writing reveals the unsettling character of the experience, designed to lessen the ocularcentricity of landscape and to awaken the other senses. Hill (2013) also chose to walk alongside other people. While focusing on understanding how legacies of the past generate affective registers capable of evoking and unsettling senses of place and time, Hill builds a narrative of the past "that attends to the discursive and embodied conditions of its existence in the present" and to "highlight the matter that brings forth memories," (2013: 385) skilfully blurring the boundaries between the present and absent as sensed.

Mobility

Fieldwork generally entails travel, and ethnography is in the end, perhaps, a lot like travel writing. Mobile ethnographies have thus begun to make sense of the itinerant and kinaesthetic aspects of fieldwork and to portray ethnographic work as happening on the move (Buscher et al. 2010). Non-representational ethnography is particularly well equipped to handle the kinetic dimensions of fieldwork. Drawing attention to movement is important not only because it evokes the perambulations of ethnographers in all their vicissitudes and complex logistical relations but also because doing so situates fieldwork in the concrete time–spaces that ethnographers actually inhabit. In fact, all fieldwork unfolds in space and time, and as a result, ethnographies are positionings, orientations, and *travails* always busy with securing the loss of old habits and coming to terms with being out of place. "Inhabiting space," like ethnography, "is both about finding our way and how we come to feel at home" (Simonsen 2013: 16). Like all forms of travel, therefore, non-representational fieldwork engages us—as practitioners and audiences—in a constant re-negotiation of difference and repetition, of the ordinary and unfamiliar.

Building on Tim Ingold's (2011) ideas on movement, we might then characterize non-representational ethnography as a practice of *wayfaring*. From this perspective, ethnographic journeys are not planned transitions from the office to the field site but wanderings through which movement speaks. These wanderings are also wonderings that seek out the interweaving storylines binding self, others, places, and times—lines that, just like ethnographic travel, are dynamic and unpredictable, with no clear roots or obvious boundaries or ends. Through journeying as storytelling, non-representational ethnographers take storylines in flight, out for a walk, along on a paddle, forming "knot[s] tied from multiple and interlaced strands of movement and growth" (Ingold 2007: 75).

Not everything that is moored is immobile. Stewart's (2014) recent examination of road registers animates the American road as "a registering form in which intensities lodged in institutional effects and lived affects, materialities and dreamworlds, differences and energies, reach a point of expressivity and become legible" (2014: 549). Stewart's masterful writing achieves this effect via experimental snapshots taken with varying rhythms, tones, and orientations. Sliding away from realism entirely, and toward what she calls *creative non-fiction* or *fictocritical*, Stewart's writing slows down and speeds up, then decelerates and accelerates again, enlivening a feeling of being on the road.

Another example of rich kinaesthetic animation comes from, once again, Hayden Lorimer and John Wylie (2010) as part of a unique trek the two undertook en route to Aberystwyth, being at times apart and at times together, and setting out from different points. Their blended narrative, denuded of the compartments typically comprising the organization of academic papers, unfolds by location—with coordinates setting the pace of their tale and the various sections of their writing. More radically experimental than most, Lorimer and Wylie's writing utilizes short sentences that give a sense of their economy of breath, echoing the brief sounds felt in the landscape, as much as the quiet through which they moved.

I fully realize that this chapter has been characterized by a high degree of abstraction. Everything that I said about non-representational or more-than-representational ethnography has been more like a series of hints than a list of prescriptions. Clearly, I do not like to prescribe what to do and how to do it, and prescriptions make especially little sense in the context of an approach that attends to be experimental. However, I am a pragmatic person as well, and I recognize the value of a few useful ... orientations, for lack of a better word. Therefore, while I end this chapter and Part I of this book here, I will pick up the thread of non-representational style once again later in this volume and provide more clarity and more examples.

Part II

Part II

5 Losing bad habits

There are many academics around the world who are truly personally invested in writing well as a way of building relations with readers, research participants, students, and peers. Academic writing as an institution, however, has traditionally been less about relationship building and more about career building. This may sound unduly harsh, but do consider this: if we academics wished for our research to truly inspire and provoke change, wouldn't we would make serious and sustained efforts to publish our work in widely distributed books, magazines, and newspapers rather than locking it in journals inaccessible to the public or in expensive books? If we sincerely wanted our books to matter to wide audiences, wouldn't we put as much effort into their publicity life cycles as we do before we hand them off to a copy editor? And if we cared more about our audiences, wouldn't all our curriculum vitaes proudly display measures of research impact, sales statistics, and reader responses?

The chapters included in Part II of this book focus on the mechanics of good writing. All of the chapters in this part of the book contain useful and practical information that should be of value to both students and professional scholars interested in honing their public ethnography writing skills. Most of this material should be familiar to anyone versed in creative non-fiction or—in all honesty—in the basics of good writing. In fact, public ethnography does not demand any particular or unique writing styles. There are public ethnographers who write introspectively and others who write reflexively yet without becoming the protagonists of their own work. There are public ethnographers who prefer to write well-developed narratives and others who trade performativity for a more factual, investigative style. Some are poetic whereas others are prosaic. Regardless of the styles they may adopt, public ethnographers invariably aim to write clearly and passionately, striving to respect their field tales by foregrounding them over citations of research literature and theory.

Writing well, for the most part, means writing simply and clearly—and this is a task that does not demand any kind of formidable talent. In this part of the book, I will focus on developing a few rhetorical strategies that can result in clear, powerful, engaging writing, but before we go much further, I want us to engage in a little bit of un-learning. Years of undergraduate and graduate education, reinforced for some of us by more years in the hallways of professional academia, have caused us to develop a lot of bad habits. Thanks to the negative reinforcement coming from conservative graduate committees and blind reviewers, we have learned to write dispassionately, anonymously, formally, and predictably. We are told there are expectations we should never violate and that there are ways of writing that make us look like journalists or novelists (god forbid!). We are rewarded for publishing in obscure periodicals that only a few readers can access or understand, and for authoring impossibly expensive books whose main value is determined by the historical prestige of their publishing press. All of these habits are rooted pretty deeply within us. So, let us begin with a little bit of un-learning first.

The eleven bad habits of highly successful academic writers

In spite of continued appeals by funding bodies, universities, and non-academy-based professional organizations to engage in knowledge mobilization, knowledge transfer, or knowledge exchange, few academic researchers have made convincing and sustained efforts to dismantle the existing dominant power architecture, which orders and organizes professional scholarly merit hierarchies along the lines of publication prestige rather than on the basis of readership size or publication impact. Hitherto, I have highlighted why academics should care to popularize their research through publication, film, and other modes. In this section, I wish to speak about some of the most common limitations of academic writing, ranging from ineffective distribution and opaque compositional style to an insistence on aligning subject matter with disciplinary and sub-disciplinary concerns and agendas rather than with elements of the dominant zeitgeist. While the list below is not exhaustive, I surmise that attention to the principles underlying these limitations will instill the impression that clear writing is not unattainable and that a few modifications to standard academic operating procedures will result in advancement of our shared collective goals of knowledge translation and knowledge democratization and, ipso facto, in cultural transformation and social amelioration.

Nice paragraph, eh? That paragraph is a clear example of what's wrong with academic writing. Ironically, you probably understood everything written in that paragraph and, being so accustomed to jargon-filled writing as we all are, you might even have breezed right through it, finding little unusual or intolerable about it. And herein lies the first problem with academic writing: its pomposity. Pompous writing makes use of big words when simple ones will suffice. Pompous writing makes things sound heavy, serious, and formal. Good writing, on the other hand, is unpretentious. It uses effective and clear words: words that are inclusive rather than exclusive; words that clarify, rather than confuse. It uses descriptive prose, has a non-formal style, and avoids jargon. Good writing employs short sentences, sentences that are easy to remember because they don't run on for four or five lines. Good writing makes a compelling and a memorable point. Then it stops and moves on.

For the second habit of bad academic writing, I am going to talk about how bad academic writing is chock full of annoying and pedantic *signposting*. Let us define signposting as the tendency to announce what is about to be said next, or what has just been said, in a patronizing attempt to guide readers in order to make sure they do not get lost. We all do it. Sometimes we don't even realize we're doing it. But you can see how annoying it is when we constantly hold readers by the hand. For example, in the definition I have given above, I provided you with an abstract understanding of signposting. I now would like to provide you with tangible examples of where signposting can be found in academic writing. Signposting can be found in introductory chapters; at the beginning and end of every section and sub-section; in summaries and conclusions. In the sentence you just read, I gave you the examples I promised I would give you. In the next sentence, I am going to conclude my argument. In this paragraph, I have shown you how annoying and unnecessary signposting is.

The third habit of bad academic writing: predictable organization. As readers of academic research, we are all quite lazy sometimes and we don't want to make too much of an effort to look for information. Or maybe we are not lazy; we are always in a hurry, and so it helps us when the information we consume comes in a predictable format. Regardless, the organization of typical academic writing is so predictable that, as authors, we have developed the habit of taking organizational conventions as law. Thus, we begin with introductions that lay out the context for our work and spell out its significance. Next, we situate research within a body of theoretical and substantive knowledge. Subsequently, we anticipate our conclusions and then we move on to engaging in more prefacing: more context, more abstract information, more background on procedures, and so on. Then the data arrive, a long time after they have been prefaced and introduced, contextualized, and justified. Then come analysis and conclusion, in that order. Such predictable organization is extremely common in journals, but even ethnographic books tend to sandwich empirical material between the thick opening and closing layers of the same introductory and conclusive matter we find in journals. But why? Do good stories—think of good novels and films—require long and pedantic introductions? Do they require summaries at the end? Would we pay money to go to the movies or read novels if they were all organized exactly the same way? What exactly do we have to lose by experimenting with different organizational formats?

The fourth bad habit I want to list is the fetishism of citations. Citing is important because it recognizes our intellectual debt to the people whose ideas have influenced us. There is nothing wrong with that, especially if the citations don't get in the way of the flow of a sentence. But often citations serve other, less lofty, purposes. We cite people who might end up being our blind reviewers—so they don't get upset with us for not citing them. We cite the people that everybody else cites because they are popular at the moment. We cite a specific journal or book publisher because we want to inflate its citation index or because we want to advertise our publishers and our own work. We cite because doing so gives us a collective identity and a sense of membership in a private club. And we cite because we talk too much and so we run out of space to complete our arguments. However, citations (especially when they consist of long strings of authors, years, and pages in the middle of a long sentence, therefore making that sentence unbearably long and hard to follow, just like this one) are unpleasant to read and often exclusive in nature since not everyone has access to a university library that provides access to expensive journals and books.

The fifth cardinal sin of academic writing is lack of narrative. Stories draw readers into a book and compel them to turn the pages. With their beginning, middle, and end points, stories give writing order and structural purpose, show action and reaction, and highlight the motives, hopes, and struggles of human conduct and ambition. Not enough academic writers are interested in telling stories. What seems to matter more is presenting arguments and generating theoretical concepts. Though arguments are important, they are forgettable without stories that underline why they matter. The abstract nature of an argument without a narrative produces writing that is dispassionate, anonymous, placeless, and timeless. It makes our work easy to forget and difficult to relate to. And it is true that not every research project yields clear and compelling narratives. But isn't the very process of doing research a story? Why take narrative out of what we researchers do?

Stories need characters. Ethnographers, of all people, should know this, but much too often, ethnographies—and this is the sixth bad habit—are just as faceless and as anonymous as other types of research. A public ethnography should strive to paint complex, nuanced, captivating portraits of its protagonists. These portraits should reveal the humanity of people: their goals and aspirations, their hopes and fears, their character and mannerisms, their appearance and idiosyncrasies. Like a good novel, a public ethnography should be personable and intimate. Nothing gets in the way of good character development more than some of the conventions of qualitative research regarding the anonymization of people. I am referring to the way research participants are reduced to lame fictitious names, the way they are so often turned into bracketed demographic variables that simply "give us good quotes" (Male, 34) or—even worse—into strings of codes and dates spat out by data-coding software (Participant #27, F, 4/10/2017). If we must use fictitious names to appease overzealous institutional review boards, fine, so be it; but let us not allow that obstacle to prevent us from describing Jane Doe's voice timbre, or the way she walks when she feels anxious, or the way she seemed to look away every time we asked her about her mother. Let us lose the habit of treating people as nothing but anonymous sources of data awaiting thematic analysis.

Seventh: one of the consequences of our fascination with argumentation at the expense of narration is our collective idolization of theoretical writing. There is nothing wrong with theory. We need theory because it is an invaluable tool to inform our understanding and imagination. But theory is often invasive. We all know it is easier to get cited for advancing theory, generating a new concept, or outlining an original analytical process than it is to be cited for telling a good story, so we sneak theory into everything. In this way, the value of our research becomes less about what we have found and more about the subservient role our empirical material plays in the advancement of theory. This makes undeveloped stories feel even worse. Theoretical excesses tend to objectify our research informants by turning their experiences and perspectives into mere vessels for conceptual development. Theory deadens stories by turning them into "cases" full of abstractions and generalizations. Theoretical argumentations also say a lot about us as writers: they show our readers that we are self-assured and disconnected know-it-alls with very little curiosity, sense of wonder, or enchantment about the lifeworld we study—the lifeworlds into which they have let us.

For my eighth point, I want to pick up a fight with our shyness. Authorship, even in the case of some good ethnographic research, is too often impersonal. We as researchers have the habit of hiding under the pretense that we ourselves do not matter. As a result, our texts often bear no imprint of our existence. As we become faceless, our style of doing research, our goals and passions, our moods and emotions, our character and mannerisms get lost underneath our data and our analysis. Obviously, this is another one of my sweeping generalizations: more and more research, especially of the ethnographic kind, is highly reflexive and situated. Yet, reflexive research is still a minority. We still know too little about authors and how their situatedness shapes the knowledge they generate. I am not advocating that we all become autoethnographers, but I am suggesting that we can all safely situate ourselves a bit more in our own work because our readers can learn a lot about our research by relating to us and our points of view.

My next point is a very simple one. We can all lose this habit in a matter of seconds without trying hard at all. When we quote from interviews with our research participants, we are told by citation style guides to "keep short quotes" within a paragraph. Just like that. On the other hand, long quotes, excerpts of more than four lines of text,

> must be separated from the normal body of paragraph by way of indentation. Indentation can occur by way of the left—just like I am doing right now—or by way of both a margin on the left and one on the right. Different citation styles will demand left indentation, or indentation on both sides. Variations among citation style guides also exist with regard to the minimum number of lines subject to indentation; for some it will be three or more, whereas for others four or more lines.

Indentation is lame. It kills quotes. It kills them, and it puts them in a coffin in the middle of the page. I have tested my students several times on whether they read indented excerpts or not, and in the majority of cases, I have found that indentation seems to give readers an excuse to skip interview quotes. Possibly this is because we all read in a hurry, but more worryingly it is because indented excerpts from data are typically preceded by short summaries of what the excerpt is all about. At other times, excerpts succeed one another in a text simply because they are examples of the same point or theme. In this way, research participants quickly become tokens of the generality of their own experiences or viewpoints, and thus their interview excerpts work as skimmable (or skippable) exhibits of an argument the researcher has already made for us in quicker and more memorable takeaways. And that's how they die.

Tenth: poor academic writing is often generated by the demands of editors, publishers, and distribution networks that work to maximize profits from narrowly defined niche audiences confined to academia and, thus, solely academic ways of writing. Clearly, we academics owe a lot to university and commercial publishers that edit and sell our work; obviously there is a steady student and faculty demand for the products they provide. However, the academic publishing complex is notoriously inefficient at reaching the broader market via "trade" publishing. "Trade" publishers deal with a multitude of readers. In order to sell their products, they advertise books widely and strive to distribute them through retail stores that will sell them at competitive prices. In order to sell a single book to 10,000 readers, that book must be produced to meet the demands of a diverse and demanding market. Academic publishers, on the other hand, make most of their business by selling to university libraries and to instructors who use books as class resources that students must usually purchase. In order to sell 10,000 copies of a book, these publishers need to reach out to perhaps 1,000 library acquisition specialists and 100 instructors who, over a few years, will compel about 1,000 students to buy that book. It's easier to sell 100 copies to one person, academic publishers will often remark, than to sell one book each to 100 individuals. The reality, however, is that few academic books sell more than 1,000 copies. Between 300 and 500 copies is the more common sales volume. With that market size, profit can only be made if hardcover books are sold at high prices—$70, $80 and up—thus excluding most non-academic readers looking for a new book to buy, even if they are very intrigued by the subject.

The eleventh cardinal sin of bad writing is rooted in a common trait we academics have: we are geeks. Let's face it, we are. Being a geek has its merits: we're focused, informed, and persistent in pursuit of our interests. Yet, at times, our geeky interests can be incredibly esoteric. The fastidious fascination we have with our topics can be so specific, narrowly defined, and obsessively detail-oriented that few other people find our research as absorbing as we do. If we truly wished to have a broader audience than the few hundreds of academy-based readers we normally get, we should give greater consideration to aligning our work with whatever is timely, newsworthy, and relevant. Indeed, the first element that "sells" a pitch to a prospective publisher keen on reaching a broad audience is a "hot" topic, not a gap in the theoretical literature. I am not suggesting that we should all limit our attention to popular topics—far from it—but I want readers to be mindful of the fact that topic selection is a vital factor in the popularization of academic research—a fact we can all consider at least sometimes.

In this opening chapter of Part II of the book I have listed some bad habits of academic writing. In the next chapter I will ... wait ... I am signposting. Sorry. Habit.

6 Sensuous scholarship

Over the last ten years, sensuous scholarship has been growing steadily across the social sciences. *Sensuous scholarship* refers to research about the human senses, through the senses, and for the senses (Stoller 1984, 1989, 1997). Building on the interpretive and phenomenological legacy in the social sciences, sensuous scholarship asks us to recognize the meaningfulness of our sensory experience of the world, to understand the skillful activities through which we actively make and remake the world through our senses, and to develop evocative strategies of representation—in other words, to write and compose sensuously.

The roots of sensuous scholarship as an organized way of knowing and strategy of representation can be found in Stoller's seminal work on the Songhay of Niger and his subsequent reflections (1989, 1997). Disgusted, literally, by flavorless ethnographic writing as well as by his own initial inability—as a young ethnographer—to apprehend the field in its sensuous dimensions, Stoller found the need to write "ethnographies that combine the strengths of science with the rewards of the humanities" (1989: 9). By advocating a focus on the sounds, smells, tastes, textures, and sights of ethnography, Stoller argued for a radical empiricism that would "render our accounts of others more faithful to the realities of the field—accounts which will then be more, rather than less scientific" (1989: 9). Taking his narrative lead from a serving of bad sauce, Stoller explained how the taste of bad sauce in a situation in which it was maliciously prepared, and later vomited up by those to whom it was served, was not a mere colorful ethnographic curiosity. Important sensory events like that cannot be easily dismissed as meaningless incidents. Stoller found that the field worker's traditional preoccupation with "big" and important topics and deep-seated truths can cause her to miss those kinds of small incidents—like the taste of bad sauce—that have great potential for shedding light on the sensory basis of culture.

Stoller's solution is to generate sensuous scholarship: a new form of "impressionist and literary tale" (cf. Van Maanen 1984). Sensuous scholarship is tasteful (Stoller 1997) fieldwork about, through, and for the human senses. It is fieldwork *about* the senses because it attempts to focus on a much-neglected dimension of life: the realm of human sensations (challenging sight as a dominating epistemology in the West, Stoller incites scholars to uncover the nuances of *all* bodily sensations). It is fieldwork *through* the senses because it is the outcome of a re-awakened and reflexive scholarly body, a body "stiffened from long sleep in the background of scholarly life" that now "yearns to exercise its muscles" and "aches to restore its sensibilities" (Stoller 1997: xi–xii). And finally, it is fieldwork *for* the senses, a kind of research that opposes the dullness of overly analytic, overly theoretical, overly formal, anonymous, and unimaginative scholarship. As he argues, sensuous scholarship offers a "tasteful" or flavorful mediation of field experiences—through the written word or other modes—which occurs through mixing "an assortment of ingredients" such as "dialogue, description, metaphor, metonymy, synecdoche, irony" (1989: 32) as well as sensations, the power of imagination and enchantment, self-reflection, doubt, and failure. Unlike bad sauce, Stoller hopes that this dish will truly appeal to audiences' palates.

While visual ethnography and related visual methods are amongst the most popular offspring of the sensuous turn in scholarship, other strategies have made great advances as well. In sports studies, for example, Sparkes (2009) has led a movement challenging the traditional disembodied approach to the sporting experience. Through autoethnography, reflexive ethnography, sensuous writing, and other modes of representation, Sparkes has pushed for greater recognition of the roles sensations play "as part of a vibrant and multi-sensorial ethnographic project" (2009: 33). Amongst such other modes of representation are practices such as *soundwalking*, through which researchers tune their ears to the tonalities of the field and the auditory aspects of social interaction (e.g. see Adams 2009). More generally, walking has led to the discovery of the sensual properties of kinesthesis (e.g. Edensor 2007). Because sensuality is so essential to the embodied and emotional experiences of place, it is no accident that sensual scholarship has found fertile terrain in human geography, which has nurtured a growing interest in non-representational theory. In Chapter 8, I will discuss non-representational writing styles that can enhance sensuous writing. But for now, let us discuss a type of sensuous writing called the *somatic layered account*.

The somatic layered account

The word *sensuous* has a twofold meaning. The first refers to the senses, as in something that is about the senses. If this were the only meaning of the concept, classic (and traditionalist) works in the anthropology of the senses, like Howes (2003), and in the sociology of the senses, like Synnott (1993), would qualify as sensuous. But *sensuous* also denotes gratification of the senses. Sensuousness, therefore, is about appealing *through* the senses and *for* the senses as much as it is *about* the senses. This is an important qualification, as much of the literature on the senses is patently *not* sensuous enough. This bias partly results from professional socialization, as most social scientists are trained to write analytically and less so evocatively—as we already discussed in Chapter 5. But it also partly results from a problem of definition: most social scientists who wish to pass as sensuous scholars feel they must provide scholarly interpretation and conceptual arguments, and these rhetorical strategies inevitably displace sensuous description.

Because so little research about the senses is also through and for the senses, it can be asked whether sensuous scholarship is merely a chimera or even an oxymoron. Must social scientists interested in awakening the senses be limited to just writing *about* them? I do not believe so, and I maintain that sensuous scholarship is always going to be somewhat Janus-faced. On one side, it attempts to gratify the senses of its audiences, while on the other, it speaks to their "minds" through analysis and interpretation. Rather than selecting one side over the other or seeing the two sides as contradictory, I believe that the authentic complexity of sensuous scholarship can only be evoked through the dialectics of analysis and description. One strategy that allows us to accomplish this is the somatic layered account.

The word *somatic* refers to the soma, the skin. *Somatic* means tactile, sensory. When added to the idea of a layered account, the word *somatic* expresses the value of sensuousness and tactility in particular. Layered accounts are not new in the social sciences. Rambo Ronai (1995) has defined the layered account as a multiperspectival narrative informed by switching between different forms of consciousness and different ways of knowing. A somatic layered account is similar to layered accounts in general, though it draws its multiple perspectives from the combination of diverse voices. Moreover, a somatic layered account draws upon multiple forms of consciousness or ways of knowing, such as the embodied, the emotional, the affective, the imaginative, the linguistic and the non-symbolic, and the intellectual and analytical. In other words, the somatic layered account speaks with both the interpretive lexicon of theory and the affective and sensuous register of sensations and emotions. It touches upon both emotion and cognition. It makes use of linguistic metaphors, but it does not dismiss the role of iconic and indexical forms of signification. It is conceptual and analytical, but it also recognizes the mystifying, more-than-representational power of enchantment.

The somatic layered account is not an attempt to set the bar lower for sensuous writing. It is not an evasion of the ambitiousness of sensuous scholarship, and it does not have different aims than sensuous scholarship writ large. As merely a specific genre within a broader category, the somatic layered account is in fact a specialized technique—one of many devices in the toolbox of sensuous scholarship. Just like autoethnography is well-equipped—amongst sensuous strategies—for detailing affect, the somatic layered account is ideal for representing and performing the materiality and corporeality of sensuous experiences.

The senses are not mere receptors of external stimuli or mere soakers-up of information about a world that is external to the body. Senses are skills: active, reflexive ways of being-in-the-world and of shaping that world (see Ingold 2000; Merleau-Ponty 1962). Human sensations are indeed actions through which we perform a self and bring a world into being. To sense is to make sense, as sensations are both interpretive and manipulative, perceptive and creative. The senses, therefore, are reflexive and performative.

In this respect, we can understand the somatic layered account as a product of two levels of somatic work. One level is constituted by the somatic work of research informants. Another level is constituted by the somatic work of researchers. A somatic layered account is thus a complex form of somatic work; it is a laborious translation that is neither a passive nor neutral record of a set of external stimuli translated into field notes. To apprehend the social and material properties of lifeworlds is to make sense of them by mediating sensations through creative metaphors. Sensations have a quality of firstness to them—that is, an immediate, carnal significance—that is so inimitable by other sign vehicles, such as language, that to reflect on them always implies skillful mediation and translation (Peirce 1958). In other words, no act other than creative interpretation and manipulation can render the materiality of the world we experience through our sensations. To feel the material world, to come to know it through our creative mediations, is therefore a form of work: a performative act.

The consequences of viewing somatic layered accounts as somatic work are important. Somatic layered accounts can not only evoke sensuality but can also breathe life into the materiality of culture in its multiple shapes and colors, textures and patterns, sounds and rhythms, tastes and odors, movements and imbalances, fragrances and painful sensations. Sensuous, performative writing can poeticize the materiality of life without pretending to duplicate it. It can give its readers, viewers, or listeners a way of feeling without actually being there. It can build—rather than flatten—the elusive character of materiality, and it can allow for embodied participation in the world of meaningful objects. Informed by radical empiricism, it can—to paraphrase Conquergood (1991)—allow for the material world to abandon being Other-as-theme and become Other-as-interlocutor, a shift from "monologue to dialogue, from information to communication" (1991: 182).

Writing somatic layered accounts

Somatic layered accounts are proportionately prosaic and poetic. Scholarly prose is important as it allows for contextualization, interpretation, conceptualization, and theorization. With Stoller (1997: xv; also see Brady, 2004), I believe that "discussions of the sensuous body require sensuous scholarship in which writers tack between the analytical and the sensible, in which embodied form as well as disembodied logic constitute scholarly argument." Such dialectics, I hope, might temper the tendencies toward self-indulgence and theoretical irrelevance, which, according to Pelias (1999: xiv), are typical of performative writing.

The second component of somatic layered account writing is poetic. As Brady (2004) suggests, the sensuous power of ethnopoetics can be easily harnessed by humanist social scientists interested in discovering the sensuality of the world. For Brady (2004: 628), poetry "opens up ethnographic inquiry to the whole realm of aesthetics." It does so through its playfulness, its self-consciousness, its counter-intuitiveness, its puzzling way of forcing the reader to question realities, its conspicuous reflexivity, and its focus on signifiers at the expense of signifieds. Poetry's metaphorical potential is no mere substitute for the descriptive prose typical of dispassionate reports. It does not aim at reproducing and representing but at producing self-consciously original creations, at evoking the reverberations of possibility, of magic, of emotionality, of storytelling. As a metaphor for sensual experience, poetry "finds the strange in the everyday, takes us to another circumstance" (Brady 2004: 630) unfamiliar to us:

Unafraid of its sensual immersions, its subjectivities, its mutual constructions of meaningful relationships, and deliberately fictionalized realities that "ring true," poetic rendering is more than another way of telling (writing or speaking). It is another way of interpreting and therefore of knowing.

Ethnopoetics shares much with other reflexive, performative, embodied, and narrative strategies. For example, ethnopoetics calls for the use of the first person singular in writing. When the "I" speaks, readers come to a deeper awareness that it is an individual who senses and who reflects. In its performative qualities, ethnopoetics allows for lifeworlds to progressively unfold through multiple accounts, to emerge as an outcome of action and interaction, of mediation and translation. In its embodied characteristics, ethnopoetics is visceral, carnal, emotional, and somatic. Its embodied nature also brings us close to the "social body" that informs and shapes the researcher's subjectivity and situatedness. Finally, ethnopoetics is narrative in the sense that it follows the logic and pathos of a story, it situates action within a temporal process, and, like a story, it introduces us to multiple characters, their interactions, and their dialogs. Ethnopoetics does not have to follow particular conventions of poetry genres. It simply needs to be a conscious poiesis: a conscious creative act.

Ethnopoetics and sensuous writing have a lot in common. I can identify at least six strategies authors can use to write ethnopoetically and somatically. First, we can capture the uncertainty, complexity, and plasticity of interaction through a subjunctive mode of writing rather than through the declarative grammar typical of detached, universalist writing common in positivist description (more on this in Chapter 8). Second, we can describe how sensations and their expressions unfold as events interesting in their own right, rather than merely identify what causes them or what they symbolize (e.g. class, status, habitus). Third, we can report on the tentativeness and fallibility of fieldwork and somatic work. Fourth, we can evoke a sense of emergence, primarily through attention to the temporal dimensions of interaction and to the dimensions of movement through spatial domains. Fifth, using dialog, we can redistribute the power of narration. With dialog, informants come to life and so do their sensations. We no longer hide their words behind our field-note excerpts or within the aseptic, ossified, museum exhibit-like frames that turn conversations into disembodied block quotes. And sixth, by clearly locating places—rather than uprooting "the lure of the local" (Lippard, 1998) and assigning them pseudonyms—we breathe life into the field through sensuous and emotional ethnographies. I will provide an example of this kind of writing at the end of this chapter.

The organization of somatic layered accounts

The traditional organization of social scientific reports leaves little space for the writing qualities I have listed above. As Stoller (1997) has argued, the formats of papers stifle creativity and imagination and often leave a bad taste in the reader's mouth. As a corrective, I propose to organize somatic layered accounts into five basic sections. Of course, I do not want to impose a new canon or formula but merely to suggest one way out of the usual sequence of introduction, literature review, method, data, analysis, and conclusion.

According to Schechner (2003), all performances unfold through three dynamic phases: people *gather* at a site, they take in the *playing out of an action or drama*, and then they *disperse*, either by returning to the places they left or by moving on. Since somatic layered accounts are meant to have performative qualities, I suggest this same sequence, where these three main stages can be preceded by a short, preface-like flashback or flash-forward and followed by a methodological summary. Far from being theoretically and substantively irrelevant, these three elements of the performance ritual give temporal and spatial dimensionality to writing. This organizational scheme can facilitate a writing style that is more sensuous than the traditional one. In fact, the succession of the three phases evokes a sense of contingency, of emergence, of locality, of narrative, and of nondeterminacy. And do not be alarmed if your research subject does not lend itself well to this tripartite structure; nearly *all* fieldwork is based on a simple tripartite structure of arrival into the field (the gathering), rapport-building and knowledge acquisition (the playing out of action), and to some degree a departure from the field, however gradual it may be (the dispersal).

Social scientific writing demands that authors take responsibility for their research and give full disclosure of their research design. I recognize the importance of this, but I advocate placing a methodological summary as an afterword that follows one's dispersal rather than inserting it as a method section in the middle of the narrative. Placing a method section in the middle of a paper is not only a major interruption in the continuity of narrative of the playing out of an action, but it also functions as a neat but pretentious attempt to separate assumptions and background knowledge from one's research experience. Using a methodological summary as a postscript allows the researcher to use method sections as reflections, rather than execution reports. Placing a method section as an afterthought borrows from filmic conventions. A method section thus becomes akin to the lines of a narrative "making of …"

Finally, I also advocate beginning research writings with short, preface-like flashbacks and flash-forwards, which allow readers to get a sense of the subject matter without being overwhelmed by it. These are not meant to resemble traditional introductions wherein authors give away the findings, lay out their theories, spell out the usefulness of their research, or make similar theoretical moves. While there is nothing wrong in principle with such introductions, I feel they interrupt the continuity of the narrative of a gathering and reduce the emphasis on sensations. Thus, instead of writing traditional introductions, I find the need to "tease" readers by revealing just a bit of the theoretical argument *and* of the embodied experiences to follow. Again borrowing from filmic conventions, flashbacks and flash-forwards stimulate the reader's curiosity and make her want to read more rather than answer all questions at once and prompt him to skip to the conclusion.

Together with these five sections of a somatic layered account are various layers of interpretation. These can range from the traditional to the experimental. Traditional interpretations are structured following the usual research conventions regarding contextualization, interpretation, and theoretical analysis, as well as concept generation whenever possible. Traditional interpretations feature citations and quotations; they aim at understanding, knowledge accumulation, and theoretical refinement. Experimental writing takes greater license in blurring the lines between description and analysis. Possibilities are legion. For example, in the passage below, Wylie smoothly transitions between affective and cognitive writing, presenting an embodied and reflexive approach to analysis:

> The pressure of the Path forced me to my feet. About five minutes' walk south from Hartland Point, having meandered through a series of sleepy, hedged lanes, it curved left, and I found myself, in an instant as it seems in memory, standing before a resplendent landscape, the best for days: the view looking south into the Smoothlands valley and the coastline carried far beyond (Plate 7). The shelving promontory is marked on the maps as Damehole Point, the first of a series of headlands knifing out into the waves. And behind the apparently nameless, faceless cliff, gathering the sunlight and becoming the configuring centre of the landscape, there is the 'strange, lonely, wild little valley' (Tarr 1996, 106) of Smoothlands. Lofty scenes are commonly supposed to inspire lofty thoughts. This one seemed peculiarly affecting and archetypal. It looked somehow too good to be true, as if it had been digitally enhanced and cleaned. It was spectacular: I was all eyes. The quotidian rhythm of walking, connoting an understanding of landscape as a milieu of corporeal immersion, is counterposed by a visionary moment of drama and transfiguration. The ambit of landscape seems to range all the way from humdrum occupancy to sublime optics. But the latter register emerges from Western visual cultures extensively critiqued for their objectification of externality and centring of the gazing subject. Sublime experience is predicated upon an initial fracture that places observer and observed on either side of an abyss. And just as the sublime beholder dissolves in dreadful delight, so he or she simultaneously undergoes an energizing apotheosis: the event of vision begins and ends with a cleaving apart of subject and world. In this way the poetic apprehension of dramatic natural scenery clarifies within a spectatorial epistemology, one which positions landscape as a slice of external reality seen from the perspective of a detached subject, a subject whose gaze is variously invested with notions of control, separation, authority and voyeuristic judgement. If corporeal rhythms immerse, then visual events, however dramatic and unforeseen, distance.
>
> (Wylie 2005: 242)

Whereas Wylie masterfully shifts voices without shifting identities, researchers also have the option to shift identities, relationships with audiences, and, thus, ways of self-expression. For example, in analyzing the performance of a technological accident, I once (2008) utilized a mock radio interview to provide embodied interpretation in the form of dialog with a radio host. Because of its oral characteristics, the dialog allowed me to break up the otherwise heavy pace of analysis and conceptualization, as well as to show how my own interpretation—in light of its diffusion through regional radio—had become part and parcel of the field tale.

MARK (RADIO HOST): "So, even though she wasn't a human being, she came off as a person."

PHILLIP: "Yes. There is a certain way in which we attribute personlike characteristics to things, especially to means of transportation. You can say we anthropomorphize them (see Gell 1998). This is not uncommon for ships. For starters, ships seem human and even have regal names. So, they're not just common persons, they are VIPs. And secondly they receive a gender, like many other material objects do. That makes it easier to talk about them as if they were human. They are not human persons, but in dramatic action they come off as if they were."

MARK: "That's true. Many refer to her sinking as her death, a tragic demise of an old lady."

PHILLIP: "Yes, her wrecking gave her the status of personhood. If you read accounts of the wrecking you'll find many instances in which bodily metaphors are used to describe her status passage from a functional machine to an abject body. That status passage revolves around her body, and our bodies, our feelings, and lived memories. The body is always at the center stage of incidents in the drama of everyday life. During the wrecking, the Queen's body loses control of itself, usurping her image of a graceful person, threatening to spoil her identity. Words like 'crippled,' 'painful agony,' are very common in many descriptions of the wrecking. And interestingly enough it seemed almost as if she resisted the stigma of wrecking and threat of abjectification. In many descriptions of the event she comes off as if she put up a courageous and tenacious fight: first to hang tight to the grip of the rocks just long enough to let her passengers off, and then to stay afloat despite her injured limbs (see Vannini 2008: 174).

There are of course countless other options, and I invite readers interested in further developing somatic layered accounts to experiment with other and better ones, because in the end almost anything, I feel, is preferable to traditional organizational formats.

An example of a somatic layered account

I feel awkward in providing an example of sensuous writing by drawing from my work because it strikes me as arrogant and pretentious. So, let me preface that I'm going to do so simply with the intent of highlighting not so much its alleged qualities but its dimensions—its organizational and narrative structure in particular. I am selecting my own writing also because I am very ... er ... familiar with the author's intentions, and I can easily identify how it came to be the way it did. Now, due to reasons of space, I can only reproduce excerpts, so

Sensuous scholarship 55

I invite you to read the full work if you are interested. But even in the limited space below, I can exemplify at least some of the points I have been making in this chapter. The work I am referring to is the book *Off the Grid* (Vannini and Taggart 2014).

The book is structured as a travelogue. It begins with my arrival on the field, it then weaves its ways across the country of Canada—where Jon and I meet people who live off-the-grid and learn from their words and demonstrations (and also from our own forays into short-term off-grid living)—and ends with a dispersal from the field originating in the departure from our last field site and our return home. In the next section, the very opening of the book, I "arrive" on the field. This "gathering" serves as the introduction to the subject.

> I stepped off the small boat mystified, with my eyes fixated on a blue heron conspicuously pretending to be ignoring us—in the way herons are wont to do—from a safe distance behind Alistair and Eleanor's home. The 40-minute glide on the waters of the shadowy inlet had been swift but smooth, punctuated by the predictable sights, smells, and tones of Clayoquot Sound: cedars overcrowding next of kin in search of gleams of sunshine, docks covered in a slimy sheen of freshly-spilt sockeye blood mixed with seagull shit, and stunted swells meeting the impassable resistance of rambling channels and coves. No element of the postcard-perfect but thoroughly familiar waterscape seemed to stand out the way the house did though, as if hovering weightlessly upon the glassy ocean surface. Feeling awestruck at the incongruous architectural sight I wondered for a moment whether the crane-like bird wasn't indeed as baffled.
>
> "He's our neighbor," said Alistair laconically.
>
> "Must be nice to have discreet neighbors like that," I joked.
>
> "Better than the otters! They're cute, but when you live in a floating home, otters are like 30-pound rats swimming under your house and chewing away your foundations."
>
> I plodded unevenly on the walking path while Alistair tied up the skiff on his own. A long but narrow—three and a half feet at most—wooden plank rendered slippery by the morning's moisture separated the front door from the mooring area. As Eleanor opened the door I cast a glance straight across the living room and out through the large window on the opposite side of the house. And saw water. Cold Pacific Ocean water drifted east, west, north, and south of every wall and every window. No driveway. No fence. No adjacent buildings. No hanging phone or cable or power lines. There it was: a rancher on pontoons, right in the middle of the wilderness. Shadowed by massive red cedars and Western hemlocks, with its image perfectly mirrored in the still, shallow, crystalline water surrounding it, dwarfed by the vertical walls of Vancouver Island's Bedingfield Range, Eleanor and Alistair's solar and wind-powered float-house only conceded ingress to the rest of the

noisy world in the form of a radio, cell phone, and internet airwaves. Aside from the ropes anchoring it on terra firma it was wholly cut off; the epitome of off-grid.

Eleanor welcomed me inside with a smile and a cup of hot coffee and invited me to tour the place. Lush indoor plants and musical gear adorned the unpretentiously snug living room. The kitchen window artfully framed distant cone-shaped mountainous islands and lazy tidal currents. A small garden patch yielded a few precious veggies in plastic pots. A motley crew of barrels and buckets collected rainwater. Despite the infrequent ripples causing the floor underneath the couch to undulate gently, the domesticity of this gently-drifting abode oozed an air of serene normality, feeling surprisingly cozy, comfortable, and safe. We could have been in any "normal" house, really.

Off-grid is an abused expression. I have heard people say they're "off-grid" if they switch off their cell phone for a day. Others think that anyone living far from the city is "off-the-grid." Some use "off-the-grid" to label people who wish to run and hide, to go incommunicado. *Off-grid*, in actuality, is a technical expression with a precise meaning. Engineers and architects—to whom the expression can be attributed—call "off-grid" those dwellings that are disconnected from the electricity and natural gas infrastructure servicing a particular region. In this sense, we cannot even say that someone is more off-grid than someone else. By this definition a home (not a person) is either off-grid or on the grid, period. Administrative bodies, such as the Government of Canada, abide by that definition too. And so does this book.

In the next section, I provide an excerpt from the end of the book. In this conclusion, the journey comes to an end, as my co-author Jonathan Taggart and I reach our final destination.

The way back

"If you don't like the weather, just wait fifteen minutes," was the locals' favorite expression everywhere we went. Newfoundlanders liked to say it too, more rightly so than anyone else. And actually they could have made the same point about their landscape: "if you don't like the landscape, just drive for fifteen minutes." Keen on seeing more of the island that had preoccupied our minds for the previous two years we left Ian and Meranda's place en route to a long loop back to St. John's, winding south around the Avalon peninsula and then up the coast through Chance Cove and Witless Bay. Despite the fatigue, the small but measurable loss in attention, the homesickness, and a shared eagerness to move on with the next creative phases of the ethnography—the writing, the editing, and the distribution—the slow drive back gave us a chance to cling on to the now-rapidly dissipating journey. Ethnographers like to wander as much as they like to wonder, after all. So as misty barren highlands sequined by stray rock gave way to rainy timberlands, and then as muffled pebbly shores of time-forgotten fishing outports gave way to dizzyingly windy cliffs seemingly plucked away from the green meadows of Ireland, Newfoundland and its skies and seas surged and transformed before us one last time.

Mid-coast, at Ferryland, we pulled over for a quick hike around the narrow cape and historic lighthouse. As our fieldwork was finally behind us we set the tripod against a sharp-pitched matted bluff and recorded a final on-camera self-interview, describing "the making of" the film in methodological detail. Like a constantly evolving landscape, ethnography jolts you at every turn. It's easy to draw an itinerary, to sketch in advance a clear sense of direction as well as a starting and an ending point, but like the undertaking of every journey the doing of ethnography never unfolds too linearly, too predictably. Sure there are lines you can draw across the map of a field, but through the actual process of wondering and wandering you always take those lines for a walk. Or better yet the lines take *you* for a walk, changing you as much as you change them.

Someone once said that the mark of a good journey is not whether it yields answers to the questions you had in the beginning, but instead whether it generates questions you never thought of asking in the first place. And so this journey did. The disenchantment and disillusion with short-sighted global economic and political leadership and with the stunted evolution of international environmental policies to meet a growing demand on the planet's resources had me wondering at the offset whether off-grid living was an answer—a better way of life than the defeatism and dependency so many of us have succumbed to. Now I knew it was at least one very small answer, a difficult but prodigious personal way forward on the path to a more responsible future. But before this journey started I never thought of asking how it might feel to detour from our broad collective path and go back, how it might feel to question the inevitability of the future and oppose, through a positive alternative, the blind march onward we collectively seem to have surrendered to join.

As more forests are slashed and burned, as new pipelines, dams, and mines are being planned and developed around the world every day to feed a growing appetite for worldwide consumption we are reminded by cool-headed politicians we can't stop progress and development. But can't we, really? Wouldn't we want to stop and turn around if we finally realized we are nearing the edge of a cliff? Wouldn't we want to go back and re-learn basic regenerative life skills made oblivious at the hands of careless concession? Wouldn't we want to re-discover the alternative hedonism of a modest and onerous consumption? Wouldn't we want to re-learn to appreciate a life lived in deep involvement with the resources made available by the places we inhabit, rather than in spite of them? And above all, wouldn't we *embrace and enjoy*—rather than *endure*—such regression? For the following twelve months, back at our respective homes, we worked on the implications of these questions—I mainly with the memories and words and Jon with the sounds and images we had painstakingly collected through our travels.

I typed the last pages of the first draft of this book during a long, foggy autumn from the comfort of my island home. On one November day, the grid that fed electricity to my laptop and heat to my living room went down. It was a planned day-long outage required by BC Hydro to upgrade tension lines crossing the water and connecting us to our nearest substation. Our island's elementary school closed and many of my fellow islanders caught the morning ferries and went to town for the day. I stayed home. No emails, no phone calls, no TV, no buzz, no noise. I read a book slowly, reviewed my handwritten notes, played a board game with my daughter, and when it got a bit chilly in the house we both went out for a long, heartwarming hike in the forest.

When dusk arrived we lit candles and huddled by our propane-fueled hearth. The grid sprang back to life in the evening, but neither of us cared much. I recalled Daniel's words, spoken on Lasqueti Island two and a half years before: "If you want to understand if you can pull it off, you should try and go for a week or two without electricity of any kind. If you enjoy it, then you can be off-the-grid." It had only been one day, and I felt I would have welcomed thirteen more.

7 Learning from documentary film

Over the last few years, I have become fascinated with documentary films, both as a viewer and as a producer. While all docs are interesting in their own ways, it is especially the work of ethnographically inclined filmmakers to which I am drawn. One of the reasons I enjoy them is because of their massively broad public appeal. Documentary films can teach us ethnographers volumes on how to better engage our audiences through intimate, detail-oriented, sensuous, and compelling narratives. Even though we may have no interest in actually making films ourselves, we can all learn so much from the choices that directors and editors make. Good filmmakers have a fantastic eye and ear for spotting and revealing details that can show—*show*, not tell—deeply insightful knowledge about both the most intriguing and the most mundane lifeworlds. And so it is to film and its pedagogical value that I want to turn to in this chapter.

Ethnographers have used the medium of film for nearly a century now. Their work has captivated audiences around the world, both inside and outside academia. However, I do not want to limit my reflections on the pedagogical value of films that are strictly categorized as ethnographic on the basis of the professional affiliation of their producers and directors. Regardless of whether or not it was made by academics who identify themselves as ethnographers, a documentary can have deeply meaningful ethnographic value if it is based on varying measures of observation and participation into the film's subjects' lifeworlds. Thus, I find that many of the widely distributed social and cultural documentaries available today through iTunes, Netflix, Amazon, Google Play, or similar video-on-demand platforms have tremendous ethnographic value and have, therefore, a great deal to teach us about conducting, writing, and sharing public ethnographic knowledge.

There are two dominant types of ethnographically inclined documentary films: observational and participatory. The observational style—the most common style of anthropological film and classically defined ethnographic film—has long been closely associated with classic disciplinary concerns and realist ethnographic practice (see Barbash and Taylor 1997; Grimshaw 2011; Grimshaw and Gravetz 2009; MacDougall 2000; Ruby 2000). It is a very unique and somewhat controversial style, the distinct elements of which have determined its wide acceptance among university-based audiences as well as its limited popularity among broader audiences.

Observational films privilege first and foremost the seemingly unmediated exposure of naturally unfolding action and interaction through extremely long camera takes, exclusively diegetic sound, and the absent presence of the camera and filmmaker. Observational films feature limited or no close-ups, no voiceover, infrequent use of title cards, and a keen preoccupation with respecting the chronology of events as they unfold in reality. "Characters" are not sought or exploited, subject-matter experts are absent, and, rather than through interviews, human subjects are portrayed communicating with one another or acting alone, as if filming were not taking place. Shooting is unpreoccupied with aesthetic concerns. The subject matter is ordinary, unglorified, taken-for-granted behavior. Editing, ideally, is merely intended to splice shots together. There is no argumentation, no re-enactments, and no clear narrative arc.

The observational approach is a fly-on-the-wall approach to ethnography, which realist ethnographers would promptly recognize as the prototypical ideal of objective research and which constructivists would immediately condemn as utter pretense (Grimshaw and Gravetz 2009). It is also a style that deeply violates—for better or for worse—contemporary cinematic and televisual format conventions for entertainment and that, therefore, receives very little attention from large distributors. Indeed, unsurprisingly, one would be hard-pressed to ever find an observational documentary film on TV channels, Netflix, or iTunes. For an example of this style, do check out Lucien Castaing-Taylor's critically acclaimed *Sweetgrass*, discussed in detail by Grimshaw (2011), as well as some of the many films by David MacDougall.

Participatory films are much more common than observational films. But let us immediately clarify what is meant by *participatory*. In contemporary qualitative research, *participatory* tends to refer to collaborative and decolonized approaches to knowledge creation, especially as they actively involve research participants in the stages of research design, information gathering, and collaborative analysis and reporting (see Özerdem and Bowd 2013). The term *participatory* does not denote that approach in the particular context of participatory documentary film, however. Though there are profoundly collaborative approaches in the context of popular documentary filmmaking (e.g. the YouTube crowd-sourced film *Life in a Day*) and in the domain of academic ethnographic filmmaking (see Gubrium and Harper 2014 for a review), *participatory* here refers to a documentary style produced through the filmmaker's *participant observation* into the subject matter he/she aims to understand (Nichols 2010). In fewer words, whereas observational films are based on the principle of a detached filmmaker who remains invisible throughout the shooting and editing process, participant documentary films are based on the principle of active filmmaker involvement.

At the center of the participatory style lies the interview (Nichols 2010). Interviews with members of the lifeworlds portrayed in the film, with the central character(s) of a story, and/or with the protagonists of an event serve as crucial human encounters between filmmaker and participants. These encounters are not meant to be objective, neutral, unbiased, fact-finding, systematic procedures.

Rather they are—as is common in fieldwork—organically emergent, deeply situated meetings between social actors whose co-presence deeply shapes each other's identity and conduct. These encounters are shaped and altered by power imbalances, differing agendas and interests, and fleeting emotions, as well as by language, class, gender, ethnicity, and many more variables. The act of filming allows for these encounters to come to life before the spectator's eyes and ears in all their partiality, contingency, and complexity.

Besides interviews, participatory ethnographic documentaries feature other material, such as *verité* footage (shot during periods of participant observation), dialog, b-roll, and—when appropriate—archival footage and extra-diegetic sound like music. Participatory documentaries may also contain graphics, still photography, and interviews with subject-matter experts who are asked to provide commentary, opinions, contextual information, and interpretation. It is increasingly rare for participant documentaries to feature a voice-of-God voiceover, so filmmakers often rely on sparsely used title cards to convey information that would otherwise be cumbersome to get across (see Bernard 2011). Participatory documentaries do not typically make use of re-enacted or staged behavior; however, at times, the presence of the camera may generate behavior or events that would not have taken place had a camera not been there.

Participatory ethnographic documentaries are recorded and edited in radically different ways than their observational counterparts. Shots range the gamut of the filmmaker's arsenal: extreme close-ups, medium close-ups, medium shots, and wide shots. Various camera angles are utilized not only to convey different perspectives and impressions but at times also to play with light or color and in order to display visually arresting imagery. Shots and countershots are utilized to give editing continuity to dialog and interaction, and the nature of cuts can at times resemble the conventions of Hollywood film. Also, in contrast to observational films, which move slowly, participatory-styled documentaries make frequent use of shorter takes and faster sequences. Editing is also done to maximize the narrative potential of film—aiming to build tension and achieve some kind of resolution at the end (see Barnard 2011).

From this description of the characteristics of participatory ethnographic films, it should be easy to understand why these documentaries are so common. Because they leave their subject matter relatively open to the audience's interpretation, they avoid the critiques—for example, of being pushy, preachy, patronizing, manipulative, pedantic, and so on—normally leveled at expository films (think of the work of filmmakers like Michael Moore). Because they focus in depth on slices of human life, they succeed at making the ordinary unfamiliar and at making the exotic mundane, just like observational films do. But by increasing the pace, by focusing on human characters, and by building a narrative arc, they avoid being as pretentiously objective and distant as their observational counterparts—thus succeeding in being more easily entertaining as well. And because they introduce audiences to filmmaking as a creative process, they are reflexive and performative but without indulging in the more self-consciously avant-garde tendencies of some performative and autobiographical films.

Learning from the participatory documentary style

Now that a somewhat detailed landscape of ethnographic film has been painted, let us reflect on what the politics and aesthetics of representation of documentary films have got to teach to the rest of us, scholarly ethnographic writers. In what follows, I will outline four qualities of the participatory style from which, I argue, we can all learn a great deal: its intimacy, detail orientation, narrativity, and sensuousness. While these qualities are not unusual in ethnographic writing and qualitative research more generally, participatory-style ethnographic film has the potential to inspire us to write more vividly without losing sight of our interpretive and analytical responsibilities toward our academic audiences.

Intimacy

Participatory documentaries have a unique revealing power: they allow us to *see* and *hear* participants vividly. Thus, participatory films enable us to listen to people's voices in their tone, language, accent, pitch, timbre, rhythm, and speaking volume. Furthermore, location audio recording allows us to hear diegetic sound—like the ambient elements of a soundscape, including noise and silence—while extra-diegetic sound like sound effects or a musical soundtrack can underscore emotional undertones. In participatory film, a camera lets us see participants' faces, bodies, countenance, poise, attire, and demeanor through powerful close-ups. In this sense, the audiovisual immediacy of participatory ethnographic film has a terrific power to facilitate the way we, as audiences, can relate to distant human beings and feel for their plight and quests, share common emotions, or perhaps even grow dislike and antipathy toward them (MacDougall 2006).

When we write, we use language to describe the characteristics of a field site, and through our words, we can paint powerful portraits of a place and its people. But the video camera has an undoubtable advantage over writing in the way it grants us iconically and indexically richer visual and aural access to the world. As MacDougall (2006: 5–6) observes: "appearance is knowledge, of a kind. Showing becomes a way of saying the unsayable. Visual knowledge (as well as other forms of sensory knowledge) provides one of our primary means of comprehending the experience of other people." This is not to say that writing cannot compete with film. Every medium is different, and I am not about to make the point that we should all become filmmakers. My argument is that by looking at how participatory filmmakers portray character, we can all learn to write more intimate ethnographies.

Examples of the participatory style's profound visual and aural intimacy can be found in two recent productions: *Up the Yangtze*, 2009 Genie Award-winner; and Michael Glawogger's 2011 film *Whores' Glory*. *Up the Yangtze* depicts the experiences of young Chinese men and women working aboard luxury cruises travelling on the Yangtze River in the shadows of the controversial Three Gorges Dam. The film focuses in particular on the trials and tribulations of teenager Yu Shui, who leaves her indigent parents' home for the first time to go to work; and

Chen Bo Yu, an overconfident urban young man whose hubris causes him to be laid off at the end of the first working season. *Whores' Glory* similarly gives us a peek behind the scenes of an underpaid, underprivileged, and often-exploited occupation: prostitution. Shot in Thailand, Bangladesh, and Mexico, the film's modest protagonists (the women) and understated antagonists (the johns) succeed one another on the screen as they go nonchalantly about their business, reflecting on the mundanity of their day-to-day commodified sexual practices and narrating their experiences with a great deal of introspection. Both films, subtitled and edited without a voiceover, are profoundly (at times, shockingly so) descriptive of the embodied activities and experiences of their participants, yielding a remarkably thick description—or as MacDougall (2006: 49) would put it, "depiction"—of intimate fragments of their lives.

It is strange to hear scholars say, as some are occasionally wont to do (e.g. Hastrup 1992), that the visual is a "thin" mode of scholarly communication. To prove the contrary, one simply has to try and describe thickly, using words, even as little as five minutes of the footage of films like *Whores' Glory* and *Up the Yangtze*. Indeed, it should be clear to anyone that audiovisual recordings are far superior to ethnographic writing in terms of descriptive "transparency" (see Geertz 1988). The typical journal article, 8,000 words or so in length, contains "data" sections that normally amount to no more than 30–40% of the total length of a paper. But as we all know, these 3,000 words or so only accommodate for about half a dozen excerpts from interviews or field notes. To boot, these passages are generally made subservient to introductory remarks that lay the context for a quote and even summarize it or paraphrase it before or after displaying it. Such a strategy often renders observation very thin and "faceless" (MacDougall 2006: 32–38), privileging telling over showing and the voice of the researcher over those of the participants, thus subtly inviting readers to skip straight to the conceptual and theoretical material (as discussed before in this book). In contrast, ethnographic film showcases participants' words, faces, and bodies (see MacDougall 2006: 16–30) in great depth—as this material often comprises 90% or more of a participatory documentary. If transcribed and annotated, a participatory documentary's ethnographic content would be ten or twenty times that of a journal article and probably roughly the same as that of a monograph. The lesson for us here is then simple: inspired by the way film describes thickly, I believe we should strive to let faces and bodies be seen more and voices be heard in their own right, less mediated and interrupted by scholarly speech.

Detail orientation

Another key characteristic of participatory documentaries is their attention to ethnographic detail. By *detail orientation*, I refer to the way in which certain shots and sequences advance a documentary's plot by functioning as strategic distractions from the main story. Details may include backstories, parallel events, or attention-grabbing close-ups of objects, places, and/or individuals' actions that reveal seemingly peripheral but actually important information about people and sites.

Attention to these details breaks up the pace of narration and argumentation, thus serving as a pacing mechanism or momentary rhythm-shifter, allowing the viewer to become distracted but simultaneously re-focused. Orientation to detail can even help organize and order a film's structure in subtle and nuanced ways.

La Camioneta is a 2012 documentary examining the contemporary transnational mobilities of material objects and people within the North and Central American geo-social context. Filmed to tell the journey of a used American school bus—as it is driven from a Texas auction lot to a Guatemalan car garage and later onto the country's rural and urban roads—the documentary winds up shedding light on organized crime's threats to public transport and civil society in Guatemala. Though detail orientation pervades the film in its entirety, one sequence in particular—during which the yellow school bus is painstakingly re-painted and re-designed through the scrupulous artistry of the employees of a garage specialized in this business—beautifully serves to connote the material and symbolic transformation of the bus's identity and its life passage to a true *camioneta*. The filmmakers could have easily edited out the garage sequence, as it is relatively peripheral to the story's emphasis on hard-hitting issues of mobility, safety, and order, but through attention to details like these, the bus comes to assume a subjectivity of its own, embodying and materializing the key turning point of the story.

A similarly profitable attention to detail is evident in another recent participatory documentary: 2012 Oscar nominee *Five Broken Cameras*. The film is a highly reflexive, even autoethnographic, account of the social upheavals unfolding in Bil'in—a West Bank town affected by the Israeli West Bank barrier and settlement process. Though the film's true concern is with land rights, occupation, protest, unrest, and state power, it is a seemingly peripheral detail that structures the story's organization into five distinct acts. The detail is the misfortune of farmer-turned-filmmaker Emad Burnat, who in 2005 bought a camcorder to tape the birth of his youngest son only to later see it destroyed—and later on, four more cameras will meet the same fate—in a street battle. Throughout the film, the periodical destruction of the video cameras used to chronicle the Israeli military's relentless crushing of Palestinian protest becomes symbolic of the futility of Emad Burnat's and his neighbors' struggles to save their town's olive groves from the barrier's construction. The breaking of the cameras further symbolizes loss of hope, as with the death of each camera, many of Burnat's friends and neighbors are arrested and shot.

When used intelligently, as in the two films above, the strategy of bringing attention to seemingly irrelevant details can make a film more memorable and its characters and events more unique. In contrast to film, this is unfortunately one of the least-often practiced strategies in ethnographic writing. Journal-length articles in particular are notorious for monotonously driving at the main argument and never going astray from it, thus unfolding without letting events and characters breathe and without much or any space at all for interesting narrative detours. In part this is due to journals' limiting word counts, but in larger part—I believe— this happens because, as scholars and even as ethnographers, we are typically praised for our theoretical, conceptual, and substantial contributions and not so much for telling a compelling and memorable story with attention to detail. If we wish to learn from ethnographic film, however, detail orientation is something we can easily integrate into our fieldwork and writing.

Narrativity

A documentary is first and foremost a story (Barbash and Taylor 1997; Bernard 2011; Nichols 2010), so the key question we must ask of a film is this: what story does a film want to tell? And even more importantly: how precisely does it create a sense of narrative? Participatory documentaries—much like narrative ethnography (see Czarniawska 2004)—want to tell the stories of ordinary people as they go about their day-to-day life. Their key distinctive style lies in telling stories through nothing but people's words and their actions, and it is in this sense that they are quite different from written ethnographies. As writers, through our own chosen words, we can re-tell an interview, recount an observation, paraphrase a research participant's experience, synthesize material or expand upon it, and thus assemble a plot that is only partially dependent on the precise form of our recorded empirical data. The writer has endless creative analytic and rhetorical strategies and sources to choose from.

In contrast, participatory filmmakers uninterested in voiceover do not have this luxury; the only material they have available to create a story is words exactly as they were spoken and images as they were shot. If a narrative element is not "on tape," it cannot be depicted. Telling a story through participatory film is thus an act of editing already-existing pieces together in order to patch a coherent whole. More than writing could ever be, the work of a participatory documentarian is that of a true storytelling *bricoleur*.

2010 Oscar nominee *Which Way Home*, for example, tells the stories of Central American children as they attempt to immigrate illegally into the United States. The filmmakers follow kids as young as 9-year-old Olga and Freddy as they travel without their parents to America from Honduras, jumping trains and struggling to stay a step ahead of law-enforcement authorities, gangsters, and petty thieves. Through the footage of their accounts and their actions, director Rebecca Cammisa assembles a story of hope and despair, courage and disappointment, and ultimately a piece of participant observation set amidst transnational political and economic forces and the ties of border-crossing family and friendship networks. Olga, Freddy, Jose—a 10-year-old from El Salvador—and teenage Honduran Kevin in the end meet different fates, which the documentary compels us to follow in a suspenseful mode worthy of the most captivating novel.

Similarly built around a sense of hope and aspiration are the journeys of the Russian teenage girls recruited by a modelling agency to work in Japan and chronicled by sociologist/filmmaker David Redmon. Redmon begins his observation at a regional modelling competition held in Siberia and organized by a former American model by the name of Ashley. Confident of her potential for success, Ashley recruits 13-year-old Nadya—a girl from a humble rural background—and a few of her newly made friends. Redmon's camera follows

Nadya's move to Tokyo, where she struggles with adjusting to a foreign culture, being away from home for the first time, and the harsh demands and modest paybacks of her uncertain occupation. As the story evolves, *Girl Model* stimulates mixed emotions in its viewers, pushing us to relate to the hopeful plight of the young girls while simultaneously prompting us to ask whether the price they pay to be successful is personally and socially worthwhile. As the story reaches its end, Redmon and co-director Sabin hint that Nadya's story will continue, maybe with different protagonists and different outcomes, but with recurring elements of deception, mistrust, poverty, aspiration, the pursuit of wealth and fame, and ultimately the bodily commodification of many young women in Russia, Japan, and elsewhere.

There are key elements of style, Stoller (2007: 180) finds, "that are necessary if ethnographers want their work to be read by a wide range of readers over a long period of time." The first is locality, or a sense of place. The places journeyed through by the protagonists of *Girl Model* and *Which Way Home*, and vicariously by us, are haunting and hard to forget. The second element, Stoller (2007: 180) continues, are the narrative events that reveal characters' identity, personality, and humanness. Through the power of stories, ethnographers can grapple with human motions and deep issues that can help readers relate to the people they encounter in ethnographic texts. Participatory ethnographic documentaries remind us writers that the power of a well-told story lies in the tension it builds, in how it compels us to want to see a narrative end and yet continue at the same time. Films like these two sensitize our creative and sociological imagination to the importance of weaving stories that speak to the critical issues of our time and the timeless human condition, bringing us to wonder about the personal and the biographical and their porous boundaries with the political and historical. "In the end," Stoller (2007: 190) concludes in exhorting ethnographers to learn from the cinematographic imagination of ethnographic filmmaker Jean Rouch, "it is the texture of the story that marks our contribution to the world."

Sensuousness

As discussed in Chapter 6, an increasing number of scholars today advocate for a more sensuous scholarship that is produced through, and for, the gamut of human sensory experience. Sensuous ethnographies are interpretive and phenomenological undertakings that put a strong premium on the meaningfulness of sensory experiences, the significance of the skillful practices through which we make sense of the world, and the importance of aesthetically rich expressions through which lifeworlds are made and represented. Film is an ideal medium for sensuous ethnographic practice (MacDougall 2006; Stoller 1992). Like the most exquisitely written ethnographies, participatory documentaries are ideally equipped to animate sensory dimensions of lifeworlds through their carnal depictions of human characters' embodied actions.

Film is most obviously a visual and aural medium, but it is also perfectly adequate for depicting sensations of touch, smell, taste, pain, movement, and balance.

As Marks (2000: 213) finds, a film's

> characters are shown eating, making love, and so forth, and we viewers identify with their activity. We salivate or become aroused on verbal and visual cue. Beyond this it is common for cinema to evoke sense experience through intersensory links: sounds may evoke textures, sights may evoke smells.

So it is by relating to characters' sensations that we feel not only for them but also with them. In the participatory documentary *The Boxing Girls of Kabul*, for example, we learn about the competitive ambitions of a small group of young Afghani women training to become Olympic-level boxers. As the camera follows them in their training centers and tournament arenas, the sounds of grunts and punches and the sights of fighting bodies evoke feelings of pain, the stench of sweat, and the violent contact of hands and faces. As the young women learn to fight and defend themselves amidst a broader conservative misogynistic culture that deeply oppresses them, their bodily sensations and their willpower to push back hegemonic forces echo the feelings of many other Afghani women who are silenced and made invisible outside the home by orthodox religious norms. Thereby boxing becomes a metaphor for protest, rebellion, and social change.

The flavors of food and the sensations associated with its procurement, production, and sharing are important dimensions of the human condition. Film cannot allow us to taste food, but it can enliven the way eating can be vicariously experienced and understood. In *Vanishing Point*, we learn about both old and contemporary ways of hunting and fishing "country foods" in the Canadian and Greenlandic Arctic. Told from the eyes and voice of Inuit elder Navarana, the film takes us westward across the Arctic Sea as the protagonist travels from Northern Greenland to Canada's Baffin Island to learn about modern life there. As Navarana learns that the descendants of her distant ancestors enjoy the flavors of the same wild foods as Greenland Inuit do, but that they practice hunting and fishing through gas-guzzling motorized boats and rifles—as opposed to the more traditional ways practiced by her people—she begins to reflect on the future of traditional knowledge and development and the fate of circumpolar Inuit.

Stoller (1997) argues that so many conventionally written ethnographies leave a bad taste in the reader's mouth, but that through a richer variety of ingredients and a greater sensitivity toward their own sensory experiences, sensuous ethnographers can aim to prepare tasteful servings of knowledge. Films like *Vanishing Point* allow us to feel what it is like to catch migratory birds with a net and unpluck their feathers for a tasty snack and to vicariously taste the flavor of the cold blubber of a freshly fished Narwhal. In doing so, they remind us that the power that sets fieldwork apart from other research traditions lies less in its transferrable generalizations and its conceptualization of generic social process and rather more in how it seduces us to travel alongside its protagonists and experience a raw sense of life together with them. Abstractions matter greatly, of course, but ethnographic film reminds us that the longer-lasting flavors of an experience are those that carve sensuous traces on our bodies.

8 Enlivening ethnography
In search of a more-than-representational style

This chapter is somewhat of a quest. After this preface, I am going to write in search of an ethnographic style that strives to do more than just *represent* field experiences and encounters. I do not pretend to have found an ultimate solution to the crisis of representation that has vexed ethnographers for three decades. Neither do I believe that these strategies will appeal to every non-representational researcher or public ethnographer. Nor am I entirely convinced that the following rhetorical choices will be appropriate for all research topics. But I hope, ambitiously, to have found at least one way to enliven my fieldwork writing enough to make it interesting to read, and it is in this vein that I share it.

In the next section, I will share a 3,000-word narrative drawn from my fieldwork on off-grid living in Canada (Vannini and Taggart, 2014). Between 2011 and 2014, my multi-site ethnography took me and my collaborator Jonathan Taggart across all of Canada's provinces and territories to document the ways of life of people whose homes are disconnected from large socio-technical networks of heat and electricity and also often (relatively) self-reliant in many other ways. The writing below is the story of an unusual field journey: a trip to an off-grid cabin in the Arctic tundra. I will tell the story of our travel and later reflect on the choices I made in telling it, focusing on the partiality, immediacy, proximity, potentiality, ineffability, fluidity, and reflexivity of my writing.

Camping, out on the land

It never fails. You're out camping and right in the middle of the night you feel an irresistible urge to go pee. The outhouse is only a few steps away, but you dread losing sleep momentum by scavenging for your shoes and headlamp. It's nippy outside but getting dressed is a hassle. But the urge is too strong, and you must eventually surrender.

It's -30°C on the Arctic tundra. You have been cautioned to be on the lookout for polar bears, especially at night. So you try and step up urination pressure a notch or two—however a futile physiological effort that may be. You anxiously scan the immense horizon glistening in the precocious pre-morning dawn. And then it happens, just like you feared it would. The light cast by your headlamp hits two beady, fluorescent eyes gazing hungrily at you fifty meters afar. Your entire life flashes before your slumbery eyes.

Iqalugaaqjuit—a "place of many little fish," in the Inuktitut language—is one of a handful of outpost camps scattered around the southern shore of Baffin Island, in Canada's Nunavut territory. Most of these outposts were built in the mid-1980s, when the Canadian government thought it behooved them to encourage—after decades of systematic eradication of traditional nomadic lifestyles—hunting and fishing and the intergenerational language and skill transfer that goes along with them.

Our *illugalaq* is a newer edifice. Built 17 years ago by Timmun and Kristiina, just like all the neighboring cabins, it serves the function of hosting its owners, family, friends, and occasional guests for short weekend or week-long getaways. "It's for our mental health," in Kristiina's words, "we come here to get away."

We arrived in the late afternoon of a cold April day. We had left Canada's West Coast with borrowed parkas and untested gloves two days before and departed Cape Dorset by snowmobile four hours earlier. Due to the unwise gear choice, the first few minutes of driving had turned out to be atrocious. My right hand had more or less frozen stuck on the accelerator handle, gripping it steady at such an angle that it worked like a human-mediated cruise control, set at precisely 21 miles per hour. Thankfully, at the first cigarette break, local knowledge saved me. Beaver fur-covered mitts had been kindly provided by Kristiina, who motherly introduced me to their superiority over polyester gloves, while Timmun inconspicuously switched on the heat on my snowmobile handlebar—a mix of old and new world solutions.

After leaving Cape Dorset we rode over lakes, ponds, rivers, creeks, and the ocean. At times we steered away from frozen waters to conquer overland trails, often none the wiser of the topographical substitutions. Other than a few stretches of pavement within tiny hamlets' boundaries, there are no roads in Canada's Eastern Arctic. Snow and ice make snowmobile travel possible during the colder months: from November to June. Boats are used to navigate the ocean separating Nunavut communities from one another and from outpost camps during July, August, and September. During the shoulder seasons, when ice is breaking or freezing up, no one other than airplanes dares to move about.

Snowmobiling is an acquired taste, much like getting lashed in the buttocks with a leather whip: once you see past the sore lower back and the bruises you actually realize that it's just another way of getting around and that in fact, for some people, it's the normal way of doing it. Given its widespread and enthusiastic uptake it makes you wonder how rougher dogsled transport must have been.

"Going out on the land," the locals' favorite expression to indicate going camping, is a bit of a misnomer. The "land" is actually snow. Some of it frozen solid, some fluffier but dry, some slushy, some icy and translucent, some resplendently turquoise even under the most timid of suns. The actual "land" is a different entity altogether, and an evanescent one for most of the year. I imagined it as a myriad of soggy colorful meadows and shallow mosquito-stocked lakes underneath all the white stuff, but only actually witnessed it as lifeless, cold granite dots littering the unimaginatively bitonous—tritonous at best on a sunny day—icescape.

Our speedometer snuck past the 30 MPH tack once or twice, but it was a short-lived thrill. Though wintery Arctic landscapes are generally easily amenable to speedy gliding, tidal forces dancing underneath the ocean constantly push and pull trails up and down, creating ridges and walls requiring twists and turns not unlike Formula 1 chicanes. Amongst them the most spectacular, though immensely vexing, are two-ton popsicles known as pressure ice. Near shores—where these small communities of Lilliputian locked-in icebergs appear, grow, shrink, and then almost vanish twice daily with the ebbing and flooding of tides—snowmobile travel is rendered labyrinthine, requiring detours, low speed, patience, and a peripheral attention to distances that is parallel in nature to the task of merging onto a gridlocked parkway.

Jon and I had been pursuing the opportunity to go camping in the Arctic since we had discovered its popularity on an earlier trip to the Mackenzie Delta, in Canada's Northwest Territories. For the thermally unadventurous Arctic camping seems like an unconscionable thing to do, but for residents of Northern Canada it is the typically preferred way to escape the hustle and bustle of growingly busy and conspicuously loud (snowmobile engines aren't as quiet as you might think) communities.

With everyone coming and going all the time even sealift—the once-a-year resupply of Arctic communities by cargo ship—"isn't what it used to be," according to Timmun. Take Iqaluit, for example, the territory's capital city. Pizza Hut, KFC, and not one but three coffee-and-donut shops of the quintessentially Canadian Tim Horton's franchise chain compete for attention with shawarma eateries, hotels, restaurants, flower shops, and crowded four-way intersections begging for the arrival of the eastern Arctic's first stop light. No wonder then that local women and men—like our friend Niviaqtsi put it—really "need a break" every now and then.

After unloading the two enormous trailer-sheds of all the camping gear—no station wagon or SUV trunk can compete with the cargo space of a *qamutiik*—we hurried to the lake to lay down our fishing net before nightfall. Though Timmun is said to have pulled it off by himself in his younger years, ice-fishing with a net is no one-*inuk* job.

You start by excavating a hole, approximately two meters wide, in the snow. With as many as two or three feet of snow cleared off the icy lake surface you begin drilling two holes immediately next to one another. You then merge the two together with a six foot ice chisel. Next, you shove an ice crawler into the hole and send it floating under the ice. This is the tricky part; you must listen for the crawler's metal hook rubbing against the ice from underneath and determine, from the snow-muffled sound transmitted above, where it lies. That is the precise spot where you want to dig and drill two more holes through the ice. If you guessed right the crawler should be there, so you fish it out and grab on to the rope that it carried from the first hole. That is the rope to which the fishing net will be tied, after being stretched from the first to the second hole and secured in both places with a simple knot around a shovel or an ice chisel. That's it. Overnight the char will magically fill the net, as if to reward you for your good effort.

Kristiina and Timmun's cabin is unpretentious and small—at 16 by 12 feet it is just big enough to accommodate cooking space, a bunk bed, and a foldout couch tucked behind the dining table. Any larger or more comfortable space would be vulgar and unfitting. Heat is provided by a combination of a propane-fueled camping stove and an electric space heater powered by a generator. The temperature inside can get as high as 21°C. The contrast with the outside requires ventilation by way of two air exchangers: simple plastic-covered openings through the wall that almost manage to arrest the unrelenting condensation. All of this makes for a visually arresting explosion of steam every time the door is opened, so that stepping outside not only feels, but also spectacularly looks just as if you walked into a meat locker.

Kristiina is a goldmine of information. Listening to her camping stories made every evening fly fast, and games of Scrabble helped when the stories ran out. Camping out on the land is a mix of relaxation and busyness, but even the busyness—directed at securing basic comforts and sheer survival—is playful enough to be a diversion from the daily rituals of life in town. Timmun and Niviaqsi, like two grown children seemingly incapable of sitting down, would spin their wheels outside the cabin as if keen on corroborating Kristiina's observations with bodily evidence.

When you camp you carry on as if you were playing house. Playing is marked by few rules. You must imagine the camp to be the human race's last self-reliant outpost and must endeavor to make your temporary dwelling as comfortable as a permanent one, but different enough from a normal home to be challenging and exciting. Good campers play the game ostentatiously, as if their skill display was subject to the scrutiny of scrupulous judges. Those new to camping, or those like me and Jon who have played the game on far away territory, mostly just listen, learn, and try not to get in the way.

The first clear night gave way to a scrimmage of early morning clouds, which then quickly dissipated as the winds rose. Temperatures hovered in the -20s with the wind chill. After a hearty breakfast of bannock and raspberry jam it was time to check the net. It was a simple enough job that even two clumsy southerners like us were allowed to help with. It was fun too. After ensuring that the first hole was free of any edge the net was pulled out of the ice in its entirety while Timmun recorded the outcome with his iPad. The fish were still alive but visibly fatigued from a long night of wrangling with the nylon net, then shocked by the sudden exposure to the cold air. We untangled sixteen the first morning, and then more at nighttime and in the following days, until we reached the contented conclusion that five dozen took enough space on our *qamutiik*.

I have camped on beaches, in forests, the desert, on volcanos, and now on the Arctic tundra but regardless of geographical features I have always found that the success of a camping trip comes down to one key variable: good food. Arctic char tastes like a genial pastiche of Pacific salmon's delicately sweet flesh and lake trout's juicy and tender meat. It is at its best when eaten raw, chunked into steaks cut sideways or into long fillets cut lengthwise and salted overnight. Kristiina taught us to make the rubbery skin optional, carve each bite sashimi-style and then dip the pieces into lemon pepper or soy sauce.

Though no more than 200 meters away from a small cluster of cabins, six in total, no *illugalaq* other than ours received visitors during the time we were there. Alleviated of the responsibility to exchange a salvo of small talk with neighbors, hunt for a wireless signal, or catch the six o'clock news, Iqalugaaqjuit felt—and the more so as times went on—like a lunar substation where could stand still and silent, or at least would be gratified by simply whispering through the ice.

The Arctic tundra has a strange way of acting. Its few visible traces—the odd raven, wolf, walrus, white Ptarmigan or fox—go about the land reservedly, looking disconcertedly surprised every time you spot them. But the Arctic tundra is not as inhospitable as it's reputed to be. Far from being a bleak, desolate, or barren wasteland, it is more like a very large pond in which it is remarkably easy to be a big fish. It is as if the tundra wished to cast a spotlight on every little animal, plant, and human life it manages to find its way there. As if it wanted to say "here you are the main feature, this is your chance to be a star."

One afternoon, as we shadowed Timmun's skidoo-powered zigzags in a fruitless search for Caribou tracks, I came to the realization that I had been wrong along about the "land." The granite rocks which I proclaimed guilty of rendering the icescape featureless with their redundant shapes and unimaginative traits turned out to be much richer upon close inspection. As Timmun exploited their patterns in the course of wayfinding through the island's interior I began to appreciate the rocks' diverse characters: the black-brown ones, darkened by a fungus named tripe; the green-brown ones, vegetated by a lichen capable of keeping Caribou alive in the winter; and the red-covered beige ones, shrouded in a bloodlike splattering of a microscopic plant whose identity I questioned ignorantly. And more than just eye candy for my color-starved sight the rocks also held enough solar warmth to serve as temporary stools in an otherwise seat-deprived place. I nodded dreamingly to the rocks, as if to apologize—they too played their part eloquently here.

Though we caught no caribou we netted plenty of fish. Eight and ten-pound char came orderly to the surface not only by way of the holes dug for our nets but also via smaller bores pierced for the leisurely pursuit of jigging. "Some people can jig from morning to night when they go camping," Kristiina pointed out after I admitted defeat, in puzzlement at the whole thing.

The excitement, I was told I would have had, all lies in seeing the fish. To make eye contact with the scaly beasts you must be comfortable enough with shoving your head down the ice hole in order to shield away the glare. Neither I nor Jon were able to lay down for too long on the snow, stomach first, and seduce the poor things with morsels of orange peel. Overcome by claustrophobia and by empathy for the Vitamin C-starved vertebrates I would spend my time wandering about the site, fascinated by the dedication of my supine fellow campers as much as by the arrival onstage an unexpected star: an overhead jet.

The Arctic is a busy place these days. Many of us have indeed travelled above it, at 36000 feet of altitude, en route to Europe or North America. I spotted my first plane the second afternoon at the lake. "Taken aback" does a half decent job at capturing my bewildering feeling. Curiously, as it zoomed by, I began wondering whether anyone from the cabin of the wide-bodied jet could see me. I knew they couldn't, but I badly wanted them to notice me. Then something eerie happened: I saw myself.

From down there I spotted myself on that very plane: pausing the movie playing on my personal monitor to lift the curtain to see where I was. And from up there I laid eyes on myself, staring from all the way below.

"What are you doing?" I asked.
"Why did you step out of the plane, don't you know you're not supposed to?"
"Why are you there, instead of home with your family?"
"What are you trying to prove?"
"Who are you showing off to?"

In my defence I mumbled away a few accounts. I said I wasn't there to show off. I said I wasn't even there because I found this place particularly comforting, at least in comparison to the cozy, private hideouts afforded by my home island's shadowy forests. I explained that maybe I too needed to be in the open, out on the land, off the grid, away from the tank farms, North Marts, and busy co-op stores of northern towns. And as I rambled on I finally found my line.

"I'm just here for the quiet."

It's loud in Cape Dorset, with its snowmobiles. It's loud in Iqaluit with all its airplanes. It's loud everywhere, with cars, ferry boats, people, dogs, and everything else clamoring for attention: "Me, me, me, watch out for me!"—everyone screams, all the time, everywhere. But instead it was comfortingly quiet there, I explained myself: a sonic emptiness, an explosion of quiet deadened by snow, chocked by ice, walled-in by rock, and finally wrapped in down and beaver fur.

As the jet quietly streaked away and the sky eventually muted its engines I was once again in possession of the power to make overwhelming noise. It was a power I regretted having to share with my camp mates and I wished that I were the only sovereign holder of silence. The only one with the sonorous might to make snow crackle, to chisel ice, and to let out a loud sneeze. I wished it were only me: the main star of a stage whose ears were all mine, the biggest fish in the largest, but most unscripted, pond on this planet. I felt the urge to bellow out a scream and witness its echo. Yet, it seemed, it would have been unfitting and I chose to hush. There and then, while camping out on the land, I had found respite from the noise of words and the cacophony of sights of our busy world.

Like all good things camping must end—for the essence of camping resides in its very temporary and transitory nature. Camping would not be fun if it never ended. Its conclusion is consecrated, for me, in a ritualistic cleansing bath of warm water and barista-prepared espresso. Camping is meaningful because it eventually stops being meaningful.

The morning we left was—as all camping departures are—dripping in mixed feelings. Niviaqsi was missing his family. Timmun and Kristiina seemed to crave the daily routines they had swept under the condensation for a while. And Jon and I longed for our homes, which we eventually found after travelling through a blinding white out.

And that famous night—the night I almost wetted myself—the beady eyes turned out to belong to a gorgeous fox, not a menacing bear.

So, yes, it never fails. You show up in the Arctic thinking hungry bears are the most fearsome thing in the Arctic. But the fear is really all in you: flying overhead, skittishly sneaking by, holding yourself back from coming down to camp and play.

The irrealis mood: beyond representation

Ethnographic representation is a unique literary style. Though it has many elements common to all non-fiction genres, it shares with creative writing several rhetorical features such as narrativity, performativity, sensuality, reflexivity, intimacy, and many more. For all but the most conservative and positivist ethnographers, the "writing up" of fieldwork has as of late taken on new dimensions, scopes, and challenges. Chief amongst these new concerns is how to deal with enlivening representation.

By *enlivening representation* I refer to a series of rhetorical options, strategies, and practices directed at making ethnographic representation less concerned with faithfully and detachedly reporting facts, experiences, actions, and situations and more interested instead in making them come to life, in allowing them to take on new and unpredictable meanings, in violating expectations, in rendering them (on paper and other media) through a spirited verve and an élan that reverberates differently amongst each different reader, listener, viewer, and spectator. In other words, by enlivening ethnographic representation, I refer to an attempt at composing fieldwork as an artistic endeavor that is not overly preoccupied with mimesis—an endeavor that is open to the potential of creation, animation, and regeneration.

But I need to be clear about something before I proceed any further: I do not wish to deny the importance of mimetic representation. I do not want to convey the idea that daydreaming or speculation can replace honest fieldwork. I am instead simply suggesting that the work of producing non-fiction and the willful engagement of creativity and the imagination are neither mutually exclusive practices nor binary oppositions.

So, how do we make representation and imagination co-exist? If we understand the "writing up" of ethnography as an approximate duplication of what occurred during fieldwork, then we ought to think of ethnographic composition as characterized by what linguists call the *realis mood*. The realis mood is a communicative mood used to indicate that something is the case. Declarative sentences are the epitome of the realis mood (e.g. "The Inuit of Canada's Eastern Arctic traditionally subsisted on hunting, fishing, and trapping"). The realis mood lies at the core of scientific communication as it allows it to be persuasive and authoritative as well as logical and definitive. My suggestion is to combine the all-too-important realis mood with another, less typically scientific, mood: the *irrealis mood*. The irrealis mood indicates that something may not be the case, or that it may not have happened, or that it may not happen at all. The irrealis mood, in other words, is a rhetorical formula used to openly create a sense of the unreal and the surreal, a sense of possibility, of condition, of wish, of fear, and of hope. There are several ways in which we can use the irrealis mood. I will describe a few.

Partiality and the conditional mood

Non-representational ethnography does not aim at comprehensiveness in the same way that traditional qualitative research does. In order to achieve comprehensiveness, realist research strategies slice data horizontally—subdividing datasets into categories, identifying themes and sub-themes within them, and selecting representative tokens as illustrative quotations. On the other hand, non–representational ethnography aims at evoking through provocative fragments rather than just reporting and illustrating through representative units, cases, and samples. Therefore, data are tackled diagonally, not in order to squeeze out representative meanings or trends but in order to create a sense of action and—whenever possible—a narrative thread. Rather than the logic of a grid made of branches intersecting through a central foundational axis, non-representational data organization and animation may very well follow instead the stage aesthetics of a lightshow—staging characters, foreshadowing events, adumbrating possibilities, beaming ideas, and all the while bedazzling and enlightening while remaining aware of what it simultaneously, inevitably, casts in the background.

A common way to achieve a sense of partiality in non-representational writing is by employing the conditional mood—one of many manifestations of the irrealis mood. The conditional mood is a common mode of expression used to indicate a possibility that is generally dependent on a condition. Conditional actions or sentiments hinge explicitly or implicitly on uncertain events, states of affairs, circumstances, and outcomes. In English, conditional sentences are generally constructed through the use of *would* or *could* and the word *if.* Utilizing the conditional mood is an important deviation from the traditional realis mood as it takes attention away from established fact, previously unfolded events, and current state of affairs and opens up instead a sense of what could happen, what might become, what could be. The conditional also creates a sense of uncertainty whenever it is used to indicate how else things could be unfolding, how else characters could be involved, or how else processes could be interpreted.

Consider, for example, how I used the conditional in my writing. I employed it explicitly in at least two sentences: "Any larger or more comfortable space would be vulgar and unfitting," and "The excitement, I was told I would have had, all lies in seeing the fish." Both of these statements open up a possibility that is indirectly revealing of an important "reality" (and absence thereof) in the field. The first one pushes us to wonder how else something could have been, thus implicitly allowing us to reflect on the appropriateness and fitness of how things actually are. The second sentence instead brings attention to an unfulfilled potential and therefore to a failure on my part to achieve a result that others might take for granted. In both of these cases, the use of the conditional allows us to imagine something that does not quite exist or did not quite occur, but it does so without being too explicit or literal. Adumbrating a possibility is important in non-representational ethnographic writing because it allows us to hint, to foreshadow, and to outline partially, without quite telling in full. Good ethnographers, of course, want to show, not tell. And good non-representational ethnographers may want to occasionally intimate instead of showing everything all the time.

Potentiality and the potential mood

Non-representational theory and research neither follow axiomatic theoretical laws, nor attempt to exercise control over its research subjects or over reasoning by way of deductive models. Rather, non-representationalists find inspiration in the generative, poietic, expressive power of the arts and humanities and endeavor to emulate their creative potential. Ambitious in its experimental drive and irreverent in its spirit to stimulate the cultural imagination and provoke change, non-representational ethnography wants to be playful, energetic, and vibrant. Rejecting the values of prediction and replicability, non-representational ethnographers are captivated by—and aim to captivate with—a transformative sense of wonder. Thus, rather than abide by traditional methodological rules, non-representational ethnographers ask themselves how to best to utilize the creative and promissory potential of innovation, strangeness, and performative aliveness. Their methodological orientation, in other words, is not "am I doing this right?" but rather "how else can I do this?" and "why not?"

The potentiality of ethnographic knowledge is best expressed through the use of the potential mood. In grammar, the potential mood refers to tentativeness and probability. A simple way to employ the potential mood is by hedging one's statements. But there are risks with doing so. Tentative writing can be weak, falsely modest, and annoyingly full of apologies, limitations, and disclaimers. Alternatively, a writer could, for example, state that something is simply "likely" to be the case. While there is nothing wrong with that strategy, it is important to remember that statisticians have made the probability of guessing right their business, and that as a result, the word *likely* carries quite a burdensome baggage. Indeed, there is an important difference between the potentiality pursued by non-representational ethnographers and by realist researchers. Whereas the latter strive to minimize the possibility of being wrong, the former pursue possibility for its very revelatory potential.

A good non-representational way to deploy a potential mood is by way of building rhetorical possibilities—possibilities that may or may not be fulfilled in the end. The building of a possibility enlivens writing by opening up a potential scenario that reveals the unique characteristics of a situation and elicits a sense of wonder. Building possibilities also animates description by creating dramatic tension and stimulating suspense. For example, the narrative description of our camping journey to Baffin Island opens precisely with a potential mood. By giving the impression that I am about to come face to face with a polar bear, the writing builds on the very possibility of that encounter. The writing's very first sentence—"it never fails"—is also a probabilistic statement as it depends for its very modality (i.e. the probability of being true) on the recognizability of the described situation. There is, at the end of the story, no polar bear. But there could have been, and most certainly the very fear of that dangerous encounter permeates more Arctic trips than our own, and it is therefore an important affective dimension of the experience of that place that my writing aimed to highlight.

Ineffability and the dubitative, presumptive, and hypothetical moods

Representational research seeks to mimic the world through realistic description. There is nothing wrong in the ethos of realistic description as long as we keep in mind that the lifeworld always escapes our quest for authentic reproduction. Our fallibility, in other words, is not a limitation but a normal and even welcomed condition that enables us to generate new realities. Ethnographers keen on going beyond representation therefore view description not only as a mimetic act but also as an opportunity to evoke multiple and contradictory impressions of the lifeworld in all its mysterious characteristics.

The lifeworld is ineffable; its fleeting dynamics, its "never-quite-so" features, its hard-to-pin-down textures constantly interrogate us. They make us wonder, they surprise us, confuse us, and enchant us. After all, the lifeworld's ineffability is the very reason why we got into the business of understanding it, and the main stimulus of our continued fascination with it. How boring would our work be otherwise, how dull would our imagination be if the lifeworld were perfectly transparent and amenable to description and explanation!

Representational writing, however, often glosses over the ineffability of life and our fascination with it. The struggle for authoritative certainty precludes and excludes admissions of ignorance, doubt, and confusion. Writing steamrolls forward as if our very questions were all answered by the time the pen touches the paper. Non-representational ethnographic writing aims to return to the immanence of enchantment, however. It wants to ask as much as to answer. It strives to wonder as much as it to respond. It relishes curiosity as much as explanation.

Three expressions of the irrealis mood allow us to evoke the ineffability of the lifeworld: the dubitative, the presumptive, and the hypothetical mood. The dubitative mood expresses doubt and uncertainty. The presumptive mood similarly connotes doubt but also curiosity, concern, ignorance, and wonder. The hypothetical mood is an explorative tone that poses possible situations, events, or interpretations. The word *if* is employed in all three of these moods. Indeed, the word *if* and its various combinations—for example, "as if," "even if"—might very well be thought as the epitome of ineffable writing. "If" is to the non-representational what "just like" is to the mimetic and representational.

My own writing attempted to be mimetic, to be sure, as much as it sought to evoke the ineffability of my field experiences. For example, I did not shy away from admitting my initial mistake about the meaningfulness of Arctic rocks or my ignorance over geological matters. Also, throughout my writing, I never ceased to wonder. I wondered about how uncomfortable dog sled travel might have been.

I imagined what the land under the ice looks and feels like. And I never pretended to appear too confident in such an unfamiliar environment, so I mumbled accounts, I failed to display skill, and I did not feel at home. And by employing a presumptive "as if" (e.g. "It is as if the tundra wished to cast a spotlight on every little animal, plant, and human life it manages to find its way there") I introduced a metaphor that allowed me to make my writing more performative and even somewhat surreal.

Immediacy and the jussive mood

Non-representational theories of time stress the multidimensionality of the present. The present time consists of repetition and difference, anticipation and transformation of the future, and the virtual unfolding of multiple happenings. Non-representational ethnography is therefore keenly sensitive to enlivening the diverse and intersecting temporalities of the present. The immediacy of the ethnographer's experiences and their evocations are informed by temporalities such as rhythmical recurrences (e.g. minutes, hours, days, weeks, seasons, years), the duration of events, the speed of various processes, the elusiveness and unpredictability of happenings, and the contested, contradictory, and conflicted practices through which virtual futures are actualized. In simpler words, a concern with the immediacy of ethnographic animation is a concern with its embodied and emplaced "live" nature—for example, the here and now of field experience—as much as with the intricacies of that present moment.

A keen concern with immediacy translates into a conscious preoccupation with the tenses of ethnographic writing. There are no easy solutions to this challenge; each project demands that we choose the most appropriate option. The present tense, for instance, is more open-ended and fluid. It allows us to write as if we were caught in the moment, as if happenings, doings, and experiences were unfolding right before us without a definitive direction or resolution. The past tense, in contrast, denotes events that have already come to an end, connoting a sense of closure and realization that may be very appropriate—and indeed ideal—for narration. Less used in ethnographic writing is the future tense, though ethnographers interested in evoking hope, possibility, and wish—but also hopelessness and destiny—may find it suitable for their purpose.

The choice of a tense is an important one, but we must realize that the immediacy of all tenses can be expressed through a jussive mood capable of evoking the linear and non-linear temporal dynamics of desire, intent, purpose, necessity, command, and consequence. Employment of the jussive mood can therefore assist in highlighting the narrative components of the fieldwork process. For example, my narration highlighted the narrative origin of our research purpose (e.g. "Jon and I had been pursuing the opportunity to go camping in the Arctic since we had discovered its popularity on an earlier trip …") and singled out that curiosity as our reason to travel there. The jussive mood is also evident in the inevitability pervading some of the situations I described (e.g. "But the urge is too strong and you must eventually surrender" and "snowmobile travel is rendered labyrinthine, requiring low speed, patience ..."), as well as in passages when the reader was exhorted to relate to an experience (e.g. "You must imagine the camp to be the human race's last self-reliant outpost ..."). Describing practices through the jussive mood also helps in making writing more interpellative and less declarative. Compare, for instance, the subtle immediacy of writing "you start by excavating a hole" with the alternative definitive declaration "Timmun and Niviaqsi began by excavating a hole."

Proximity and the admirative mood

Non-representational ethnography is embedded not only in time but also in place. Emplaced ethnographies pay attention to how embodied experiences of the field are colored by the many properties—the sights, sounds, textures, smells, tastes, temperatures, movements—of place. These and other spatialities of the field must be tended to, reflected upon, cultivated, and carefully evoked by non-representational ethnographers whether their research focuses on geographical issues or not. Ethnographic representation, therefore, deeply relies on proximity. The proximity of the ethnographer to people, places, weather, events, animals, inanimate objects, practices, and assemblages allows ethnographic writing to be close at hand, intimate, involved, and momentous. Proximity allows for reverberations to be compelling, personable, eventful, and idiosyncratic.

There are many ways to express proximity. One of the most obvious is the admirative mood, a mood that is constantly present throughout much non-representational ethnographic writing. The admirative mood is chiefly used to express surprise, wonder, and enchantment. It is a mood often found in writing that details experiences of discovery and exploration. In my writing, the admirative mood is evident in several passages, such as my description of pressure ice movements, as well as my wonderings about the character of the tundra (e.g. "The Arctic tundra has a strange way of acting ..." and "I began to appreciate the rocks' diverse characters ...").

It is easy to fall prey to romanticism while using the admirative mood. Fieldwork, after all, is travel, and travel lends itself quite well to the lyrical contemplation of an over-enthusiastic explorer. At times, such admirative proximity is appropriate and appreciated, but at times admirative ethnographic composition can slip into corny travel writing (something of which we—in the eyes of the beholder—are all invariably guilty at times). A possible way to free oneself from the trap of romanticism is by using another few dimensions of the admirative mood: irony, paradox, and sarcasm. My writing, for instance, employed an admirative mood toward quite a few paradoxes, such as Timmun using an iPad to record the outcome of a traditional practice. I also employed a diffused sense of irony to remark on the unfamiliar character of the place.

Thus, one way to employ the admirative mood without engaging in excessive romanticism is by employing humor. Humorous situations are pervasive in everyday life and fieldwork alike, and they are especially poignant when one comes face to face with new places, new situations, and new acquaintances. Yet humor is conspicuously absent from too much ethnographic writing. Conveying humor through irony, paradox, and sarcasm can allow ethnographic composition to be admirative without being obsequious, reverential, or much too easily enthralled or amused. Humor can help in making oneself and informants less superhuman, more "real," and easier to relate to. And it can serve the purpose of conveying the quintessential ethnographic stance toward making the familiar extraordinary and the extraordinary familiar. In sum, admirative moods can help ethnographic audiences to feel as if they were there too, as proximate to the field and as full of wonder, surprise, and exploratory spirit as the ethnographer him/herself.

Fluidity and the subjunctive mood

Fluidity refers to the property of being easily subject to change, to being in a constant state of process. Rather than through frozen and static models, non-representational theory and research view subjects of their inquiry through the lenses of transformation as a regular—not an exceptional—feature of life. Therefore, the focus is kept on adaptation, alteration, malleability, diversity, versatility, variability, and evolution. Ethnographic research in particular does not unfold in linear ways, and it allows itself to be capricious, inconsistent, mercurial, unsettled, unpredictable, dicey, haphazard, ambivalent, desultory, and skittish. As a result, ethnographic compositions should avoid conveying impressions of an overly linear undertaking and should instead aim to enliven various forms of change.

Fluidity is achieved through a style of writing that enlivens the alterations and adaptations of fieldwork. A kind of irrealis mood that can be used to animate a sense of fluidity is the subjunctive mood. The subjunctive mood expresses emotion, wish, judgment, opinion, or the need for outcomes that have not yet occurred. When used in subordinate clauses (e.g. "I suggest that we leave before sunset"), it can it can be used to convey the expression of past or present desires without actually referring to whether these were fulfilled. When used in counterfactual dependent clauses, the subjunctive can have an even more powerful effect by highlighting doubt and uncertainty (e.g. "if it had been sunny we might have been able to reach our destination faster").

Using the subjunctive mood can help ethnographers shed light on the constant malleability and open-endedness of their work. It can serve the purpose, in other words, of highlighting how realities are not determined in advance by blueprints, cognitive schemata, and pre-planned outcomes. It can animate how people change their minds, how they do things—or choose not to do something they could have done. For example, my writing uses the subjunctive to denote how I acted toward the silence of the tundra: "I wished that I were the only sovereign holder of silence" and "I wished it were only me: the main star of a stage whose ears were all mine, the biggest fish in the largest, but most unscripted, pond on this planet. I felt the urge to bellow out a scream and witness its echo. Yet, it seemed, it would have been unfitting and I chose to hush." Through such rhetorical choices, I aimed to enliven the fluidity of the moment, how things could have been.

Reflexivity and the desiderative and volitive moods

Non-representational ethnography shares with other post-structuralist research a strong disinterest in absolutist, universal knowledge. Because no research is value free, the knowledge generated by non-representational ethnographers is personal and situated. Without becoming self-obsessed or indulgent, reflexive ethnographers position themselves squarely in their own research, sharing their work as both a personal narrative and an emotional, embodied, and intellectual perspective informed and shaped (and not "biased") by experiences, dispositions, objectives, sensations, moods, feelings, goals, and skill. By being reflexive on how their presence colors the object of the inquiry, researchers' interpretations become more, not less, robust in light of their open-endedness.

Volumes upon methodological volumes have been written on researcher subjectivity reflexivity, situatedness, and positionality, and there is neither reason nor space to rehash those arguments here. What is more compelling here is a discussion of how reflexivity can be stylized through the use of the irrealis mood. Amongst others, there are two types of irrealis mood that can be utilized to animate reflexivity: the desiderative and the volitive mood. The *desiderative* mood expresses wishes and desire. Typically employed verbs are to want, wish, long for, ache, crave, fancy, prefer, yearn, and related synonyms. For instance, in my writing, I conveyed how toward the end of our camping trip, "Niviaqsi was missing his family. Timmun and Kristiina seemed to crave the daily routines they had swept under the condensation for a while. And Jon and I longed for our homes." And I also conveyed how I craved peace and quiet—a desire that was quite revealing of the significance of camping for both myself and the others. A closely related form of the desiderative mood is the *volitive* mood, which is similarly used to express wish and desire as well as fear.

Reflexivity can be used to add context and perspective to an interpretation. A unique way of exercising reflexivity in a typically irrealis and non-representational mood is by doing so through wish. Wishing colors an interpretation though an emotional and affective tinge that lessens the cognitive weight of analysis. Take, for example, how I wished to have been spotted by airplane passengers. Though I knew this was unlikely, that very wish allowed me to see myself from another position and another emotional and intellectual state. Of course, I never saw myself from that airplane, nor did I question myself the way I wrote that I did, but through that wish, I introduced a reflexive perspective marked by the mood of the moment.

Non-representational theory is becoming more and more accepted, and its principles are growingly clear and popular. Yet non-representational writing continues to be much too often an expression of disembodied minds overly focused on developing theoretical ideas and ontological abstractions. Non-representational ethnographic writing, by invoking the power of volitive and desiderative reflection, can help in countering these trends. A volitive and desiderative mood can animate writing by highlighting the uniqueness of each writer's fears, wishes, and desires and can make each of our writing styles more unique, less derivative, less mimetic of one another's work.

9 Writing in magazines and blogs

In spite of the ongoing growth of the sheer number of genres and modes of communication available to ethnographic researchers, many ethnographers still rely exclusively on the prototypical media of their scholarly trade: the book and the journal article. It is safe to assume that all of us academics are quite aware of the limited access the general public has to these media. Yet, as many of my colleagues often remind me when I present my thoughts on these issues, writing is something quite habitual to most of us, something that we have learned to do very efficiently in the limited time that most of us have to dedicate to research. So, in this chapter, I want to consider a couple of easy and practical options available to writers in order to make their research more widely accessible. My primary objective is to examine the process of communicating ethnography through popular print magazines, web-based magazines, and blogs, but in addition I will be spending a few introductory words on how to generate hypermedia books.

I am going to reflect on a handful of very practical considerations that ethnographers might want to entertain whenever they attempt to popularize their work through writing-based communication channels. Such considerations are so practical that they may seem to be common sense to those who have already enjoyed some success in this publishing realm. However, I want to take nothing for granted in this book, and I am going to share everything of practical value that I know. My reflections pertain exclusively to my own personal experiments in ethnographic knowledge mobilization, but are intended to stimulate others to tackle similar challenges and hopefully avoid my mistakes. Fiction and creative non-fiction writers might find my recommendations overly basic, but my concern in this chapter is with inciting those academics who have never tried this route, and encouraging them to embark on this journey with the right tools.

Composing ethnography for magazines

Many different kinds of magazines around the world generally publish good writing, dedicate a great deal of attention to human-interest content, and can reach wide audiences—ranging from a few thousands to millions. Popular magazines can therefore constitute an appealing medium for ethnographic work. However, ethnographers for the most part have yet to learn how to take advantage of this medium's potential (for an exception, see Zompetti 2012).

Writing for a magazine generally begins with a pitch to an editor. Unlike the academic journal article submission process, submitting a pitch to a magazine requires some basic "marketing" know-how because the query has to be enticing enough to capture the attention of an editor with multiple competing choices on her desk. Several websites explain in detail how to do this, so I won't discuss the art of pitching in too much depth, but in essence, I will say that in my experience a magazine pitch

- should be concise but sufficiently descriptive (a 150–200-word email is typically what I submit);
- ought to be relevant to the audience of the magazine;
- is ideally timely in that it addresses a topic of contemporary interest;
- establishes the credentials of the writer.

I find the last point to be especially important. Magazine editors receive frequent pitches by freelancers from all kinds of backgrounds. Academics and advanced students have professional status and expertise that set them apart from the rest of freelance writers and should not be afraid to begin their pitch by explicitly articulating those credentials. If I have writing samples available, I make sure to send them as part of my pitch, but at the same time I do not want to convey the impression that my research on the topic I am pitching has been published too much before (editors like some degree of exclusivity). Once a pitch is sent, the writer needs to wait for an editorial response—which can be nearly immediate or may take up to 3–4 weeks—but, unlike journal submission, multiple magazine solicitations can be made simultaneously.

Once a query is accepted, the writer is given a deadline and a maximum word count, and from there onward, the process unfolds like any other editorial process. Accompanying photography can help a pitch, but not necessarily if it is not of sufficiently high quality or if publishing space is unavailable for pictures. Finally, editors may issue formal contracts, make more or less detailed promises for payment, or guarantee no payment. Some academic writers might see getting paid for one's writing as a welcome change from actually having to pay fees to be published, whereas others might view profit-making as inappropriate (more on this later).

Magazines are periodical publications containing a variety of thematic content. While the word *magazine* has traditionally referred to print publications, magazines increasingly duplicate content on the web—or publish exclusively online—so the distinction between printed and web-based publication is no longer of immediate consequence for content producers. Magazines' thematic content is enormously diverse, of course, a fact that creates an interesting opportunity for ethnographers. Ethnographies are as diverse in content and subject matter as life itself and are therefore amenable to being shared through a vast variety of magazines. Ethnographers would do well to consult the magazine shelves of a library, bookstore, or news kiosk or to do internet searches to get some inspiration and ideas for new publishing outlets.

In addition to considering subject matter, ethnographers interested in magazine publication might also be able to make their research relevant to publications that cover a geographical area where a particular fieldwork project has unfolded. For example, my research on off-grid living took place across all of Canada, in all ten provinces and three territories. As a result, I was able to pitch stories to magazines not only in light of the subject matter of my work, but also because my fieldwork was conducted in the communities where a particular magazine was read. A word of advice: it is important to start from smaller publications such as hyper-local magazines and only gradually work up enough confidence, skills, and credibility to submit to more prestigious and national and international titles.

Most magazines have a distinct audience characterized by people with similar demographic and social characteristics. This is what makes them appealing to advertisers, obviously. This is also something that can make them useful to ethnographers keen on sharing a message amongst a particular public. Being able to share insider knowledge or common values with an audience might enable an ethnographer's message to be better understood, well received, and perhaps even more potent. Being able to speak a similar "language" with an audience might also come in handy if an ethnographer has to counter a particularly tight space allocation, which might otherwise make it difficult to explain technical terms or provide much context.

A key difficulty of writing for magazines is the limited space. A typical magazine article ranges from 700 to 1,500 words, and only rarely do writers receive more than a space allowance of 2,000 words. This may seem incapacitating to an academic accustomed to 8,000-word limits and up. In my experience, limited space is no reason to give up. An 8,000-word journal article is typically filled with many sections (e.g. introduction, literature review, conclusion, references, etc.) that can make the actual ethnographic content quite limited (e.g. 2,000 words or less). Because magazine editors typically treat an ethnographic article as a "human interest" type of story, their interest primarily focuses on the "data" and a brief argument framing the story. As a result, my magazine pieces generally follow an easily replicable format squarely centered on the story and argument that my "data" allow me to tell without having resort to complex academic concepts requiring long explanations.

Take, for example, the article "Bamfield's Unlikely Off-Gridders" (Vannini 2012b). In the magazine lingo, this piece is called a *profile*. Profiles allow readers to become (relatively) intimately acquainted with one individual (or a couple, in this case) and the immediate circumstances at hand. While a 1,300-word article cannot provide an in-depth portrait of a human being, the content is actually longer than that generally reserved for an informant in a typical journal article, where persons are reduced to fictitious names and anonymous places, one-letter identifiers for race and gender, their age, and a four-line quote. When they are compared this way, a magazine piece might actually feel more intimate than a journal article, despite the limited word count.

Now, let us examine the magazine article format in some detail. Generally, a magazine article begins with a *hook*, like "Jan and Nelson aren't the typical off-grid couple." This hook teases the reader into wanting to know more, in this case into wanting to know what makes Jan and Nelson atypical. The actual *resolution* to the hanging interrogative does not come into focus until about two-thirds of the way into the article, when the reader's attention is finally pointed to Jan and Nelson's "birthdays," and their actual age isn't revealed until the very end of the writing. Now, this format is meant to "seduce" the readers into staying with the piece; their curiosity is what, ideally, keeps them going. This is quite different from a typical journal article characterized by an introduction that gives away the entire content by way of a detailed preview and summary.

Another example of a hook is what I call a *puzzle piece*. A puzzle piece is essentially a question—which either the writer or an informant asks—with no immediately available or even relevant answer. Take, for instance, the puzzle piece I used in "Cutting the Cord," an article published in *Canadian Geographic* (Vannini 2012c): "What happens when you apply heat and cold to a Peltier Junction?" A puzzle piece of this kind is not meant to capture the reader's interest in the actual answer—after all, the reader of this magazine may or may not be interested in physics—but is rather meant to perform an old trick of the ethnographic trade: making the ordinary unfamiliar. By catching the readers by surprise, hopefully enough interest is sparked to keep them going, and eventually other pieces of the puzzle are added. It's a bit like partially concealing a photo, evoking curiosity in the rest of the hidden image, and then eventually revealing more bits one at a time.

Between a hook and a resolution stands what ethnographers would call *thick description*. In this sense, magazine editors are no different from academic gatekeepers: they expect more showing than telling, sufficiently detailed context, and a detailed-enough portrait of people and relevant actions. Now, as ethnographers, we know very well that 1,000 words are not enough to provide a thick description, but by foregrounding important details and backgrounding less relevant others, by evoking rather than systematically describing, and by hinting rather than exhaustively categorizing, much can be done in a few words. Indeed, it helps to think of a magazine profile as a *fragment*: a small piece of a broader puzzle, but still a piece warranting attention in itself—kind of like a subsection of a research paper. That fragment might hopefully be good enough to incite the reader to want to learn more—from a book, for example, which can be cited as part of an author's bio. In this sense, a magazine article is like a trailer for a film—a piece of a much bigger product.

There are other important differences between ethnographic magazine writing and the more traditional fare. In the above-mentioned pieces, for example, I adopted a few rhetorical devices that not every academic editor would go for. For example, the two articles begin with a focus on me as a writer. I generally do this because much ethnographic writing resembles the popular trope of travel writing. By writing as if my work was a kind of travel writing (and, in a way, all ethnography is), I position my story around my process of *discovery*. Discovery is the broad format for which my ethnographic work—and arguably much of ethnographic research in general—is commonly accepted in magazines. By presenting fieldwork as a process of gradual discovery, I also avoid coming across as an annoying know-it-all who has all the answers before a trip can even begin.

Next, in the opening, close attention is paid to the where, when, what, how, and why of a story: the key elements of the introductions typical of journalistic writing. Within the opening paragraphs, therefore, I stage a scene that tells the reader where I am, when I find myself there, how I got there, and what I'm doing. I pay no attention to the typical demands of academic introductions that would expect me to state my thesis, make explicit the worth of my work, cite my influences, and offer a preview of my writing. If I ever need to cite someone, I try to do so subtly.

Following the points above, in contrast to academic writing, I offer no signposts in any of my magazine writing. *Signposting*—as discussed earlier in this book—is what we do (constantly) in academic writing when we tell our readers what we are about to argue, how we are about to organize our work, what section comes next, or what we just discussed or found. In other words, when writing for a magazine, I just try to bring readers along on a voyage without regularly stepping to the side to inform them of where we are going.

In academic ethnographic writing, my personal idiosyncrasies are generally silenced; in ethnographic magazine writing, I feel I am expected to bring color to my character and make the situation in which I find myself interesting. This is what almost any creative non-fiction writer does as well in order to make a character relatable or at least memorable. Thus, in "Cutting the Cord," I am a clumsy handyman, and in "Bamfield's Unlikely Off-Gridders" I am a wonderer and a wanderer. The focus is never on me as a protagonist, however, but merely as a travel guide and fellow discoverer.

Short informant quotes are necessary in magazine ethnographic writing. They are intended to evoke a sense of dialog and are meant to lend character to a human subject. They are, therefore, aimed at creating a scene and are not used as verbal data to closely analyze. As a result, I choose bits of dialogs that contribute to the narrative unfolding of a piece, and I paraphrase what I cannot otherwise display. As opposed to academic writing, I also take part in conversations by asking questions and taking turns at speaking. Conversation is an important part of storytelling, so I am not afraid to hide questions or comments that my reader would typically say in the same circumstances if she were there. I do not hide my emotions.

Short and vibrant sentences and paragraphs replace the verbosity of academic writing. Indeed, at times, a single sentence can constitute a paragraph if it represents an important narrative element and I want to bring attention to it. I also write with a thesaurus at hand to keep my word-choice fresh, and I make sure that the important conceptual keywords are prominent but easy to understand. Look, for example, at the emphasis "self-sufficiency" receives in "Cutting the Cord."

I do not abstain from making some generalizations and engaging in argumentation. I do so in order to contribute to the sense of discovery typical of a piece and not in order to contribute to theoretical understanding or generate a new concept. Magazine editors, unlike journal editors, are interested first and foremost in the story, in the "empirical evidence," if you will. A story has to have a message, and that message can and should be told in few, simple words. Conveying a message this way actually even helps me as an academic writer too: whenever I become able to tell what my research is about in few and simple words that everybody can understand, I end up understanding it better myself!

Academic writing most often assumes a position of certainty. The academic ethnographer is competent and secure in her arguments. As a magazine writer, I try to mix interpretive authority with awe. Awe, naiveté, and a sense of wonder—I believe—must be present in magazine ethnographic writing because those are arguably the affective forces pushing a reader to want to "travel" with me in a particular lifeworld. Both the articles I mentioned are, in fact, underscored by a certain "How in the world do these people do what they do?" tone that is typical of the ethnographic imagination. Affective modes, of course, must be driven by the particular content of a study.

For all my writing—academic and popular—I use the present tense. The present tense allows for writing to be situated in a clear temporal and spatial frame, as if it were happening as the actual experience unfolds. The present tense, especially in its subjunctive mode, also allows for relations and actions in the field to unravel in an open-ended manner, without a determinate or even probable end. The past tense, while it is a definite aid in longer narration and while it is *de rigeur* in reporting the past, has a tendency to make events, experiences, utterances, and actions factual, as if closed to interpretation or alternative ways of unfolding. As well, ethnographic magazine writing, in contrast to ethnographic academic writing, should in my mind allow for no tense shifts of the kind that are customary in academic writing ("I will show how ...," "I collected data by ...," etc.).

Finally, whereas academic ethnographic writing generally ends by fizzling out with a litany of apologies for limitations, suggestions for future research, synopses and repetitions, magazine writing should end with a proper *denouement*. A *denouement* is a narrative resolution, a way of "untying" the narrative thread. Different resolutions are demanded of different kinds of narratives, of course, but in general I prefer to bring the spotlight back onto my informant(s) and let him/her have the final word. For that, I choose a quote that encapsulates the wisdom of the lessons his/her ways of life teach us.

Multimodal content for blog and hypermedia books

Magazines accept more than just writing. Photography can accompany printed pieces, and audio and video content can supplement web-based pieces. This can give visual, audio, and multimodal ethnographic data great exposure. Audio, photography, and video can deeply enrich the ethnographic offering of magazines, complement writing, and provide newer opportunities for ethnographic composition. I want to highlight a few reasons why this should be considered extremely valuable.

First of all, web-based magazine written content can generate interest in and can direct web traffic to additional audio and visual creations. Uploading a video on YouTube or Vimeo, or an audio file on SoundCloud, is easy enough these days that any ethnographer with web access can do it. The internet is full of interesting content, and audience attention is hard to get. Thus, embedding a video in a magazine article can help with directing general audiences' attention to these other media.

Second, magazines can give exposure to ethnographic photography in different ways than journals and books do. For example, the article "Off-Grid World" published in *Yukon: North of Ordinary* (Vannini and Taggart 2012) features photography that most journal editors would have discounted for its lack of un-analyzed visual data content. The magazine editor, on the other hand, sought to publish photographs that were aesthetically rich and painted a beautiful picture of the places we visited. Because the quarterly publication is Air North's official magazine, the photos were seen and appreciated by tens of thousands of passengers from around the world.

Third, web-based magazines (or traditional magazines with duplicate web content) allow informants to speak in their own words and with their own voices via audio clips. For example, in "Living Off-the-Grid in BC" (Vannini 2012d), I uploaded on SoundCloud short audio segments from interviews and hyperlinked them. Readers interested in hearing bits of conversations as they actually unfolded can follow the hyperlinks and listen on their computers. These "digital audio footnotes" also let me, as an ethnographer keen on sharing richer data, publish longer excerpts than I can otherwise do through short transcribed quotes. Besides relaying the words as spoken, these clips also convey interesting elements of the soundscape in which an interview takes place.

Blogs

In the Internet 2.0 world we live in, the prospect of self-publishing by creating a personal website or maintaining a blog is certainly tantalizing. Yet, in my experience, most of these publications have a limited audience, and without constant publicity efforts and regular updates, they risk quick obsolescence and eventual oblivion. This does not mean that ethnographic blogs are inefficient uses of academics' time. Rather, it means that blogging must be done strategically and systematically. In this brief section, I want to highlight select ways in which a blog can be useful.

A blog is essentially a journal, not unlike a field journal or research diary. In most cases, ethnographic projects consist of long periods of data collection in the field followed by long periods of analysis and composition. The very extension over time of an ethnographic project makes it a perfect candidate for blogging. Obviously, a field journal contains private matters, whereas a blog features only the information that can be filtered to the public but, aside from this important difference, a personal journal and a blog can be similar in many ways by serving as outlets for sharing ideas, raw observations, fieldwork updates, key readings, fresh discoveries, news about publications, and some "behind-the-scenes" methodological narrations. Whenever a comment feature is enabled—or at least whenever the blogger is easy enough to contact by email—these "write-as-you-go" fragments of the ethnographic life can serve as "trials" for working arguments, writing styles, and so on, to which an audience can give feedback.

In my experience, my blog on my off-grid project has also benefited me in other ways. First, by posting a FAQs page, I could quickly direct colleagues, prospective informants, and members of the media to what I had been doing without repeating myself too much over time (journalists, in particular, tend to ask the same questions and expect fast answers—nothing pleases them more than seeing a list of FAQs!). This FAQs page has made it easier for many newspaper journalists to interview me with very quick turnarounds and to gather the necessary information about my research as well, reducing the likelihood of misunderstanding.

Second, by posting information about the field sites I would be going to visit in advance of my travel, I was able to recruit additional research participants, who contacted me to ask me to visit them.

Third, by aggregating on my blog all the various radio and newspaper appearances, as well as providing links to magazine articles or media material co-produced with my collaborator, I provided enough content—and regularly updated content as well—to attract and maintain a sizeable readership over time. This audience had enough time to accumulate over the months and years, so that the publication of the book and film eventually appealed to them as a familiar and long-awaited offering.

Finally, and I believe this an especially important point, by seeking aggregation with the *Huffington Post* (Vannini and Taggart n.d.), I gathered a larger audience than my blog alone could have conquered. The *Huffington Post* publishes magazine and newspaper-style articles as well as numerous blog posts aggregated from a variety of users who take advantage of that site's great traffic. Amongst others, anthropologist Paul Stoller (www.huffingtonpost.com/paul-stoller/) has taken effective advantage of this medium. The sizeable audience of the *Huffington Post* gave me enough reason to invest time in more elaborate written and even video posts which—by virtue of cross-links—could then generate more traffic for my own blog as well. The *Huffington Post* is only one of many blog aggregators out there. Seek your own; they will produce much greater traffic than you could on your own.

Blogs in sum—at least in my experience—are largely a labor of love with uneven and unpredictable use value, but through the application of a few strategies and some care and attention, they can offer a big payoff in return for a small investment.

Hypermedia books

Year after year, ethnographic research is increasingly communicated multimodally in new and creative ways. One of the many ways in which multimodal content can be shared is through hypermedia books. A hypermedia book is an assemblage of different materials shared through multiple media, at the center of which lies a book. Think of a hypermedia book as a volume that, in addition to sharing written knowledge, serves a wide offering of information, each piece told through its most ideal mode and disseminated through its most ideal medium. In this way, a book becomes the center of a network of multimodal knowledge.

Since 2010, I have been serving as series editor for several books published by Routledge under its Innovative Ethnographies list. The series description reads:

> No longer insecure about their aesthetic sensibilities, contemporary ethnographers have expanded upon the established tradition of impressionistic and confessional fieldwork to produce works that not only stimulate the intellect, but that also delight the senses. From visual to reflexive ethnography, from narrative to arts-based inquiry, from hypertext to multimodal scholarship, and from autoethnography to performance ethnography, fieldwork has undergone a revolution in data collection practice and strategies of representation and dissemination. Innovative ethnography is a catalytic field of experimentation and reflection, innovation and revelation, transformation and call to action. The new Routledge Innovative Ethnographies book series publishes fieldwork that appeals to new and traditional audiences of scholarly research through the use of new media and new genres. Combining the book and multimedia material hosted on the series website, this series challenges the boundaries between ethnography and documentary journalism, between the scholarly essay and the novel, between academia and drama. From the use of narrative and drama to the use of reflexivity and pathos, from the contextualization of ethnographic documentation in felt textures of place to the employment of artistic conventions for the sake of good writing, this series entertains, enlightens, and educates.

Innovative Ethnographies titles live simultaneously in books and on the web. In its book medium, such ethnographies unfold exclusively through writing, with the occasional exception of just a few black-and-white photographs. On the web, these books are then enlivened through all the modes of communication that the internet can currently support, chiefly audio, video, photography, drawing, maps, and interactive dialog (through blogs' comments). Hypermedia books in this series, however, do more than simply refer their readers to web pages. Thanks to the hypertext functionality of e-books (every book in the series is published in both paper and electronic formats), readers can click hyperlinked parts of the book and seamlessly navigate content on the web.

I myself have written two hypermedia books and found the process and the final products rife with simple and practical opportunities to animate ethnographic content. For my research on ferry mobilities, for example, I relied extensively on hyperlinks to allow readers to map the BC coast's numerous islands and remote communities. I also relied greatly on short audio clips to convey the atmospheres of ferry boats and terminals, as well as to paint portraits of my informants through the sound of their voices. A few years later, I turned to video and photography—thanks to the work of my co-author Jonathan Taggart—to portray the off-grid places and homes I visited, giving readers/viewers intimate access into households' everyday lives.

In both cases, I personally found the process of linking books and the web very easy. While I concentrated on writing the book, a student or a technical expert I hired had the job of assembling all my non-written material into a website. This was possible because I had budgeted some of my grant money for this task, but in all honesty I alone--if necessary--could have put together a basic website using Word Press or a similar web builder for less cost. All authors of the books published in the Innovative Ethnographies series have the option of creating their own website or working together with one of my own graduate students and a basic web-building tool (Drupal). In my case, once my website was ready, all I had to do was to hyperlink all the relevant passages of my Word document (it's a simple thing to do; if you've never tried, just right-click a word and create the link you want). I simply ensured that all the chapters of my book had an approximately equal number of hyperlinks and that the sheer number of hyperlinks wasn't overwhelming. Linked material has to be relevant and interesting and achieve something that writing cannot achieve on its own.

Thanks to Google Analytics, I am able to tell how much traffic these websites get, and it's quite considerable—for academic research, at least. For instance, lifeoffgrid.ca regularly receives about 3,000 unique visits a month, even now that over three years have gone by since the publication of the book. Thirty thousand users a year is not much compared to a high-traffic website, but it is most certainly far more than the number of copies the book has sold. In this sense, the website accompanying a hypermedia book serves not only the purpose of extending ethnographic content multimodally but also the double purpose of advertising the book and making its basic findings accessible to people unwilling or unable to buy it. And all of this can be done at a relatively low cost.

Risks, warnings, and limitations

Ethnographers have a lot to gain from reaching wider audiences. Writing for the audiences typically reached by magazines can allow ethnographers to engage in public education, can increase the potential of our work to achieve social and cultural transformation, can guarantee our fieldwork greater levels of visibility, and can even teach us new "tricks" by exposing us to different media formats, genres, and technologies. It can also expose us to some level of risk, and I feel compelled to conclude this otherwise optimistic and encouraging chapter by outlining some limitations of this kind of communication.

The first risk is misunderstanding. By writing in popular magazines, an ethnographer risks being seen by the general public as simply another type of journalist, and this may affect our legitimacy and may expose us to unwarranted criticism. General audiences may not understand or appreciate the level of rigor followed in all interviewing and participant-observation procedures, the amount of fieldwork undertaken, and the depth of theoretical and epistemological preparation typical of the ethnographic trade. This may subject our position in the academy to crude criticism ("How is this science?!"), for example, or similar misplaced disapproval.

The second risk is of an ethical nature. By writing for limited circulation journals and books, ethnographers are protected by narrow exposure. Things change when "they read" what "we write about them" (see Brettell 1996). Having suddenly gained a new audience means we must become a lot more sensitive to delicate issues of representation, which may at times influence our arguments and even dull our critical edges. Magazines also generate much greater personal exposure for our informants than our typical writings do, which can increase our potential to do harm. For instance, for all my magazine writing, I have not used fictitious names for my informants (magazine editors abhor fictitious names). This is something that I cleared well in advance with all my informants, but it is something that must be dealt with very gingerly in different cases. To lessen the risk, I ask informants for explicit approval of my writing in all its various media. I share with informants my initial submission and the copy-edited version of the article and ask them to check on factual accuracy and the appropriateness of my representation. All of this is, of course, done in compliance with my university's Human Subjects Review Board.

Finally—but I fully realize that many more risks could be listed—there is always the risk of sensationalizing a story to make it more interesting. Academic audiences may or may not care to read good writing; what they care about, after all, is not entertainment. Magazine editors generally want to sell audiences to advertisers in order to meet a bottom line. Our work thus risks being featured alongside articles on losing weight quickly or on crooners' beautiful homes. To compete with this more traditionally popular material, ethnographers may feel pressured to make rhetorical choices that exaggerate their field stories. Furthermore, there is always the risk that getting paid for our work might deepen these vicious tendencies.

In spite of these and other challenges, I do believe that ethnographers have a lot to learn from reaching out to broader audiences. I have personally gained great satisfaction in seeing that my writing is read, for the first time, by friends, relatives, and neighbors and in hearing that they understood and appreciated my narratives and arguments. I have also been able to give exposure to my university, something that administrators have greatly appreciated. Most important of all, I feel I have served well the cause of public education by stressing, in my case, the importance of issues like energy conservation and sustainability through positive stories. I'll admit it has been a fun learning experience too.

Part III

10 Multimodal ethnography

Traditional ethnographies are for the most part unimodal, that is, they are communication products that make use of only one mode of communication: writing. Modes are not the same as media. Modes are the *ways* in which people, objects, or animals communicate. Speech is a mode of communication, for example. Gesturing and singing are other modes, and so is writing. Media are the *channels* carrying our communication modes. For instance, a book—which is a particular medium—can carry writing (a mode), but so can other media such as a newspaper, a website, or a peer-reviewed journal. Television is a single medium, but it can transmit several modes of communication such as recorded or live dialog, still images, moving images, and writing.

There is nothing wrong with unimodal communication—indeed, it has served our species very well for the purpose of communicating complex and abstract ideas clearly. Unimodality, however, is only one option that we have for communicating. There are other options, and as academics, we sometimes tend to forget that these options exist. There are now multiple and growing possibilities for combining ethnographic writing with other modes for different analytical purposes (e.g. see Dicks, Soyinka, and Coffey 2006) or for the sake of broader knowledge mobilization. As more communication technologies become cheaper and user friendly, and as the distribution of their content becomes more democratic, these options demand we take them into serious consideration for all of our research projects. To be clear, I am not suggesting that ethnographers abandon writing or that they take on other modes of communication simply because they are available. But I believe that multimodal communication can serve the aims of public ethnography very effectively, and it can attract newer and younger generations of makers and consumers of ethnographic knowledge. Thus, whenever it makes sense for it to be so, I believe that public ethnography ought to be multimodal.

Multimodal ethnography can be many things. Visual ethnography, for example, can be a combination of writing and photography. Such has been the most typical multimodal research in the social sciences. But other multimodal possibilities exist. Writing, for example, can be combined with video. In this case, an ethnographer can write a paper and produce a short video or feature film that can be distributed through a website. By doing so, a researcher can easily satisfy both career imperatives (which often demand that research be written and published in a peer-reviewed printed journal because, well, academics are great at demanding social change but pretty bad at enacting it themselves in their own world) and calls for public engagement (e.g. by uploading one's video on a popular website like YouTube or Vimeo). Indeed, even a photography-based ethnography can be shared in similar ways, with a paper ending up in a journal and photography being distributed through a website like Flickr or a personal photoblog. Since print journals often severely restrict the number of publishable photos, and since they can only reproduce them in black and white, publishing them independently on a website makes sense. Of course, the need to publish photos or a video separately from a written article ceases to exist when a journal is published on the web. In those cases, whether a journal is published in HTML or PDF version, photos and video can be embedded directly into one's writing.

While photography needs writing to convey a more contextualized message, video is immediately multimodal when it conveys multiple forms of communication such as speech, gesture, movement, and other sounds. Think about how many words it can take a writer to describe an object, or a person's facial expression, or a place, and compare that with the number of seconds it can take video to convey that. But video's role in ethnographic research is not just to allow ethnographers to accommodate for larger quantities of their thick descriptions to be shared or to render sensations, practices, and experiences otherwise difficult or impossible to capture through writing. Video can also be used as a secondary multimodal technology to reproduce and report on other multimodal research productions.

For example, some public ethnographers have lately made effective use of theatrical performances to share their research (for a review of these projects, see Tedlock 2005). The work of Soyini Madison, for example, has shed light on such diverse issues as the struggle for clean and accessible water, the struggle between traditional religion and modernity in Ghana, and the oral histories of University of Carolina laborers and service workers. Performances like these can benefit from a secondary, wider audience if cameras are employed to record live theatrical shows. Video can also be used to report—in journalistic style—on other kinds of multimodal productions. For example, some researchers organize exhibits, gatherings, festivals, and other events that are essentially bound by space and time— that is, by the necessity of being there in person. Video can be used to record these events and share them widely via the web or television. As local TV stations continue to struggle with budget cuts and find themselves limiting the original content they can produce, it becomes easier for research teams to have their productions (which represent "free content" for TV stations) featured on television channels, either as a short story as part of a newscast or as a full-length special feature (perhaps for a community or public-access channel). In these cases, the video does not need to capture every single message the research intends to convey. Rather, a short video can simply be used to "advertise" the complete project (e.g. a book or article), which remains accessible elsewhere.

Whether it is a still photography–based essay, a documentary video, an event or performance, or a short video reporting on such an event or performance, I believe that multimodal products resonate well with public audiences for at least four reasons. First, multimodal communication products such as video and photographic essays can be easier to find than most traditional academic products. Journals (except for the few that are open access) demand expensive individual or institutional subscriptions. Single-article downloads can be pricey too. Books, which can be equally expensive, are also rather hard to find for most people, as they are neither marketed widely nor sold at large commercial bookstores. On the other hand, accessing websites is inexpensive. By placing a multimodal ethnographic research study on a high-traffic website, or at least by carefully selecting strategic keywords and re-publishing non-final versions of peer-reviewed work on a personal or university site or a widely used one like academia.edu, an ethnographer can reach out to more people.

Second, multimodal communication products borrow from genres familiar to the public. Consider how widely read current affair magazines are in comparison to peer-reviewed journals. As discussed before, despite the fact that many magazines welcome submissions from freelance writers (such as academics and students), they are hardly ever the target of academics' submissions. A photo essay article about one's research study, properly "translated" for the magazine format, would undoubtedly be more appreciated by general audiences—indeed better understood—than a long and complex peer-reviewed journal article. As discussed earlier in this book, of course such a magazine piece would not need to replace a journal article—it could simply be produced in addition to the former as a way of publicizing findings more widely. The same could be said about producing a video. Documentaries are widely consumed these days on the Internet, Netflix, and satellite and cable TV and through DVDs. Multiple publics *enjoy* watching a documentary video much more than they might enjoy reading a journal article on the same topic. The fame of documentarians like Michael Moore—judged in comparison to social scientists who write on the same topics—is indeed quite revealing of this phenomenon.

Third, multimodal communication products can make our research more visible and more accountable to our very own informants. Much too often, people donate ethnographers their time, stories, and experiences without receiving anything in return. We have all heard informants complain that nothing came out of their research participation even when a peer-reviewed journal article or two were published on the subject. On the other hand, the ability to share one's research with informants—and, through their preferred social media, all of their personal networks—by the means of an accessible multimodal product can somewhat repay our debt to them. I, for example, have shared research back with my informants by publishing their photographs on the website that accompanied one of my books or my making available short videos about them, which they could then share through their social media.

In spite of all these benefits, not enough academics take advantage of the multimodal potential of ethnographic research, so why is that? Some might say it's because of lack of money to buy the necessary gear. I don't believe that argument. If we all had as little as 10% of the money that we have spent over the years going to conferences around the world, we would have all the gear we need to produce professional content. A high-end DSLR camera with a few accessories costs as little as a single international conference trip. Staying home instead of flying overseas to a conference can buy us not only a camera but also maybe even a tripod, a high-end sound recorder, and a lavalier microphone. It's really up to us to determine what is more valuable: a few sandwiches in between conference sessions and another line on a CV, or a great gear set that can unlock a multitude of possibilities and opportunities?

The real argument against producing multimodal content has nothing to do with lack of money to buy gear, in my mind, but rather a lack of skills. I myself was never taught how to produce multimodal content in graduate school. Sure, there are now more advanced and forward-minded courses and programs around the world than there were 20 years ago, but I would be willing to bet that most of the people reading this book have never taken such a course. So, what I want to do in the rest of Part III of this book is to share basic and practical knowledge with you on how to do video and audio recordings and how to take better photographs. My intent is to keep things simple and practical: I am going to eschew entirely epistemological reflections (why is it that we know so much about the representational validity of photography, for example, but that we wouldn't be able to define what "aperture" means?) and focus on *doing* multimodal ethnography. Let us begin by making a shopping list of what we need.

The right gear for the job(s)

Over the last year, I have been filming a documentary on artisans and the value of handmade work. It's one of those projects I call "professional development work." Throughout my career, I've taken on quite a few of these. They are short (never more than a year), local (so I don't spend much money on travel), and focused on developing a new skillset for me. I find it easier to develop new skills during these types of projects because external pressures are low to non-existent, and typically the absence of grants to support these projects makes it possible for me to shed the weight of outside expectations entirely. Anyway, one of the things I learned on this project is that tools matter. In the particular case of my project on artisans, I wanted to become more familiar with a new video camera, and there is no better way to do so, I thought, than using it.

There are specialized tools for everything, and each artisan can probably write volumes about the significance of every tool they own in relation to each of the tasks typical of their job. In particular, during the filming of my ethnography, I recall a woodworker who told me that every craft comes with its own set of hammers. Mind this: there isn't a hammer for every single form of craft, he said; there are multiple hammers for every type of artisanal work, and then, within each category of work, there are multiple specialized hammers for each task. Despite this, most of us—lacking specialized knowledge and familiarity with tools—still only know the word "hammer."

My point is that we should have the same attitude toward the production of multimodal ethnographic work. Each task has its precise tool: a specialized tool that works best under certain circumstances and with precise demands. A photographer or filmmaker, for example, will tell you that every particular set of shots will demand a particular lens. And often that lens will even need to be equipped with a particular filter for the job. Makes sense, right? I highly doubt anyone is disagreeing with me, so I will really get to my point now: don't you even think for a single second that you could use your smartphone to produce professional multimodal content. It would be like a woodworker picking up the first hammer that she sees at the dollar store. I heard this attitude countless times from non-technically literate colleagues and students: "a smartphone can do everything these days." Sure. That's what advertisers of smartphones want us to believe. It's just the same way a pick-up truck can get you on the very top of that snowy mountain and a cold can of beer can turn you into an irresistible sexual magnet.

In preparation for writing this book, I have checked out a few books on "doing ethnography" of this or that kind, and I've never found any of them where tool selection seemed to matter. I believe it matters profoundly, and that is why over the next few pages, I will ask you to open up a web browser, do some shopping around for the best prices, and build a wish list. Since in the next chapters I am going to cover audio, video, and photography production, I am going to limit my coverage here in what follows to the right gear for those jobs. And because gear changes quickly, I am going to suggest a mix of individual models and the broader type of tool they exemplify, so hopefully my presentation will still be useful in a few years from now.

Audio

A high-quality audio recording is a must for both audio and film documentarians. Audiences will forget shaky images, limited dynamic range, unimaginative compositions, and all sorts of visual shortcomings (have you ever watched the successful doc series "The making of a murderer"? That's exactly my point …) but will not forget poor-quality audio. Indeed, if there is a gatekeeper involved—like a producer or editor—your work marred by poor audio will be rejected outright and will never air. And if you upload it yourself, your listeners will simply click away after a few seconds. Making great audio capture even more essential, the post-processing of audio is quite limited in the extent to which it can fix recording problems. Not even the best audio editor in the world can turn a recording made with a low-quality tool into a good-sounding output.

The great news is that good audio recording is not terribly expensive at all. An excellent digital recorder capable of producing professional broadcast content will only cost around $320, and microphones for various jobs will cost even less than that. My personal recommendation for an audio recorder is the ZOOM H5. There are other brands and models in that price range that will do the job, of course, but the H5 has proven its value to me. It can provide high-quality field recordings and serve as a voice recorder. It can be mounted on a camera and works well handheld. It can record multiple tracks in .WAV format up to 24-bit/96kHz. It's easy to use, it comes with a variety of available accessories, and it works like a charm with or without external microphones attached to it. And because it records on SD cards, it's super easy to grab one of those cards out, stick it in your computer, and start editing right away.

Though you could get excellent quality sound out of the X/Y input of the ZOOM H5, in most situations, you will want to use external microphones to record voices, especially in a one-on-one interview situation. There are two kinds of microphones you will want to add to your shopping list: a lavalier and a shotgun. Maybe you won't need both at first. Some people favor "lavs" and other people like shotguns, and no-one has a definitively better argument over their counterpart. Lavs are easy to work with. Clipped on the chest of an interviewee, they will record human voices beautifully and work better in windy conditions than shotgun microphones. Shotguns need to be handheld with a grip of some sort that will prevent them from picking up handling noise (I personally like a very inexpensive "pistol grip"). They also invariably need to be covered with a windscreen when working outdoors because they are very sensitive to wind rumble. And they need an operator who will point them at the source of sound. But once those variables are in place, they will record possibly better-quality sound than lavs do, they are much better at separating the human voice from a noisy background, and they work in those situations where attaching a lav to someone is not possible or desirable.

For a high-quality and inexpensive lav, I recommend the Microphone Madness MM-MSLM Omnidirectional MatchStick. It's around $130 and it will never cost you a penny in batteries because it's powered by the devices it's attached to. It can plug into your ZOOM X/Y input and even directly into your DSLR mic input. As far as shotgun microphones go, my vote goes to the RØDE NTG2. It's light, has an outstanding signal-to-noise ratio, can work handheld or be mounted on a camera with a cheap accessory, and uses an XLR connection that guarantees reliability and clean transmission into either your ZOOM recorder or camera (if your camera has an XLR input jack; otherwise you will need an adapter). Its normal cost is around $270. So, there, you've spent the same amount of money you would have spent on a round-trip domestic airfare to that conference, and you're now in the position where you can record the best-sounding professional audio documentary.

Photography and video

Good cameras are more expensive than audio recorders, but the positive thing is that a single tool can do two jobs: photography and video. That's right, I don't advocate buying dedicated cameras—cameras that can only shoot stills or camcorders that can only shoot video. A single tool can do both jobs, and that is definitely the way to go for someone who is building a brand-new toolbox for themselves or for a university department. Personally speaking, in all honesty, I own two cameras: one that shoots only digital film and one that I now primarily use for still photography (as well as video, whenever my larger and heavier digital-film camera simply won't work). But owning two cameras, while necessary whenever two are needed at the same time, is a bit of a luxury for the beginner and probably too overwhelming of a chore anyway.

There are many good cameras on the market, and it's not terribly fair to recommend one brand over another. Another option that has arisen lately is the availability of mirrorless cameras. Mirrorless cameras are smaller and lighter than DSLRs and are therefore preferable if weight is not an issue. Personally, I like a heavier camera over a lighter one because I can grip it better—weight makes an object more stable (that is another strike against smartphone cameras, by the way). The most outstanding mirrorless on the market these days is the Sony $\alpha 7$, which retails for as little as $1,000. Sony now makes newer versions of that camera, and the original model has gone down in price to as low as a grand; newer versions are pricier. It shoots outstanding video and good stills, and it works amazingly well in low light. A comparable DSLR for that price would be a Canon 80D, which in my mind shoots better stills but not as good video. If you can spare another $2,000 or so, then you should consider buying a Canon 5D or one of the newer Sony $\alpha 7$ models, as the price difference is entirely justified.

Now, choosing a camera means committing to different lens mounts, and therefore it is a decision to be made very carefully. Chances are you will change cameras in the future sooner than you will give up on your lenses, so choosing a Sony mirrorless, or a Canon DSLR, or a Nikon DSLR is a decision that will impact what type of lenses you are committing yourself to, because lenses are not always compatible across brands. I have no recommendations on the matter. Take time to investigate each option and determine which lens family appeals to you more.

When it comes to buying lenses, I recommend buying one at a time, over time, as money becomes available (as you skip more and more unnecessary conferences over the years, perhaps?). The first lens I would recommend is an eclectic "normal" zoom lens, which is a bit of a jack of all trades. My normal lens is a Canon 24–105mm, which serves me very well for both wide shots (in the 24–35mm range), medium shots (in the 35–60mm range), and profiles and close-ups (60–105mm). It's the lens I have on my Canon 5D MkIII nearly all the time, and I wouldn't trade it for anything. I shoot a lot of "run and gun" footage where I am basically following around a subject who is busy with a variety of tasks, and the 24–105mm allows me to get everything I need without stopping to change lenses. Having image stabilization is extremely important, so I recommend buying lenses with that function (look for the letters IS in the name of the lens). It will cost around $1,000.

There are two or three other lenses that you will want to put on your wish list over time. They are less necessary, and I have known of photographers and filmmakers who do excellent work without them, but they are useful if you can spare the money. The first is a telephoto lens. Any lens over 150mm is a telephoto lens that can bring a subject much closer than it appears to the naked eye. Anything over 200mm is considered "super telephoto" and is probably overkill for those of you reading this book, unless you are keen on shooting sports action or wildlife. In my experience, a 70–200mm is an excellent choice because it also allows you to zoom back to 70mm, which is not too far from a normal field of view; with a couple of steps back from the action, you can always get a medium shot. I find that a 70–200mm allows me to capture close-ups of research participants who are not too comfortable around the cameras. They see that I'm five or ten meters away from them and they relax, perhaps even forget about me, even though I am getting a fantastic visual of their facial emotions in detail.

The next and last lens I will recommend is a landscape lens, like a 16–35mm zoom or a 16mm or 20mm prime. I shoot a lot of landscapes, and they simply don't look as full and as enveloping at 24mm as they do at 16mm or even 20mm. Besides, if you ever have two cameras running at the same time during an interview, you can use a 16–35mm lens on a camera for a wide shot, while the other camera zooms in around 70–105mm for a close-up. It's the best of both worlds. Both the wide lens and the telephoto lens I mentioned will run around $1,000 or slightly above. All these prices, by the way, refer to lenses with image stabilization and USM (Ultra-Sonic Motor). It's possible to buy cheaper lenses without those features and save money. On the other hand, you could find ways to spend even more money by buying lenses with a higher f-stop. The prices of the lenses I have been referring to are for lenses with a f/4.0, which is plenty adequate. Lenses that allow for wider aperture (all the way to f/1.8) are more expensive but perhaps also not necessary for most of us. We will talk more about f stops and aperture later.

A final word on prime vs. zoom lenses. Zoom lenses are more versatile, obviously. You can shoot up close and zoom out a second later without stopping to change lenses—what's more convenient than that? On the other hand, prime lenses typically produce higher-quality images and are cheaper. Their only trouble is that you will likely need a set of them, and you will nearly always have to carry them all with you. There isn't a single winner in this battle, and most professional photographers and filmmakers will own both zoom and prime lenses. I am a fan of zoom lenses, though I also own a Canon 50mm f/1.8 STM lens that works like magic every time I need to shoot an interview in low light. And it only cost me $250. So, if you want to own nothing but prime lenses, be sure to buy at least four: a wide angle (16mm), a normal (35 or 50mm), a profile (like an 85mm), and a telephoto (150mm or up).

A few final "accessories"

Hopefully you haven't busted your budget yet, because I have a few more items to add to your shopping list. Even though I call them "accessories" these are really essential pieces of gear. The great news is that they're not as expensive as cameras and lenses are. So, the first item is a sturdy tripod. Tripods are absolutely essential pieces of equipment if you want to avoid shaky footage (and you do). They are especially important for ethnographers who plan on shooting interviews, because it is virtually impossible for anyone to handhold a small camera steady for longer than a few minutes and outright impossible to do it while simultaneously asking questions and listening. Clearly, they are not as essential for photography as they are for video, but even photographers are known to use their tripods regularly, for example for long exposure, time lapses, and for most situations in which a super telephoto lens is mounted to the camera (shakiness is magnified as you zoom farther).

A photographer's tripod is not the same as a videomaker's tripod. Photographers don't need to pan *while* they are shooting, whereas someone recording video does. Because of this, photographers' tripods tend to have smaller, cheaper, less efficient tripod heads. If you are doing video, you will need a tripod head that offers some resistance as you pan vertically and laterally, and you will also want something stable enough to support the weight of your camera and whatever you may have mounted on it. Tripod manufacturers specify the maximum amount of weight their products will support, how much their tripods will weigh, and how long they are when extended and when folded. These are all key variables to consider. A long tripod (when folded) may be unable to fit in normal luggage and may thus be problematic to travel with. A heavy tripod may be cumbersome to carry if you have to walk around quite a bit as you shoot. Personally, I find that a good video tripod, with a good video tripod head, should cost around $300–400.

Just a quick note: some people find that a monopod works well for them. A monopod allows you to put the camera down (though you still need at least a hand to hold the monopod) and stabilize your image as you shoot. A monopod also allows you for more stable footage—compared to working handheld—as you walk or move around with the camera. A monopod is also faster to move around and set up than a tripod, it takes less space, it's lighter, and it folds into a smaller size. It's also cheaper than a tripod. However, with a monopod, you can't pan up or down at all, and even lateral pans will be somewhat awkward. I myself have sometimes screwed my video tripod head onto my monopod in or order to pan better, but the result is never as good as what you get with a tripod. Do consider what is best for you.

A great tool to stabilize handheld-captured footage is a loupe or viewfinder. Photographers are typically able to stabilize their images better than DSLR filmmakers because, by bringing their camera close to their face and looking into the viewfinder, they essentially create a third point of contact between their bodies and their cameras. When you shoot video, you need to monitor the LCD screen of your camera, so you can't have that third point of contact—unless, that is, you buy a loupe-style viewfinder. For about $100, a viewfinder can give you that third point of contact and not only stabilize your footage but also give you the necessary cover around your LCD screen while you shoot outdoors (it's extremely difficult to see anything on LCD screens when the sun shines on them). As if this wasn't enough, good loupe-style viewfinders magnify the image of your LCD screen and allow you to judge focus infinitely better than just by looking at a naked LCD screen. It's an absolutely essential piece of equipment for DSLR filmmakers.

The last thing I will mention is a decent filter for your camera. Whether you are doing photography or video you will want to (1) protect your expensive lenses and (2) protect your images from being washed out by excessive light. The best filter for most of us is a variable density neutral filter. A neutral filter does not have any tint; it is faithful to color and light temperature as perceived by the human eye. The variable density part is the exciting stuff. With a variable density filter, you can rotate its rim until you feel that you have darkened the image enough. There is nothing more useful than a neutral density filter on a sunny day, especially as you attempt to maintain a constant shutter speed and a low f stop (again, we will talk about these things in another chapter). Don't cheap out on a filter. You don't want to invest over $1,000 on a lens and then slap a $20 piece of crap in front of it! After, would you buy a fancy sports car and put bicycle tires on it?

So, by now, you hopefully haven't gone broke and you can actually afford batteries, memory cards, and storage drives and even spare a few dollars here and there for upgrades and the occasional extra toy. And obviously, you will need a decent computer to handle all this, something with at least 8 gigs of RAM (though 16 is better) and with the necessary software (we'll talk about that later too). And hey, I never said this was cheap, but I did argue that it's all worth it!

11 Working with audio

Audio documentaries are an increasingly common way to share research with broad audiences. There are several reasons for their proliferation. Radio stations—traditionally the main media for the dissemination of audio documentaries—have multiplied exponentially with the shift to internet-based and satellite broadcasting. Surely there are still AM and FM dial-only radio stations, but with more of us listening to our favorite channels on the web and XM radio, stations' reach has expanded and transcended local boundaries. Another reason for the popularity of audio documentation is the vast popularity of "podcasts" on the internet (podcasts *are* nothing but audio documentaries). Varying in length and in the way they are shared—ranging from news network productions uploaded on highly trafficked websites, to independent content shared via user-generated websites and blogs—audio documentaries are an intriguing way to share knowledge with people around the world.

In the pages that follow, I am going to outline a few practical tips on how to create audio documentaries, beginning with topic selection and moving on to audio data collection (i.e. production), editing (i.e. post-production), and finally on to distribution. Much of what I will cover in my discussion regarding production and post-production will also be directly relevant for the production of sound for video content as well, so this chapter very much serves a double purpose. I will write this chapter on the basis of the assumption that you will be working with professional gear, such as the tools I covered in Chapter 10. Many smartphones nowadays offer audio-recording tools, though even with the use of dedicated lav microphones attached to them, smartphone audio recording is not advisable except for desperate circumstances when nothing else is available at hand.

Before we begin, I should issue a few words of caution. Audio production can be a very complex undertaking, and it is no accident that entire degrees and programs of study are dedicated to it. However, when broken down to its most basic components, and when it is well done, audio production with the right tools can yield clean recordings that are easy to edit and share and remarkably pleasant to listen to in one's home, car, and anywhere a pair of headphones can be taken. What I am hoping to do in this chapter is simply to give you an introduction to this skillset, so you may develop an interest in the subject and learn more on your own later. Those of you using this book to teach a university course might find it valuable to use this chapter as the basis of a course assignment, which should be an especially useful exercise to be undertaken in order to get over the inevitable anxiety that students may feel when dealing with this for the first time. That assignment might consist of a producing a short audio documentary that draws from two or three interviews, field recordings, and perhaps a short voiceover. Such an audio documentary might in the end range in length from 8 to 15 minutes.

When is audio documentation ideal?

Audio documentation is ideal whenever a research topic and its corresponding lifeworld have pronounced sonic qualities. You might be dealing with music-related topics, for example. Or perhaps your research deals with soundscapes, either directly or indirectly. There are also times when audio documentation may not be an immediate choice and yet, upon due consideration, it will reveal itself to be an ideal mode and genre of communication. Narrative, for example, is a great subject matter for audio documentation. When people share stories in the context of a research interview, all they typically communicate are verbal recollections. In the absence of photographs or archival footage of any kind to illustrate such recollections, video would be a very limited mode of communication because it can do very little beyond showing a "talking head" telling a long story. Audio documentation, on the other hand, can liberate our eyes from being stuck on a screen and allow us to imagine the elements of a story freely, working as a "theater of the mind," as it were.

Audio documentation is also particularly useful when certain topics make other modes of communication less powerful than they could be. For example, during my research on ferry travel, I found that video would have revealed "too much" of my subject. Video images seemed to "flatten" my representations of mundane travel experiences, taking away the extraordinary value of the daily practices I wanted to describe. Video made mundane experiences look even more mundane, in other words, whereas audio documentation left a lot more to the imagination. Video also showed too much of the places I wanted to describe with evocative language. A combination of still photos and audio clips instead lent the subject a vastly more captivating feel that allowed readers and listeners to wonder more on their own.

At times, audio may simply be more practical than video. For instance, certain university human-subject review boards can be quite conservative toward the use of photography and video because these modes cannot protect the anonymity of research participants. In cases like these, audio documentation can serve as a viable alternative. Of course, research participants can also be identified through their voice, but the lack of images can offer a relatively lower degree of visibility, or it can at the very least give a higher impression of anonymity. Audio documentation is also better equipped than video to handle certain delicate topics for which being on camera might feel overwhelming to some people. Many people, it seems, are more at ease talking about intimate subjects with a voice recorder in front of them more than they are with a camera. Moreover, despite the omnipresence of cameras in everyday life, there are still many people who simply aren't comfortable being in front of a lens. Audio recorders, in my experience, tend to make such research participants feel a lot less anxious, and this in turns always yields more authentic and more deeply personable data.

Recording sound

Recording high-quality sound requires forethought, good gear, and common sense. Unlike video recording, I find that recording sound does not require nearly undivided attention and a lot of experience. It is, in other words, something that can be more easily handled on one's own, without the need for assistance during an interview. It is also something that requires less expensive gear and something that most people can learn to do entirely on one's own. Though I can only provide a brief introduction to sound recording in this section, I really do believe that, by following my advice, you will do very well and even surprise yourself with the professional quality of your recordings.

Let us begin with the settings. Your ZOOM H5 (or similar) recorder should be set to record in the .WAV format. Never record .MP3 files. Sure, they will be smaller in size, but the quality of your recording will be much lower. A 1TB hard drive these days costs around $80 and it will hold tons of .WAV files, fully warranting your investment. Also, be sure to record in the 24-bit, 48kHZ format. This is something you can "set and forget"—there is no need to change this setting every time you use the recorder. I also recommend that you replace the 2GB SD card that comes with most recorders with a much higher capacity card, like a 16GB one. While 2GB is more than enough for the length of a typical interview, having a 16GB card will enable recordings much longer than 120 minutes and will ease all your anxieties about needing to copy files after every interview. Once you have familiarized yourself with the instruction manual and you know how to operate the basic recording functions of your recorder, that's it; you are set to start attaching microphones.

As I said before, your basic choice is between a lavalier microphone and a shotgun. For most interviews, I find that lav microphones work very well. They are more unobtrusive than shotgun microphones and easier to forget for interviewees who might find an interview situation somewhat intimidating. Whereas a shotgun mic pointed at you constantly reminds you that this is not a normal conversation, a mic clipped on a shirt is out of sight and out of mind. Shotgun microphones work better than lavs in noisier environments, however. I also prefer a shotgun mic whenever I interview more than one person at a time. In those cases, I simply sit or stand at the same distance from every interviewee (this is very important, or I will record voices higher or lower in volume in relation to my distance from each interviewee) and I turn my pistol-grip mounted shotgun toward each person as they take turns speaking. If you do indeed make use of a shotgun mic, do not forget to buy a pistol grip; it is a simple but effective tool for avoiding microphone handling noise.

Whereas you will always be the one holding shotgun mics, lavs must be clipped onto your interviewees. Clipping a lav microphone can be a socially uncomfortable task in some cases. In my experience, most people are more comfortable doing it on their own rather than having me do it. Because the microphone wire must be hidden under the shirt whenever filming takes place, it's much less awkward for the interviewee to place the microphone themselves than to have me place my hands under their clothing (no kidding!). To show people how to do this, I normally demonstrate the task on my own shirt and then ask them to do it. Not everyone feels comfortable clipping a mic on their own, though. Many older people, in my experience, prefer when I do it, and in those cases I will do my best to avoid awkward bare-skin touching by using my mic's long wire to go behind their back, over their shoulder, and then partly around the neck, making sure the wire is well hidden behind them. Whether you clip it or they clip it, be sure the mic sits about 20–30cm or so from the mouth and away from layers of clothing that it may rub against. Do not worry if a mic is visible on camera; as long as the wire is not exposed, it is all fine. If you are not filming, a wire can be fully exposed to view.

When attaching a microphone to your recorder, be sure to pay attention to what you are doing. Lav microphones must be either inserted into the X/Y jack of the ZOOM H5 or into an XLR input (depending on your lav mic type), either channel 1 or 2. Shotgun microphones typically have an XLR connection, so they must be inserted into either XLR input channel 1 or 2. The silliest mistake to make with all these things is to insert a microphone and then forget to turn the "on" button of its corresponding channel. So, right after connecting a mic, turn on the relevant channel and test the sound levels right away. If you have connected a mic into XLR channel 1, for example, ask your interviewee to say something (I typically ask them to count to 20 in their normal voice) while you rotate the gain dial corresponding to channel 1 to get the best recording volume. Then be sure to turn the dial for the channel that you are not using all the way to zero. If you have connected a lav mic into the X/Y jack of your ZOOM H5, there is no need to turn the XLR dials down to zero.

The best recording volume is right around -12db. By this mean that as your interviewee speaks, his/her voice should peak around that level. It's perfectly ok if their voice occasionally reaches around -9db at the highest, or around -18db or slightly lower when their voice goes down. The human voice naturally goes up and down, but as long as your recording captures most of it around -12db, everything will be fine in the end. If you're going to mess up your levels, it's much better to record low levels than high levels. Turning up low levels in post-production will introduce a bit of noise, but that is probably not the end of the world. On the other hand, recording "clipped" sound (sound that occasionally hits the 0db mark) means recording unusable, distorted sound. A final recommendation on this subject: do not obsess over the gain dial. Unless conditions change dramatically during a recording, it's ok to set the gain dial right and then just monitor it every now and then without touching it. There is no need to "ride" the gain by adjusting it every few minutes or, worse yet, every few seconds.

If you have ever recorded interview sound (and most of you probably have), you know the basic no-no's: don't record in loud environments that will make it impossible to separate signal from noise (coffee shops are among the worst places for an interview); don't forget to carry extra batteries with you; don't neglect to check that your recorder is still working (do this every few minutes with a quick glance); and stay away from windy environments (if you must record in a windy setting, do try to turn your interviewee's back against the wind to use their body as a shield, and perhaps also hide their lav mic under a layer of their clothes).

If you are using a shotgun mic, don't forget to point it at the interviewee's mouth at all times and to sit or stand relatively close. Shotguns are very sensitive to wind, so if you are conducting your sound recordings outdoors, be sure to invest a few bucks in a fuzzy windshield cover (also known as a "dead cat"). Many documentary filmmakers use their shotgun attached to a boom, but I find that this draws excessive attention to an interviewee. Booms are not only obtrusive, but they also require the presence of a boom operator, whereas a pistol grip is something I can hold on my own if I happen to be conducting an interview all by myself.

By the way, don't forget to press "record." Seriously (I have, at least once...).

Believe it or not, at its most basic level, this is really all there is to the basics of recording high-quality interview sound. You will also find that the same fundamental rules apply to recording field sounds, away from the rather controlled environment of an interview. Same formats, same levels, same precautions—nothing much changes at all. The only thing that might occasionally change for me is the use of microphones. Clearly, I never use a lav to record field sounds, typically employing either my shotgun microphone or the X/Y recording input of my ZOOM (I just cover the X/Y mic with a dead cat to protect it from wind). Something I do whenever I record field sounds, soundscapes, or anything of that sort is to speak into the microphone before every recording to indicate to myself later on (when I copy and name files later at home) what I was actually recording. There is nothing worse than recording interesting soundscapes somewhere, recording a few times throughout the day, and then later on to forget what exactly you recorded, why, when, and where.

One more thing. Before or after an interview, it is very important to dedicate a few seconds to recording so-called *room tone*. Room tone is essentially the ambient sound of the environment in which you are conducting an interview. Every environment, even when it may seem very quiet, has a certain sonic texture. Maybe its texture comprises car traffic in the distance, urban crowds, birds chirping, or kids playing in a nearby room. Whatever it is, record it for about 30 seconds. Ask your interviewee to be absolutely quiet for 30 seconds, be sure to do the same, and just record it. It will come in handy later when you have to fill gaps between clips in an interview (more on this later). This is a simple task and there is not much to it, but be sure that your room-tone recordings don't happen to record any music playing in the background, or you will be forced to use the same short song clip over and over.

Recording sound for video productions

Recording sound for video requires only a few extra tasks. Most professional makers of video and film record sound externally to their camera. Most cameras, in fact, feature poor microphones, and it is highly unadvisable to use them at all, especially for interviews and dialog. To get around this problem, all you have to

110   *Working with audio*

do is record dialog sound separately, in *addition* to on-camera recording, and then synchronize external and internal sound tracks during the editing process. After synchronization, the internal sound track is going to be discarded whereas the external one is going to be kept. It is important to do this right or you will have off-sync sound: audio and picture ahead of or behind each other.

Synchronizing sound is quite an easy task nowadays, but you will want to follow my advice to make sure you avoid surprises later. Synchronization software like Plural Eyes (my recommendation) which works by matching the graphical wave patterns of your on-camera audio and your external audio. This software is powerful and intuitive, but it greatly benefits from a little help during the recording process. There are many ways to help it along the way, but my favorite is easy and super practical. After pressing "REC" on both the camera and my ZOOM (this doesn't need to happen exactly at the same time), I snap my fingers. And then I begin my interview. A simple finger snap is a loud enough noise to create a steep spike in my sound recording, and that spike is then used by Plural Eyes to match the two separate tracks.

Now, if you have followed my advice and bought a DSLR or mirrorless camera, you will find that you will be unable to record one entire interview on camera without pressing record again after 30 minutes. That is because most cameras have a 30-minute recording limit. However, there is no need to stop the recording on the ZOOM and immediately re-start it after you re-start recording on your camera. But it's still a good idea to snap your fingers once again after you re-start the recording on your camera. Doing this will leave you at the end of the day with two, or three, or more video clips and one single uninterrupted sound recording, but if you remembered to snap your fingers each time you re-started your camera recording, your synchronization software will line up each video and audio track together effortlessly, leaving just a few gaps in between the video tracks when you were probably excusing yourself to your interviewee for the shortcomings of your camera. If you forget to snap your fingers (or clap your hands), your software may still be able to synchronize your audio tracks, but its success rate might be decreased, and you might end up having to manually sync the odd clip or two (ugh!).

There are times when you will rely on your camera to record sound without the benefit of an external microphone. This is perfectly acceptable any time you are recording b-roll or any kind of action other than an interview or extended dialog. If you make use of the camera-mounted shotgun microphone I recommended earlier, or a similar one, you will find that its recording quality is going to be invariably good. The only trouble with recording on-camera sound is that the on-camera microphone will likely record camera handling noise since it sits so close to your hands, but that is something you can cut around in the editing process if you are careful to not move your hands too frequently. On-camera microphones will also work well enough for impromptu field interviews, though chances are that unless you are recording your interviews with the very same shotgun microphone, there will be a marked difference in the texture of your recordings. There are worse problems to deal with, and unless you are planning on becoming a serious filmmaker who aims for very wide distribution, this is probably something to not lose sleep over. As long as you avoid recording anything with your DSLR's puny little built-in microphone, all will be well.

The basics of sound editing

If you have followed my advice thus far, you should have access to good-quality audio material that is free of problems. On the basis of the assumption that you will have at least three types of audio material to work with—interview files, field soundscapes, and room-tone clips—I will now give you a few pointers on how to assemble a simple but well-done audio documentary. I will also assume that by now you have moved all your sound files into various folders separated by categories that make sense for your project and that you have backed up all your files on a separate hard drive. So, let's get to it!

The initial post-production phase of audio documentation has a great deal in common with the initial steps of qualitative data analysis of the thematic kind. The first step is to transcribe your audio material. Transcription is not absolutely mandatory, but it makes your work easier and better organized. When you transcribe interviews for audio or video editing, make sure to mark recording time in your transcripts, noting time every 30 seconds or so. The second step is something with which you are likely extremely familiar: thematic analysis. There is really no difference between thematic analysis for paper writing and thematic analysis for audio-documentary production. No matter how you like to conduct your analysis, you will end up with a collection of excerpts—at this point perhaps simply nothing but a list of highlighted passages in your transcripts—that give a vivid impression of the themes you have decided to cover. However, how you have made those selections is up to you, and since this is not a chapter on thematic data analysis, I will simply move on by assuming that you have made your list for good reasons and that you are happy with it.

So, now that you have your excerpts highlighted on paper, what do you do? Well, if you haven't done this before, it is now time to determine how long your audio documentary should be. You might have chosen excerpts that, when simply added together, add up to a 30-minute documentary. But is this what you need? Is a 30-minute documentary going to serve your purpose well? I really don't have the answer. The answer depends on your chosen topic, your intended audience, and your distribution channel. If you have a group of aficionados in mind—members of a subculture, for example—who are going to captively listen to your documentary no matter how long it is, then maybe you can afford to take 30 minutes of their time. If you are self-distributing on the internet, you also don't have to worry about precise time constraints. But if you are working with a distribution channel like a radio station and with a "general" audience as your target, then you'll want to keep your content shorter—much shorter. How short is really up to you and your gatekeepers. What I can tell you here and now, however, is that the content that you have highlighted, set aside for the world to hear, and quickly added together to get a sense of how much content you've got, is at this stage likely to be twice as long as it should be.

Yes, twice as long. I am serious. I cannot even tell you how many times I have found this to be true. I always start with material that I think is absolutely great, only to realize, cut after finer cut, that I can manage to get across the same essential content in half the time I started with. And shorter is often better because it's easier to share, appreciate, and remember. And if you think that you simply cannot afford to cut out half of your good material, ask anyone not connected with the project to help you out. Chances are they will have a much more objective and wiser perspective than you, given your personal investment in the project. You will resent them for their frank opinion now but will thank them later.

Now that you have made your nearly final selection on paper, it is time to head to your computer. There are dozens of audio-editing software packages available nowadays, and it is up to you to choose whatever you can afford and are willing to learn. Most of them work extremely similarly, and once you have learned the basic principles behind one, you have learned the basic principles behind them all. This might entail heading to YouTube to watch a few tutorials uploaded by people who know their software well. It is amazing how much you can learn from these videos, and there is no substitute for them. Because so much work at this point is software-specific—what and where to click, drag, and so on—I will keep my presentation generic and let the YouTube videos of your choice take care of the rest. Personally, I work with Adobe Premiere Pro CC for my video work, and now that Adobe Premiere Pro CC has essentially incorporated Adobe Audition, it makes sense to assume you might be working with it too, or at least with something very similar.

Your workflow at this point will consist of three-point editing and timeline assembly. First, you bring up a file you need. You then identify the passage you want to select by dragging the timeline to the relevant spot of that file and mark "in." Let us say, for example, you want to select an interview excerpt like this one: "I was born in 1971. That was a difficult time for my family and for my country. And so, hum, you know, I didn't really have an easy childhood." The words "I was" comes at 03:48 in your interview file and the end of that excerpt—after the word "childhood"—comes at 4:01. So, what you need to do is direct the playhead at 3:48 of the source file and mark "in" by pressing whatever button you need to use in your preferred software. Then move the playhead over to 4:01 and mark "out." Congratulations! You just got your first except cut. Now simply drag it onto your project timeline. Repeat the process for the next excerpt. And the next. And so on, until you have all your excerpts cut and placed in the order you want them on your timeline.

However, do not attach each clip to the one preceding it and the one following it. Doing so would be like writing a paper in one big whole paragraph. You need breaks in order to achieve good *pacing*. Pacing is what gives your audio (and video too, incidentally) good flow. It makes your work stand out as having good rhythm. It's what saves your work from droning on and on. You will find that as you build your timeline, your excerpts need to be separated from each other by pauses as short as a fraction of a second to a few seconds. I typically like to assemble my clips together with pauses of 2 seconds for excerpts that logically follow each other well, 5 seconds for excerpts that represent different subthemes, and 10 seconds or more in between the end of one master theme and the beginning of the next. What I do to fill those pauses between clips is dependent on the project, but typically I will use anything except for more speech. I may use music, room tone, field sounds, soundscape elements, maybe sound effects—basically anything that the project demands. Regardless of how I fill those pauses, I want to avoid producing an audio documentary that is wall-to-wall talk. Chat-filled documentaries will tire your audience to death or force them to tune out.

Your next step in the audio-editing workflow consists of cleaning up your cuts. Personally, I like to clean up my clips right on my project timeline. Take, for example, the except we selected earlier: "I was born in 1971. That was a difficult time for my family and for my country. And so, hum, you know, I didn't really have an easy childhood." "Hum"s and "you know"s do nothing for me and, likely, your audience, so I like to cut them out. In Adobe Premiere, I turn my cursor into a razor and shave that stuff out, then *ripple delete* the gaps. A ripple delete is a deleting action that gets rid not only of unwanted material but also of the unwanted gap that the excited material's exit has caused. I will clean up all my clips like this as much as I can, making sure that I make my timeline leaner without introducing any problems as a result of my cutting. By the way, you will find that razor-cutting like this, and ripple-deleting, works best *before* adding any other sound tracks to the mix. Your interview and dialog track should be the first track you work on, and until you are happy with it, you might want to restrain yourself from adding any other tracks and working on them.

I will now share with you a trick that by itself is almost worth this entire chapter. After you have cut your clips, added them to your timeline, and cleaned them of any unwelcome distractions, you will find that some of your clips—probably most—can sound quite unclean. That is because when people talk, they often blend words together. When we hear someone talk, our linguistic competence allows us to mentally separate words that have blended into one another, thanks to our understanding of the context in which they are spoken. But when you cut words out of their context, you will likely run across words that have blended into each other and will be somewhat difficult to understand. So, for instance, when you cut off "you know," you might have found that the sound "ou" in "[you kn]ow" is now blended together with the word "I." So your "I" now sounds more like "ou-ai." And that's just awful to hear. There is another problem. Cutting sound clips generally has a tendency to introduce little clicks and bops—digital noises that makes your audio track sound jittery and jumpy, as if it was cut and pasted (indeed it was!). So, how to get rid of all these problems? With a simple audio transition called *constant gain*.

Constant gain is essentially a very short but incredibly effective audio fade. Drag it from your effects panel onto *every* sound clip, both at the beginning and end of every clip. It's time consuming, but it's worth it. Trust me. Now, chances are that the default duration of a constant gain is simply too long. A constant gain is effective when it is three frames long, or just about 0.1 seconds. So, you will need to change the default duration in your software settings or simply change the duration of a constant gain every time you apply it. The constant gain will take care of all your clutter and make your chosen clips sound natural and smooth-flowing.

After applying constant gain to the beginning and end of all your clips, and obviously after having cleaned all your clips, you should now have a timeline that you are reasonably happy with. Now it is time to listen again, and again, and again. You might even want to ask other people to listen to your work-in-progress and give you advice. This is the time to shift clips around, order, re-order, and do whatever you need to do to present the best possible story your material can allow you to share. As an ethnographer, you are a storyteller, so I won't spend any time in this chapter discussing storytelling. No one could really advise you on how to tell your story; the story you share is the result of the creative, empirical, ethical, and theoretical choices you wish to make. You may, for example, choose to add a voiceover you recorded. Or you may simply let your interviewees tell the story without the mediation of your voice. These are decisions you should make carefully on the basis of your goals and style.

Now that you have achieved your narrative goals with track 1, it is time to add more tracks to the mix. Every track after track 1 should contain material that was recorded with a clear purpose. You may lay down a music background in track 2, for example. Next, you might add room-tone clips on track 3, soundscape recordings on track 4, and so on. Staying organized while doing this is crucial. Most editors like to keep sounds recorded with different microphones on different tracks. This enables them to apply effects to entire tracks, for example, and to stay on top of potential problems before they spill out all over a timeline. A good editor is first and foremost a well-organized editor.

A quick note on music: avoid copyright headaches. Stay away from music tracks that were produced with commercial purposes and choose instead creative commons-licensed music. There are several websites where you can select such music. These websites—and even each specific composer—will list what they wish from you. Sometimes it can be a few dollars; sometimes it can be nothing but credits. Be sure you keep a record of where every track came from and what kind of agreement is in place for you to use it. If you ever work with a radio producer, they will want to see that neither you nor they are infringing copyright. And if you happen to have friends who are musicians and are willing to compose a little bit of music for your documentary, this might just be the time for them to pay you back for that time you helped them move.

The next step consists of mixing your tracks. Mixing, at the very least, consists of balancing every clip so that each one plays at the desired volume, standing above or below the others in relative volume as desired. My suggestion is to ensure that every one of your dialog clips plays at about -12db. At times, this will mean raising or lowering their input a few decibels. Clips other than dialog and interviews should be set lower than -12db so that speech is not drowned out in music, soundscapes, or noise. I like to keep most of my non-speech clips to levels lower than -18dbs, though I will raise their volume (gradually, not suddenly) every time they fill in a gap in my dialog track. Music, for example, can be faded up and down to accommodate substantial pauses in the dialog track, and so can soundscape clips and similar material. Whenever I fade music up to fill a gap, it must go no higher than -9dbs.

Track volume is additive, so if I play three different tracks at the same time, each at -12db, I will end up with a very loud master track. You will want to avoid reaching levels higher than -6db at any point in your master track. Make the necessary adjustments to avoid this and therefore to avoid clipping master audio. By the way, -6db is a ballpark figure. Computer playback can probably survive as high as -3db without significant distortion, but playback in a theater or projection room will probably be distorted, or too loud, above -6db.

The last tip I am going to pass along has to do with sweetening your speech track. This explanation could get extremely complicated, so I will keep it as simple and practical as I can. Here is the idea. Human speech occurs at specific frequencies. Music, natural sounds, industrial noise, and any other sounds also occur at their specific frequencies. What you will want to do as an ethnographic audio documentarian is to privilege the human voice and make it stand out against the other tracks. This is what parametric equalization is all about. I really won't bother you with how it works, but here is what I'm going to advise you do. Take the effect called "parametric equalizer" and apply it to your speech track. Not to each clip, but rather to the entire track as a whole. Then change its parameters. In Adobe Premiere Pro, I recommend you use the "voice enhancer" preset. Your speech track will suddenly sound a lot better.

Last, you will want to even out your voice track. As we speak, our voice goes up and down naturally, but when we record someone's voice and broadcast it, we will turn those normally occurring fluctuations into something quite unnerving. To compensate for this, drag the effect called "single-band compressor" over your speech track (again, not on over every clip but rather the whole track). A compressor levels out the natural ups and downs of a voice and makes listening to it much easier. In this case as well, you will have to edit its parameters. I recommend using the "voice leveler" preset in Adobe Premiere Pro (or Adobe Audition). There; your speech track will now sound as professional as it can sound—if you did everything right up to this point, that is!

Exporting and sharing with the world

All you have left to do at this point is to listen again and again until you are perfectly happy in every possible way with your work. It is absolutely invaluable to receive advice from friends at this point and listen to their reactions very carefully, even if you disagree with them. They, after all, might very well be members of your audience. After you feel you've done it all, it is simply time to export your track. Exporting sound (and even more so, video) is a task that can get geeks like me going and going forever. Codecs, formats, 16-bits, 24-bits, all this stuff is enough to make your eyes bleary. So, don't stress out about it, and instead simply take my word for it. In Adobe Premiere Pro, simply export your work as a .WAV file set at 48kHZ, 16-bit. It's the best your listeners are likely to be able to play back on the radio on the web. It'll be a hefty file, but it is nothing that is too hard to handle through online distribution. It should also be light enough in size that it can be copied onto a thumbdrive for easy playback in classrooms and conference rooms.

Now that your file is ready for playback, it is time to spread joy to the world. Distributing an audio documentary can take many forms. You may upload it on a media-sharing website like SoundCloud or a similar one. You may upload it onto your project's website or a site that collects audio docs like yours. You may submit it for the consideration of radio-station producers (who may end up being interested in just a few minutes of it, or the whole thing). Or you may even combine it with paper-based publications.

For example, throughout my work on off-grid living, I created a multitude of short clips, corresponding to select interview excerpts, which I uploaded on SoundCloud. Then, I created hyperlinks throughout the various papers I submitted to journals, thus enabling my readers to actually listen to interview excerpts, rather than just read them. This is something that added a very valuable sonic component to my writings and that allowed me to share more empirical material that I would have otherwise been able to do given the restricting word-count limits imposed by nearly all journals. I never got more than a few hundred playbacks on these clips, but I really do believe that they added empirical, narrative, and multimodal depth to my writings.

Short clips excerpted from your audio documentary can come in handy for use on social media as well. Most people today will be more inclined to play a short (60–90 seconds) clip shared on Facebook than they are to play something considerably longer. If you have several of these clips to post on your project's Facebook page over time, you will keep your audience engaged longer and likely attract more people along the way. If all you have is a massive 30-minute doc, you most certainly can't keep posting it and posting all the time to keep the discussion going and the interest alive very long.

Short clips are convenient for another reason too. Most radio stations will balk at the idea of playing a long audio documentary that a freelancer has submitted. Even though you may give it free of charge to them, it will likely be difficult for a radio station to find a dedicated slot for your program in their daily schedule. But a short clip (up to 150 seconds) is another story entirely. In my experience, I have found that radio-station producers were happy to play a short clip I pitched to them and then invited me to their studio for an interview that ranged in length from as few as five minutes to a whole hour. There is nothing that will set your pitch apart from others more than a nicely produced clip; radio producers will likely call you again in the future to see if you have any new projects to share! And while it is true that you can't really achieve any kind of depth in a short clip, even when accompanied by an in-studio interview, you can easily use radio appearances of this sort to draw attention to your full documentary. Simply use the radio appearances (especially if they are advertised or uploaded online) to keep the drum rolling on your social media of choice. And remember, if your ethnographic work has a broad regional or national interest base, you can pitch different (or the same) clips to different radio stations around the country and soon attract a wide audience of radio listeners that you would have had a very difficult time reaching through social media alone.

I hope this chapter has inspired you to give audio documentation a try. Producing and editing audio is less complex and intimidating by far than producing video, and it can serve as an intermediate form of skill development if you plan on making use of video-based distribution later in your career or in a later phase of your research project. Remember that there is nothing like learning by trying, so do not hesitate to produce more and more work even if your first attempt falls short of your expectations. You can always fail better next time.

12 Working with images

There are essentially two ways to work with images, whether still or moving. The first of the two is simpler. It requires turning the camera on, clicking the button that will record video or take pictures, turning the camera off, and then uploading those pictures to a website or another medium. This is how I took most of the photos for my *Ferry Tales* project, and it is also how most photographs are taken by the greatest majority of people with their camera phones. There is essentially nothing wrong with this approach if you believe that images should be a non-mediated, or practically non-mediated, way of representing a social reality. If you believe in the value of this approach for the purpose of doing visual fieldwork, then you believe that any active intervention on the part of the photographer would constitute a distortion of reality, a distortion motivated by bias, premature interpretation, or artistry. If you hold such approach to be the best way of working with images, then you might as well stop reading this chapter now (but then again you probably quit reading this book a long time ago …).

The second way of working with images is more complex. Its difficulty comes from the recognition of the fact that the very act of framing a slice of a social reality with a camera, freezing it in a still or moving reproduction, and relying on the automatic visual configuration of the camera as enacted by its manufacturers undoubtedly *is* to all intents and purposes a subjective interpretive act. If you recognize that photography is indeed an act of mediation, then it behooves you to learn the multiple possibilities in which such mediation may occur. As you become aware of all the possibilities, and how to precisely actualize them with your camera and your editing software, you will likely learn to appreciate photography (whether still or moving) as a mode ideal for storytelling. Images—as creative signifiers of a corresponding signified social reality—are very much like words: semiotic resources that allow storytellers to enliven or animate the subjects, contexts, and happenings of their narrative. The words you choose to compose an ethnography are your choice, and so are the images you choose.

How precisely do you then turn to photography as a storytelling medium? Fundamentally, the answer is twofold. First, you can use images to convey a specific type of content. Second, you can use images to enliven a specific type of content by way of particular forms. The focus of this chapter is on form, and in particular on how the form(s) and styles of image making can allow us to generate stories. Learning photography could take years, so in this chapter, I will have to limit myself only to the basics of working with images. I will begin with camera operation and then move on to exposure and finally to composition. Most of what I will say here will work for both still photography and video, because working with image forms is essentially identical in most cases. Whenever there are differences between still photography and video images, I will underline them, so please read this chapter carefully.

Meet your camera

The only way you can compose the story you wish to compose, in the precise form and style of your choice, is to become intimately familiar with your camera. Over the last few years, I have met many students who were all too eager to learn how to work with images. "What's the best resource I should read?" these students often ask me. My answer is invariably the same: "Your camera's instruction booklet." It is an intuitive answer, but not everyone is willing to accept its truth. I myself must have read twenty or thirty books—and countless papers—on visual ethnography and visual methods before I actually read the instruction booklet of my camera. Becoming familiar, intimately familiar, with your gear is as important as a woodworker becoming familiar with the types of wood available to her and to the many tools for cutting it and shaping it. It is entirely pointless, in my opinion, to work with visual methods without first working with the basics of camera operation. The results of such approach will be as advanced of those of a woodworker operating with an unspecified kind of wood and the one and only tool her workshop automatically defaults to (does this make any sense? No, that's my point).

Reading a camera's instruction booklet will tell you precisely what *your* camera can do and how. I cannot do that here, but I can share with you what I know about the functions and features common to just about all (decent) cameras. So, at best, this chapter is going to help you make sense of your instruction booklet and hopefully give some conceptual depth to it. Before I get to my first piece of advice, let me stress this: knowing your gear intimately well will mean that the very moment you need to use it in the field—that very moment when you cannot afford to take 20 seconds to figure out how to do something with your camera— you will be able to pull the trigger. As an ethnographer, you know that things happen fast, really fast, when you're doing fieldwork, and you know very well that your brain is always in overdrive when you need to be focused on doing so many things simultaneously. If you know your gear and you are simply able to turn to habit to get whatever you want out of your camera, then the task will be simple. If you do not know your gear, you will have to take 10 minutes to fix a problem or look up a function, and you cannot afford this time. Remember, the first step of taking images creatively is to rely on your aesthetic choices, not the automatic mode chosen by your camera manufacturer. So you will need to act quickly, and effortlessly, to execute the choices you would like to make.

The first step at this point is to spin the function wheel of your camera away from the automatic mode (if your camera only allows you to take pictures in automatic mode, return it to the store and get a better one). As you leave the automatic mode behind for good, you will learn that you have four basic options. In no particular order, they are *shutter priority, aperture priority, fully manual*, and *bulb*. In shutter priority, you get to choose your camera's shutter speed. Your camera's brain takes care of the rest of the exposure settings on the basis of what it considers ideal. In aperture priority, you get control over aperture; your camera does the rest. In fully manual mode, you get control of everything: shutter speed, aperture, and ISO (though good cameras in this mode can give you control over shutter speed and aperture while choosing the ISO automatically for you). Finally, in bulb mode, you get to control everything, but you also enable the camera to take very long exposures (1 second and longer).

There are a few more functions I recommend you take control over. The first is white balance. Every source of light has a certain temperature. A tungsten bulb is a warm source of light, a cloudy sky on a winter day is instead a cold source of light, and so on. Your camera changes the color temperature of the tint of the images that it takes by compensating for how warm or how cold the light hitting the sensor is. So, for example, if you are taking images in a room lit by a tungsten lamp, your camera will add a cold (blueish) tint to the exposure to compensate for the tungsten lamp. As a result, your whites will look white, and not red or orange. Fortunately, you don't need to memorize the color temperature, measured in degrees Kelvin, of every source of light. Click the white balance button of your camera and select the image that corresponds to the source of light you are dealing with. Most cameras will have white balance pre-sets corresponding to tungsten, neon, mixed artificial and natural light (typical of a domestic setting by a big window), sunny skies, and cloudy skies. Be sure to change the white balance whenever conditions vary or you move around. And if you ever need your images to give off an especially warm or cold feeling, then you can alter the white balance accordingly. Selecting the "sunny skies" white balance setting for a cloudy day, for example, will make your cloudy atmosphere feel even colder.

Subsequently, you will want to learn what "style" of images your camera wants to take by default. Style refers to a combination of sharpness, saturation, contrast, and color tone. Cameras are typically set to take pleasing photos, and manufacturers give us the option to select among profile styles, landscape styles, and so on. Each profile style comes with a certain combination of settings. Forget all this and take control of your colors. Select a flat or even a superflat profile by turning down sharpness, saturation, contrast, and color tone. As you do so and take a shot, you will see that the resulting photograph or video recording will be quite unappealing in its flat, un-vibrant feel. And that's great. When you take a photos or video recording with sharpness, saturation, contrast, and color tone set at anything but low value, you essentially "bake in" those variables. When you go and edit your photos, you will find it much more difficult to alter them as you wish because your camera has already pre-selected so much information upon capture that is now nearly impossible to alter it during editing. When shooting in a flat or superflat profile, instead, you capture more information that is a lot easier to change later on. Sure, it will be more work for you in the editing room, but your images will end up looking like you want them to look, rather than the way your camera maker wants your images (and everybody else's in the world) to look.

The next function you should take control over is the type of the images you record. Forget .jpg for still photographs. Sure, you can take thousands of .jpg pictures even with a small memory card, but they will all be cheap and hard to work with. Select, instead, RAW pictures. RAW photos are great to work with because you can change just about anything when you go to edit them. So, if you forgot to set the white balance or change your ISO, for example, no worries; you can fix it later at home. You can't do that with .jpgs. And yes, a bigger memory card is totally worth all this. If you are working with video, you will only be able to record RAW footage with more expensive cameras or with DSLRs that have undergone serious amounts of hacking. If there is a hacker in you, look up Magic Lantern on the web and good luck.

Most of you working with DSLR cameras won't have a great degree of control over the type of video files shot by your camera, and we won't worry so much about that now. Most cameras nowadays shoot in h.264, which is a pretty mediocre codec, but it's easy to work with. What you can gain control over, however, is your camera's focus. Switch on the manual focus now. It's your story, after all, and you're the one who should control what to focus on. As for those of you sticking to still photography, automatic focus might be a more practical decision for now, until you become fussier about your work. That's it, then; you're now in charge of your own camera!

The basics of exposure

The concept of *exposure* refers to the specifics of the interaction between film—or a sensor, in the age of digital cameras—and light. Exposure can be a rather complex subject at first, so I will do my best to break it down into digestible bits and only focus on what matters at the introductory level. Readers who are interested in the intricacies of exposure will need to do some digging on their own time. What matters to me here is to convey how a solid understanding of exposure can empower a visual ethnographer to tell a better story, a story told through images that are both coherent and well lit. So, let us work through the subject by breaking exposure down into four parts: aperture, shutter speed, ISO, and frames per second.

Aperture refers to how open or closed a camera lens will be or, in other words, to how much light a lens will let through to the sensor. Why does this matter to us? Because by letting in more or less light, the *depth of field* of our images changes, and depth of field is quite possibly the most powerful tool we have in visual storytelling. To explain what depth of field is, imagine a market square full of vendors, patrons, stalls, and lots of products for sale. As a photographer, you are standing near one of the four corners of the square. Let us imagine for a moment that you are interested in conveying the social organization of the space of such market. In this case, you need a shot that will capture everything your eyes can see. Such a shot should have everything in focus, from the vendors right in front of you to the stalls situated at the other end of the square. This shot will then have a wide depth of field. Depth of field, or aperture, is measured by your camera in f/stops. F/stops higher than 8 and reaching all the way to 22 or higher (22 is one of the most common limits) will capture in focus nearly everything your eyes can see.

Let us now imagine that you want to draw our attention to a particular vendor—just one single person. In this case, any other element in the photo would be distracting, so you want to keep the vendor in focus and everything else out of focus. The way to do this is by narrowing the depth of field. The f/stops you will want to select are between 1.8 and 5.6 (most lenses will stop at 4, but some will allow you go down lower). If there are objects or people present behind, or in front of, our vendor, they will go out of focus—ranging from a soft blur if they are nearby to almost complete oblivion if they are far away. This is a very powerful way to capture a viewer's attention, isn't it?

In general, close-ups are best captured with shallow depth of field. Medium shots require intermediate f/stops ranging from 5.6 to 8. Wide shots, on the other hand, benefit from apertures ranging from f/8.0 and above. Learning this simple but effective rule will go a long way toward enhancing the coherence and narrative power of your images. I should point out, however, that how shallow or deep your depth of field will be will also strongly depend on the type of lens you are using. If you are shooting with a wide-angle lens (anywhere in the 16–24mm range), it will be very difficult to achieve shallow depth of field. On the other hand, if you are shooting with a telephoto lens (100mm and up), you will find it so easy to reduce your depth of field that you will risk getting unwanted soft focus even on the subjects that you wish to have in focus (patience and precision will solve this problem, but sometimes a higher f/stop might be necessary too). Do keep in mind that higher-end cameras will typically allow you to photograph at a shallower depth of field than cheaper ones.

Let us now move to *shutter speed*. Shutter speed refers to how quickly your lens will open and close to expose your sensor to light. This matters to us for two reasons. The first reason is more conceptually compelling, and the second reason is more procedural. Let's look at the first reason. Let us imagine that you want to record the image of a fast-moving subject. Two fishmongers might be entertaining the market's patrons by tossing fish at each other as a way of drumming up business, for example. You want to take a photo of their interaction, and you wish for the vendors and the fish to be in focus, right as the fish is in mid-air. To do so, your lens will need to open and close fast; a slow shutter of speed would otherwise give you a flying blurry fish. Try setting up your shutter speed at 1/250 and see what happens. Your lens is now opening and closing in one 250th of a second. Is that fish in focus? Probably, though if you want an even sharper focus you could try an even faster shutter, like 1/500. Experiment with the different results with different moving subjects.

Taking sharp-focus images of objects or people in movement sounds pretty appealing, but it may not always serve a story well. If you freeze objects and people in time, you will find it difficult to convey that things are actually moving at all. Sometimes a slight amount of blur is desirable, both aesthetically and narratively. You might want to photograph a vendor buying produce and walking around the market, for example, at a slower shutter speed like 1/50 or 1/100. In bulb exposures, you might even leave the sensor exposed for a second or even for minutes (we won't cover this here but do understand that this is a key tool for certain types of storytelling as well) in order to exaggerate movement so much that it becomes a blur. Just like different types of shots demand certain types of aperture, the various speeds at which subjects move will demand certain shutter speeds. Normal action will typically require 1/50 or 1/100, and anything faster—from a runner to a race car—will demand faster shutter speeds if you are to have any hope of capturing something in focus.

Those of you working with digital video get a major break when it comes to shutter speed. Unlike still-image photographers, you are capturing several frames a second, ranging from 23.976 to 60 and above (more on this shortly). As a result, you want your shutter speed to be synchronized with your frames per second rate (or *fps*). The rule is to take your frames per second and multiply that value by two. So, if you are shooting 30 frames a second, you want your shutter speed to be 1/60. If you are shooting 23.976 fps, you want it to be 1/50 (it's an approximation). If you are shooting 60 fps, then you want it to be 1/120. You get the math. Since most videomakers will shoot the same fps pretty much all the time, it quite easy to set one's shutter speed to the desired value and then forget it; it's one less thing to think about.

Now, what frames per second value should you choose? It depends on what story you want to tell. Video will look more film-like at 23.976, 24, and 25 fps. Video will look a lot less like film and more like video at 30fps. Traditionally, television has shown us images at 30 fps and movies at 23.976 fps. Now, if you want to shoot images in slow motion for dramatic effect or to break down complex movements, then you will want to shoot at 50, 60, or 120 frames per second and then slow down your footage when you play it back to 23.976, 24, 25, or 30. So, for example, if you shoot footage at 60 frames per second and play it back at 23.976 fps (a very popular way of doing slow motion), then your recorded action will play at 40% the speed of the original. Now, if you want to avoid committing more numbers to memory and you are shooting for the internet and digital projection in rooms and theaters, simply set your camera to shoot at 23.976 fps and its corresponding shutter speed: 1/50. It will work like a charm.

The last variable to think about is *ISO*. ISO refers to the sensitivity of film to light or, these days, to the sensitivity of a sensor. Low ISO values make your sensor very insensitive, and high ISO will render it very sensitive. Unlike aperture, shutter speed, and frames per second, ISO is not a terribly creative tool to play with; get your ISO wrong, and your images will look desperately dark or bright. So, if you are shooting in bright environments (like on a sunny day) choose a low ISO, somewhere between 100 and 200. A cloudy day or shaded area might require something around 200 and 400. Shooting indoors, depending on how much light is actually available, will require an ISO ranging between 800 and 1600. If you are feeling already pretty overwhelmed by all this information, do take it easy on

124   *Working with images*

yourself and let your camera set the ISO automatically. It is the one thing that it will do better than you in most cases.

Just about the only time that your camera will choose a bad ISO for you is in low-light conditions when you really don't care to have your entire image exposed in its true colors and details. Let's say you venture into an indoor area of that farmer's market in search of a butcher's stall. The butcher's corner happens to be dark and cold, and you want to portray the place by focusing your image on the white stained coat the butcher is wearing, her sharp knife, and the red meat she is cutting. There are dark walls around the butcher's working zone that matter very little to you. Your camera's ISO of choice will likely be one that captures detail in the white coat the butcher is wearing *and* those dark surroundings. But an ISO of 6400 is ridiculously high, and it will make your image look very unpleasant. Setting your ISO to a value like 1600 and no higher will instead render the dark, unimportant parts of your image black (with no details), but it will allow you to capture your subject in a more ideal and pleasing light. Choosing the ISO on your own will also be necessary every time there is a stark difference between foreground and background. Let us say, for example, that you are shooting an interview under the shade of a tree, and in the background you have a sunlit beach. Your camera will choose an ISO that is a compromise between the shady foreground and the bright background, but your interest is in the interviewee, not the beach. So you will want to raise the ISO to get good clarity on your subject's face, even if that will cause your background to become blown out in white.

Avoiding underexposed and overexposed images

If all there was to exposure was a creative combination of various values of shutter speed, aperture, and ISO, no amount of creativity would ever cause images to look terribly dark or bright. The reality is that when we expose our sensor to light, we risk exposing it too little or too much. Underexposure (which results in excessively dark images) and overexposure (the opposite) arise as a result of poor combinations of the variables of shutter speed, aperture, and ISO we have chosen. Think of the three variables, plus frame rate in case you are doing video, as a blanket. The blanket is meant to fit the bed precisely, but as we pull one corner one way, the other three corners will move with it, and they'll have to move carefully or they will leave the mattress exposed.

Perfect exposure will only happen over time through lots of practice. For now, do consider the following four pointers. These are not the only problematic value combinations you will encounter, but they are also the most commonly experienced and quite possibly the easier to understand and solve.

1   As we discussed before, in order to obtain shallow depth of field, you will need a low f/stop. A low f/stop will bring lots of light onto your sensor, and in order to avoid overexposing your images, you will need to decrease your

ISO or increase your shutter speed (the latter is an option, not necessarily advisable to those doing video). This seems easy enough, but what if you can't lower your ISO because it's a very bright environment you are shooting in and your ISO is already at its lowest? The problem is easily taken care of if you have listened to my advice and purchased a variable density filter. Rotate the filter and your exposure will darken just like you want it. Simply be careful, though; the shallower the depth of field in lower light, the harder it will be to get the focus right.

2. The opposite problem might be harder to solve. Let us say you wish to capture a deep field and you want everything in focus. Your f/stop therefore needs to go above 8.0. To compensate, your shutter speed should decrease (however, remember that if you are doing video, you can't mess with it too much), and your ISO should increase. If a decrease in shutter speed solves the problem without introducing too much motion blur in your still image, that's great. If not, the ISO will need to go up. However, remember how high ISOs will likely ruin images? Anything over 1600 is risky, so you will either have to reduce your ambition and go down in f/stop value or (if you are taking still images) switch your camera mode to "bulb" and take long exposures of 1, 2, or several seconds.

3. Another problem I will consider is slow-motion footage. Who doesn't like to capture slow-motion footage to break down the elements of a movement or to dramatize action? Trouble is, capturing footage at normal speed and then slowing it down while editing will make the original footage look jerky because your 24 frames per second will now play at, say, 12 frames per second, and it will start to look like a quick slide show. So, in order to do this right, you will have to start capturing footage at 50 or 60 frames a second. As we already mentioned, this will mean doubling up your shutter speed. So now you have darker images, right? What do you do? Raise the ISO if you can, absolutely. But what if you can't because there isn't enough available light? Well, you could buy a portable light and mount it on your camera (not a bad tool to have) or—if you have skipped enough conferences already—shelve the idea and stick to slow motion only in brightly lit environments.

4. The last problem I will bring up is noisy footage. Let us say you are shooting in a poorly lit environment, either inside or outside. You have decreased your f/stop in order to avoid a high ISO. You do not have a flash or a light for your camera. And you are unable to flick on a switch and cast more light on your interior setting. What do you do? You will have to come to terms with using a high ISO. This will likely introduce great amounts of digital noise over the images. Some people don't mind digital noise as much as others. Personally, I think that it looks like a computer vomited on an image, and I will try everything I can to clean it up. One of the best solutions is to de-noise it using a software called Neat Video. As long as you are patient and take the necessary time to apply Neat Video, and as long as your images are cleanable to begin with, you should be able to clean up most of the mess.

The basics of composition

Composition refers to the geometrical relations among the subjects present within an image and their relations with the frame within which they are contained. Though composition is an important subject, it is not something I want to dwell on for too long. Ethnographers have a practical rapport with composition; their reason for creating images is to give their viewers a feel for naturally unfolding action and social interaction, and this task requires that they shoot whatever will help them answer a research question. The reality of doing visual fieldwork is that most of us will have no control over the environments and social situations we shoot. Manipulating the subject of our images would make no sense and so we typically shoot—whether stills or video—in a "run and gun" type of style that consists of moving around quickly to cover our subject as best as we can. In light of this, there are only a few rules of composition that are necessary to respect.

Let us imagine our image frame as a rectangle (long gone are the days of shooting a square frame) whose proportions are 16:9 with its vertical sides, in other words, shorter than its horizontal sides. Let us now draw two horizontal and two vertical lines across it, like in the following picture.

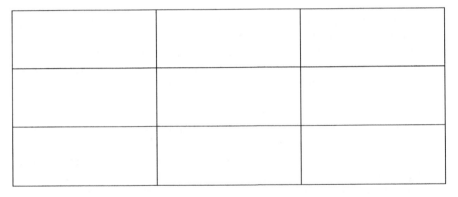

The two lines above have divided our frame into three horizontal thirds and three vertical thirds. This is the basis of the so-called *rule of thirds*. The rule of thirds gives a simple system for balancing our compositions. According to it, the subjects of our image should be situated on or along the points of intersections of our lines. Linear features should flow from section to section.

For example, let us imagine we want to take the image of a person. Instead of smacking our subject right in the middle of the frame, by applying the rule of thirds, we would typically place her along the vertical line on the left of the frame or the vertical line on the right. In doing so, we should take care to place her eyes right around the point of intersection of the left or right vertical line, with the higher of the two horizontal lines.

Placing a subject on the left side or right side of the frame is not an arbitrary decision. When speaking or interacting, people typically are oriented toward the right or the left, however mildly. If our subject is oriented toward her right, then you would want to place her on the right side of the frame. The opposite orientation clearly calls for the opposite course of action on your part. This will make it possible for us, the viewers, to get the sense that we are not missing out. Try and place a subject leaning (i.e. looking, moving, etc.) right on the left side of your image and observe the results. You will feel like your subject is looking away, speaking with someone, or moving away toward something we can't quite see.

There is a very practical application of the rule of thirds in visual ethnographic fieldwork. Most people do not enjoy looking straight into a camera. Let us take the example of an on-camera interview. I have interviewed hundreds of people on camera, and I cannot even begin to convey how strongly they relax when, before the interview begins, I tell them to look at the interviewer and not the camera. In a case like this, the camera can be placed essentially in front of the subject. The camera operator can also sit or stand next to the camera, roughly in front of the subject, whereas the interviewer or researcher can keep to the left or the right of the camera. As this happens, the subject will typically look and act at a slight angle, away from the camera and toward the interviewer or researcher. At that point, a balanced composition simply needs to make room either on the right or the left side of the subject's body, depending on whether they are leaning right or left toward the interviewer.

Relatedly, it is important to leave the right amounts of headroom. Let us recall that it is important to place our subject's eyes right at the intersection of either the left or the right vertical line with the upper of the two horizontal lines. In keeping our subject's eyes there, no matter how much of the rest of his body we are capturing, we will need to make some necessary "cuts." Let us imagine we are capturing a close-up of a person's face. Given the widescreen image captured by a 16:9 aspect ratio when capturing a close-up, and putting our subject's eyes where they should be, we will crop off a bit of our subject's head. This is both normal and desirable. Capturing an entire head in a close-up, without any cropping, will result in placing our subject's eyes too low, and that will look very unappealing. On the other hand, you will find that there is no need to crop heads when taking a wider shot that captures an entire person's body.

The last thing I will mention about the rule of thirds refers to the z axis. The x and y axes refer to the horizontal and vertical lines of our frame. The z axes are the two lines that cut across our frame diagonally. Even though images are two-dimensional, by shooting while taking into account the z axes, we add a considerable amount of depth to our compositions. This is not only pleasing but also puts action into a much greater context. Get on the web and Google-image "rule of thirds"; you will see dozens of examples of how everything that I have talked about works in practice.

Conclusion

In this chapter, I have covered a lot of material that is quite possibly foreign and complex to most of you. Some of you might even be wondering what the point is in putting such painstaking care into taking aesthetically conscious images.

Well, I feel that I always put painstaking care into choosing the right words and in crafting aesthetically sensitive writing, so I don't see why my attitude to images should be any different. In addition, I can share a valuable practical methodological discovery. Time and time again, I have found that my research participants feel validated and even proud of their participation in my visual research when their images are pleasing. Making someone look terrible, or perhaps simply uninteresting and unappealing, on screen brings embarrassment to them, which is a type of harm we must avoid. Taking good images matters, and it will make it much easier for people to become interested in taking part in your next project if they can see what good work you have done before.

I have purposefully left out of this chapter the topic of image editing. If you have listened to my advice and taken images that are flat, you will need to color correct them and grade them according to the styles of your choice. This is where software like Adobe Lightroom or Photoshop for still images and Final Cut Pro or Adobe Premiere Pro for video (or better yet, for the sake of color grading, DaVinci Resolve) will come in handy. However, it is pointless for me to cover this subject in this mode of communication, a book, when user-uploaded YouTube videos will do an infinitely better job at showing you what buttons to click and what the results will be. If I have made you at least a little bit enthusiastic about capturing good images, you will now find that the next step is to join the rest of us image geeks on the internet. See you there.

13 The basics of shooting and editing video

In a not-so-distant past, the production of ethnographic film, just like all other sorts of documentary films, required the involvement of two distinct groups of people: a production team and an editing team. The shift from actual film to digital video, and more notably the astoundingly fast growth of non-linear editing (NLE) digital platforms, have made it possible for a solo-working ethnographer to shoot, edit, export, and share both short and long videos. These revolutionary changes, however, have not necessarily been equated with a growth in quality among the large mass of videos being made around the world today. While there now exist more beautifully filmed and intelligently edited ethnographic films than ever before, there is now also an ever-expanding amount of poorly shot and amateurishly edited products.

The reality is that in order to reach a wide popular audience, ethnographic video producers need to compete with scores of professionals and hobbyists who are amazingly talented at telling stories about the various lifeworlds they are personally involved with. The average viewer has no easy way of distinguishing which of the thousands of factual content videos available online or on various on-demand platforms were made by professional ethnographers and which ones were not. To that viewer, what matters is production value, educational value, and entertainment value. No matter how methodologically solid our ethnographic fieldwork might have been, no matter how conceptually sophisticated, no matter how ethically sound and empirically relevant our content, if we choose to share with the world poorly shot and roughly edited video, we will reach no more than a few dozen viewers. Thus, producing and editing good content is absolutely essential for a public ethnographer.

In this short chapter, I will share a few tips on how to get started on the way to shooting and editing decent video. Reading the next 5,000 words or so won't turn you into a professional filmmaker, but if you follow my tips, you will start to form solid habits and strong skills which you may then further develop on your own in the future. Some of the advice I will share may sound obvious and overly simplistic, and yet it is absolutely essential to follow, so it bears being stated and always remembered. The good news is that if you mastered the content I shared in Chapter 12, what I will say in this chapter will undoubtedly come across as intuitive and even easy. So, assuming you understand the basics of exposure, all you have to do now is shoot editable content and then edit it. Those shall be the two main sections of this chapter.

Shooting video

Let us start by understanding the three types of content that most of us public ethnographers are likely to shoot. First, there is *action* footage. Action footage consists of more-or-less naturally unfolding action (the presence of the camera may make that action very unnatural indeed, but we won't worry about that effect here). Action footage may comprise people interacting with one another, going about their routine business or unique cultural rituals, or even demonstrating something for the sake of the camera. Second, there is *interview* footage. Interview footage consists of a sit-down or stand-up conversation between the researcher/videomaker and research participant(s)/interviewee(s). Third, there is *b-roll*. Essentially, b-roll is all kinds of contextual footage that is neither action footage nor interview footage. B-roll is used for its imagery during the editing process in order to illustrate, expand, or contradict whatever point we, or our research participants, may be making. It may also be used to facilitate transitions, plug holes, create mood or atmospheres, and so forth. Whatever you shoot will end up in one of these three categories and, for the sake of staying organized, you will want to create three folders in your hard drive corresponding to these three basic categories. Creating subfolders for each root folder, using categories the project demands, is also extremely important to quickly retrieve material later.

Action footage

Action footage is arguably the most important material you can shoot during audiovisual fieldwork. As you shoot action, you essentially play the role of an observer, though to varying degrees, your very presence in the field with a camera will inevitably turn you into a participant as well. Having said this, this is the most important tip I can share with you regarding action footage: capture it. Just don't miss it. There are no substitutes for action and no repetitions are possible, so if you don't capture it the first time around, it is as if you weren't even there in the first place. Capturing it—as much as possible of it—means essentially three things: being prepared, being attentive, and being able to anticipate action.

Being prepared means doing your homework in advance. If you know that you are going to be shooting action tomorrow, then today is the day to make sure you have enough batteries and that they are all charged and ready. It means making sure you have enough memory cards and that they are all empty and ready for recording. It means having the right gear in your camera backpack. It means knowing your gear and having clean lenses and filters. It means creating a plan of action in your mind, perhaps consisting of a list of shots you absolutely need. And so on. Being prepared today for the shooting tomorrow means rehearsing in your head how you will confront different situations as they arise. Will it be dark where you will be shooting? Will the light change? Will there be noise? Where will you position yourself? Can you use a tripod, or will you need to shoot handheld? Will there be space for you to move around? Will everyone be comfortable with your camera's presence? Today, not tomorrow, is the time to prepare yourself and your gear and rehearse your role.

Being attentive is absolutely necessary to ethnographic fieldwork of all kinds, so I won't spend paragraphs upon paragraphs explaining to you what you already know about observing action in the process of doing fieldwork. What I will do, however, is advise you on how your camera should be attentive. When you edit video, there are three types of shots you need: wide, medium, and close-ups. Just like the grammar of writing requires that we use subjects, verbs, and objects to create a sentence, the grammar of editing requires we also use three components. If we only use nouns, for example, our writing turns into a list. The same happens to our video if we use too much of the same types of shots.

Wide shots are shots that allow you to see a lot of what is happening. You may have a wide shot of action unfolding in a public square, a sports field, or a single room—size does not matter. What matters is that you see an action as a whole in its context. Close-ups, on the other hand, allow our eyes to focus in on details. You may have a close-up of a person's face to show the emotions they might be feeling, or you might shoot a close-up of a carpenter gripping a hammer. The third type of shot will likely be your most common: the medium shot. Medium shots show action and movement closer than a wide shot but wider than a close-up. A shot of a person from the waist up as they are doing something with their hands, for example, would be a medium shot. Being attentive in the process of shooting action footage therefore requires paying simultaneous attention to the big picture, to details, and to everything in between and capturing all three types of the needed shots when they matter most.

Finally, you need to be able to anticipate the kind of action that is about to occur. Anticipating action means being ready to shoot from the right position, the right angle, and with the right gear moments *before* something is about to happen. The key difference between doing observation without a camera and with a camera is that when you do observation without a camera, an event will be relatable with words simply because you lived it. When you do observation with a camera, no event will be relatable if you didn't shoot it at all or even if you shot it poorly because you weren't ready for it. Therefore, anticipating means staying a step ahead of the present time and gearing up for it.

Anticipating action is absolutely necessary, not only because you need to capture just about everything, but also because you need to capture something that is easy to edit. What does this mean? Let me give you a golden rule of shooting for the sake of easy editing: make sure every one of your shots is at least 10 seconds before you move the camera or reframe your shot. A 10-second shot without camera shake, zooming in or out, or exposure changes is a *usable* shot any day and any time. Any less than 10 seconds will make you wish it was longer when you try to edit it.

A derivation from this golden rule is that you might want to get 10-second variations of the same content. Let us say, for example, you are filming a logger who is sawing down a tree. Have the camera locked in for 10 seconds for a wide shot, then 10 seconds for a medium shot, then 10 seconds for a close-up shot. This could be the very same clip—you don't need to press record and stop three times. This will give you 30 seconds of great material to choose from in the editing room. You could even have 30 seconds of the same basic content approached three ways: first locked in, then with the camera gently panning left, then panning right (or maybe up, and then down). You could then do it one more time with a simple locked-in shot, then a gentle zoom out, then a gentle zoom in. If you anticipate that the logger is going to be doing the same thing for a while, this is the time to get variety. But if you anticipate that the tree is about to fall, then safely get out of the way and find a vantage point where you can get a wide shot of the tree falling down … but not outside your frame!

Anticipating action also means adjusting exposure before shooting. If you know the tree is about to fall down, you will likely need a wide shot. A wide shot—say, with your zoom lens set at 24mm—will need a high f/stop and a higher ISO. Anticipate and prepare accordingly. You might even want to film the tree falling down in a high frame rate so you can play the event back in slow motion. Anticipating events will allow you to not miss a beat. Now, if you are filming by yourself, with a single camera, chances are you won't be able capture absolutely everything, but if you follow my advice, you will capture as much usable footage as possible.

Interviews

Compared to capturing action footage, recording interviews is easy. When recording an interview—which is normally a relatively planned and structured encounter between you and an interviewee—you will likely have a great degree of control over the situation. This means that through good planning, you can be nicely prepared to record your interviews without any hiccups and, as you interview your research participant, you can dedicate more of your attention to listening and less to the camera or to anticipating what is about to happen next. Having said this, it is necessary to make no mistakes, or you will waste your time and your interviewee's time.

There are two things you cannot get wrong as part of an interview: focus and sound. Let us start with focus. Focus is something that can never be fully fixed in post-production: it has to be gotten right. Before you start an interview, do beg for your interviewee's patience for a few seconds. Zoom in all the way to the subject's face and, if you can, use your camera's magnifying function to make sure the focus is right upon magnification. I like to look right into the subject's eyes, get them in perfect focus, then zoom back out to a medium shot framing around 50mm. I typically use an f/stop between 4.0 and 5.6 in order to blur out the background; that way, the viewer can focus on what the soccer coach is saying about her players and not get distracted by those players kicking a ball in the background. If this is a sit-down interview, I likely won't have to worry about focus anymore. If it's a stand-up interview, I will want to make sure that my subject is not moving around or she may get out of focus. If that happens, I fix my focus immediately.

If you have read Chapter 11 carefully, you will understand the basics of sound recording. After a brief sound test, I press "record" on my camera and sound recorder, snap my fingers to facilitate synchronization later, and I am in business. Every now and then, I glance at my voice recorder to make sure the levels are peaking around -12db and, when absolutely necessary, I will beg for my interviewee's patience if we need to pause for a loud motorbike riding by or something like that. I know documentary filmmakers that are manically controlling about sound in interviewee settings. They will walk into someone's house and shut off their refrigerators, re-arrange furniture to avoid reverb, ask the children to go play outside, and do all sort of things to avoid background noise. As an ethnographer I find that background noise is quite revealing of a place's atmosphere and therefore interesting in its own right. So, as long as it doesn't destroy my interview, I don't worry about it so much.

A few words ought to be spent on lighting and composition. I personally hold the belief that interviews are the least visually engaging content you can shoot, so I don't obsess over how beautiful my framing will be. Talking-head content is nothing but talking-head content, and it's not worth staging a scene by moving furniture around or re-decorating walls. There are, however, a few things I am mindful of. For example, I like to avoid plain white walls as a background. No one looks alive against a white wall. I also like to avoid a busy background. If I have to shoot an interview in a beautiful locale, I still want to make sure that my viewer's eyes are going to be focused on my interviewee and not on the dolphins frolicking in the background. Moreover, I like to conduct an interview in a place that is not annoyingly busy. Coffee shops, means of transportation, and streetsides are the worst for that.

My main visual preoccupation is always not so much what is in the background, but my interviewee's face. There are a few things I want to avoid so as not to do poor justice to a subject's face. For starters, I want to avoid a foreground that is excessively darker than its background. To avoid this, I never shoot with a window visible in the background (unless it is not so bright outside and it is quite bright inside). I also try to avoid situations where the interviewee is sitting or standing in the shade while the sun shines brightly in the background (shooting in the early afternoon is especially bad for this). If I have to do an interview outside around noon and it is sunny, I will move into the shade or the sun will cast racoon eyes on my interviewee's face. I also like to shoot with the sun to the left or right side of my interviewee's face—never directly in front of them (or they will squint all the time) or behind them (in order to avoid a silhouette effect). If the sun or a bright source of interior lighting are to the right of my subject's face, I want to make sure I leave room on the left of their face and vice versa. This ensures that the side of the subject's face that is more visible to the camera is better lit. Finally, I am personally against the idea of an interviewee removing hats or sunglasses for an interview (some documentary filmmakers will insist these come off)—I'd rather have my research participant feel comfortable and fully themselves than resentful of me. After reading all this, I know what some of you are thinking: "what do I have to care so much about how someone looks? I am not shooting commercials!" You are not shooting commercials, but you do have to care about how your research participants look because—chances are—they are not like you. Most people—almost all—do care. And if they're going to feel ashamed about the way you made them look, then you are doing harm to them.

Now, if you have managed to get focus and sound right, and you haven't chosen the worst lighting in the world, you have yourself a perfectly editable interview, and the rest is just the cherry on the cake. If you like cherries, here is how you collect them. First, try to get a few different shots of the interview. You might wish to re-frame before you're about to ask a question, for example, and get an equal number of questions answered on wide, medium, and close-up shots. Assuming that you set up the camera on a tripod right in front of and at the same height as your interviewee's eyes, you might occasionally vary the angle and move the camera and tripod completely (in all likelihood, you will only do this if you have a second camera or perhaps a colleague who does the interview while you focus on the camera exclusively).

Second, get a few contextual shots. Get an establishing shot of where the interview is being held, for example (a wide shot of the park you are in, the building you are in, etc.). Then get shots of things that are in the proximity of the interviewee: books on a shelf, a painting on the wall, and so on. Taking these shots is typically done after the interview if you are alone working with one camera; if you have a second camera and a colleague taking care of the dialog, you can do these things while the interview goes on—provided you don't get in the frame of the main camera and you don't make any noise. Finally, get a few shots of the interviewee's hands as he speaks. A lot of people speak with their hands, and it is easy enough to film them with a second camera or—if you only have one—while the interviewee drifts away on an irrelevant tangent. Shots like these are gold to cover up jump cuts when you edit the interview.

Third, if your interviewee has time and is comfortable around you and the camera, you might want to supplement the interview with additional material. For instance, after filming interviews for *Life Off Grid*, Jon and I always asked our research participants: "what would you be doing right now if we weren't here?" Their answer might be: "I might be cutting wood," or "making supper," or something like that. We would then ask them to do just that, while we filmed them for a little bit and even continued the conversation about what they were doing.

Finally, the last cherry on the cake is still photography. If you have a second camera, take a few still pictures of your interviewees. You may use these on your project's social media page or website, in a book or articles, or for any other reason—as long as you receive informed consent for all this.

B-roll

The notion of b-roll dates back to the principle that dialog and action were—and to some people still are—primary, and that anything else was secondary. But to think that anything other than action and dialog (or interview) material is secondary in importance is a mistake. For ethnographers, context means everything, and context is often revealed through the backgrounds of action and speech. B-roll, which focuses on context and its details, is therefore of crucial importance. B-roll is also extremely important for the sake of good pacing. No one can or should edit a documentary that is full of action and/or dialog. The pacing of such film would be breathless, relentless, frantic. B-roll allows the pace of a film to slow down so that the viewer's mental energy can be recharged and then re-focused. So, by this token, b-roll is essentially anything that I did not include in the two categories I described earlier in this chapter, and especially visual material that can be easily shown without its original sound.

Capturing b-roll is much easier than defining it. This is because normally we are under no time pressure to record it. Let us say, for example, that you are filming a documentary on environmental conservation at a particular park. You will need images of that park, and lots of them. So you might find yourself exploring it on foot, carrying your camera around and setting it up on a tripod to get a good and interesting shot any time you feel the need. Indeed, you might even have the time to set up your camera on a slider if you have one, calmly adjust exposure, experiment with a few different ways of framing the subject, or maybe slowly pan in a few different ways beside getting a locked shot. Because you have time, generally speaking, you might even change lenses and filters, try a few creative shots at various angles, wait for the light to be ideal, and so on. And since you are calm and relaxed, you will even remember to get lots of different types of shots: wide, medium, and close-up. Yes, recording b-roll is fun and often a nice way to decompress after a long day of meeting people.

There are only a couple of tips I want to share about capturing b-roll. First, avoid unnecessary camera movement. Camera movement needs to replicate the natural movement of the human head and eyes. So, if you have a non-moving subject, should your head and eyes move? Probably not. Our head and eyes might move if we want to see how tall a tree is, for example. Or they might scan a landscape left to right, and right to left, if the vista is wide. But do yourself (or your editor, if these are different people) a favor and be sure to always record a locked shot as well if you choose to record a panning shot. Besides, camera movement needs to be smooth. If your camera is set on a (good) tripod, your vertical or lateral pans will likely look nice, but if you are filming handheld, try to keep your panning limited and extremely slow. My second and last piece of advice about b-roll is this: you can never have enough of it. If you dislike talking head videos (and you should!) you will resort to b-roll to illustrate, expand, or contradict spoken words. Having a full folder of shots to choose from will make your editing process a lot easier.

Editing

Now that you have filled your folders with all sorts of video (and sound) material, it is time to start editing. In all truth, the editing process should have already been started. Just like data analysis begins right as data collection starts, the first phase of the editing process should begin as soon as the first batch of files are taken off the camera's memory card and copied into their respective folders. This first phase of editing is called *logging*. Logging consists of reviewing each clip and writing down on a worksheet what it contains. You might want to write down next to every file number things like clip length, the names of the people and places portrayed in it, and the precise content it captured, and you could even make all sorts of notes about the types of shots it contains, its audio content, and its overall quality. Logging essentially allows you to archive and categorize all your material, so it is best that you do it as your data collection unfolds. That way you know what you have and what you don't have before and not after you leave the field.

The process of logging is also the time when editing starts, albeit still in your head. As you review your files, you start envisioning how your story could unfold on the basis of what you are shooting and what it feels like to watch it. When I log, I start to form ideas on how certain clips can be used, what material reveals itself to be more or less useful, and the numerous (at this point) kinds of options I have for assembling together the story. Logging is not a lot of fun, but it also allows me to assess the quality of what I am shooting. In a way, logging my clips allows me to grade my own work by spotting the mistakes I make and by learning from them. This is why logging must take place right as data are being collected. Imagine how terrible it would be to shoot for a year, open the files for the first time, and realize that either your camera's settings were off somehow or that the images that you thought were in focus on the camera's LCD screen are actually off focus now that you look at them on a big computer screen (a common occurrence).

As logging goes on and eventually ends, it will be the time to create a *paper cut* of your video. A paper cut consists of a Word document divided into two columns (well, there are different ways of doing this, but this is one of the most common). On the left column is the content of your video as you imagine it will be assembled, more or less clip by clip. On the right column are the names of the files the content described on the left corresponds to—perhaps with a few notes as well. Some paper cuts can be extremely detailed and other types can be looser—this depends on whether you are the planning type or the impulsive type who envisions things on the go—but all kinds of paper cuts rely essentially on your knowledge of the footage, your imagination and storytelling intents, and transcripts of dialog and interviews (an absolutely essential resource). A paper cut should also give you a very precise grasp on how long your video should be. In my experience, however, videos tend to be a slot shorter on paper than they are in the end, so be mindful of this if you have tight limits to respect.

Now that you have deeply familiarized yourself with your transcripts (and therefore engaged in a bona fide thematic data analysis), categorized your files, imagined your video in your mind, and written down extensive notes on how it will all be assembled (as part of your paper cut), it is time to start cutting. This is where some of you will get excited and others will be daunted or even terrified. It is understandable. Though editing video through NLEs has become more and more intuitive, it is a specialized skillset that takes some time to master. It is also time consuming and resource intensive (you will need the right software and a powerful computer). Should you be of the opinion that it is perfectly acceptable to task a professional editor with putting together your video, now is the time to do it—now, that is, that you have learned from your shooting, that you have familiarized yourself with your content and the options it has opened, that you have analyzed data, and that you have cut together your documentary on paper. In my mind, to task an outsider with assembling your work without engaging in all these tasks yourself would be tantamount to returning home from the field, handing someone your field journals, and asking them to write your ethnography. Paper-cutting is absolutely essential to retain a sense of authorship over your video.

Making the cuts

In the limited space I have here, I cannot describe the editing process in great detail. It is a subject that would require a single book, or more, to fully outline. It is also a process that is quite variable from NLE to NLE. For example, even though I am very familiar with Adobe Premiere Pro and DaVinci Resolve, it would take me weeks to learn how to use Final Cut or another software. So, what I am going to do in the last remaining section of this chapter is share a few fundamental rules of the grammar of editing that we should all respect (until we become so good at it that we can actually break them).

The cuts you make are driven by your story. How you make them is also a function of the chosen form of your story. If you like long cuts, that is your choice. If you like the fast-pace feel that short cuts give you, that is also your choice. Everyone has their style, and here I am simply going to relay a few basic rules that we should all take into account. The first rule is that of variety: a selection of wide, medium, and close-up shots will advance your story much better than a series of shots that are all the same. There is no rule on whether you should go from medium to close-up or close-up to wide, but generally you will find that most movies use a wide shot to establish a context, a medium to describe an action, and a close-up to reveal a detail and emotion and to transition to a new sequence. The second rule or guideline is to advance the variety agenda even more. Now that you have created variety within a sequence, be sure to create variety across sequences. In other words, do not show the same content, in the same form, over and over. The videos that are most difficult to watch are those that show the same thing (interview talk, for example, or long cuts of observational footage) minute after minute after minute. Keep it lively. Change it up. Think of video editing like song-writing: you can't have the same basic rhythm all the time without any change.

The third piece of advice I will share is to work with audio and video tracks independently whenever you can. When you unlink audio from the video track, you open yourself up to a world of possibilities. You can use interview words to set a mood relayed through images shot elsewhere, for example. You can use images to contradict words. You can use sound recorded in the field separately from video to enhance the feel of the images you shot with your camera, and so on. Just remember to show us who is talking every now and then, so we don't get confused or we don't forget.

Fourth, use title cards sparingly. I have seen the work of many students who felt compelled to make an abstract conceptual point with their videos and, upon realizing that the images and audio they had weren't enough to advance their argument, they decided to write the point of their story on title cards. When used very sparingly, title cards work, but use more than a few and suddenly your video will feel like a classroom PowerPoint presentation. Let the words and images tell the story, and if you feel like a point needs to be underscored or better conceptualized, then write an article to accompany your video.

It would be easy to go on forever in this section, but I want to limit myself to a small set of rules (or guidelines) that feels manageable and easy to remember. So, I am going to share two last bits of advice. My penultimate tip is to embrace silence. Because interviews are the most obvious material that beginner documentarians will shoot, it is somewhat instinctual to resort to interview words and interview words alone to advance a story. These types of videos, however, featuring wall-to-wall talk, are very hard to digest. Just like you might find it difficult to listen to every word of a lecture for 15 or 30 minutes, do keep in mind that it's even more difficult to stay focused on speech if words are being relayed while competing imagery takes our attention away from them. Pause. Breathe. Silence (or better yet, non-verbal audio) is golden.

And finally, have someone else—several honest friends—preview your work right as you go from a rough cut to a fine cut to a final cut. Prospective viewers' responses are invaluable because they are not as familiar with the material as you are and are therefore apprehending it for the first time in a completely different light than you are. Listen to their words. Even though what they say might hurt your ego, they are likely right. Learn from their feedback and make the necessary adjustments, both now and for any future project.

Save and export

Be sure to make back-ups of everything along the way—hard-drive failures are not unheard of. Working with footage contained on portable hard drives external to your computer helps reduce the chances of crashing, and it speeds up the workflow, but you will want to have back-ups of back-ups and save different versions of your fine cuts at the end of every working day (in case tomorrow you realize that the version you completed the day before yesterday worked better than the version you cut yesterday ...).

Once you feel you are really done, you will want to export your video in a format that is easy to watch. The choices for different codecs are overwhelming, so I suggest you ignore them until you become a more advanced filmmaker and export everything for now using the h.264 codec. That will create an MP4 file that is played by all computers and is easy to share on the internet. If your computer gives you the option, and you have shot in full HD at 1080p or 1080i, select your target bit rate to be somewhere between 15 and 20bps and your max bit rate to go no higher than 25bps. Choose two passes as you export, rather than just one. Congratulations; you are now ready to share your work with the world.

14 Sharing videos

The potential for the dissemination of ethnographic knowledge via film to broad public audiences is enormous. However, all too often, the creation of an ethnographic film is viewed as the end point of a project, and not enough attention is given during production and post-production to the broadcast quality of the picture and sound—a shortcoming that, in the end can deeply affect the extent to which a film can be disseminated and appreciated. Having already discussed how to boost a project's production value, in this chapter, I want to share a few pointers on selecting among various film distribution avenues while weighing their pros and cons.

How to aim for wide distribution

Where precisely a documentary film is shown is largely determined by its production value. The higher the quality, the higher the chance a film will be selected for film-festival screenings or television broadcast and the greater your chances of making future films. From the get-go, it is important to anticipate your audience and aim high while balancing these ambitions with the realities of your budget, funding, and project parameters.

Publicity

During production, do not forget to collect dynamic, eye-catching *still* images that reflect the heart of your project. These stills can be taken during production or taken from the video footage if necessary. Filming at high resolution makes it easier to reproduce high-quality video stills. Also, don't forget to invest time in creating a strong poster, postcard, and/or website for the project. If you anticipate festival screenings, a postcard is good way to inform potential audiences at the festival itself. Write a succinct one-line synopsis (logline) and a 25–50-word synopsis. Edit a trailer. Spread word of your film through social media and send media releases to all media outlets potentially interested in talking to you and/or your participants about your film.

Clearly, this is a lot of work. Production photography, graphic design, written material, a trailer … this is more than most people can handle on their own.

Fortunately, universities offer us plenty of opportunities for collaborations with faculty and students across campus. In my experience, students are keen to work on collaborative projects that can enrich their resumes, give them a chance to show off their skills, and expand their networks. So my advice is to share tasks and delegate work that you, on your own, are not able to do or simply do not have the time to do. At times, these collaborations also bring about fresh ideas and original perspectives on the value of an ethnographic film, revealing connections that may not have surfaced before.

Film festivals

Ethnographic film festivals for makers and researchers of ethnographic films and topics are uniquely meaningful venues to learn about colleagues' work, share one's research, and develop valuable friendships and collaborations. Thousands of cities and towns the world over organize film festivals that attract dozens of filmmakers and industry professionals and hundreds of spectators. Film festivals showcase between a handful to well over 100 films that range in length from short to feature; in genre from experimental to documentary to narrative; and in theme from none to specific, such as LGBTQ, race, environment, outdoors, and so on. Film festivals also differ from one another in terms of prestige and status. Sundance and the Toronto International Film Festival generally attract large-budget films produced by well-established production companies. Though these festivals are always on the lookout for dynamic independent films, the competition among thousands of submissions is steep. Other, less internationally prominent, festivals tend to be more open to small productions and even student films. It is important to keep in mind that all ethnographic films are documentaries, so they should be submitted to festivals specializing in both ethnographic and documentary film in general.

The process of submitting films to festivals can be resource intensive with regard to money and time. Submission fees range from a few bucks to over 100 dollars, while travel to one's own film screening is usually the onus of the filmmaker. The efficiency of online festival submission websites, such as Withoutabox, FilmFreeway, and FilmFestivalLife, can save significant time. Filmmakers can input extensive information about their film and upload on a secure, private screener to these sites, choose from hundreds of listed film festivals to submit their film to, and pay festival fees by credit card. I suggest prudence when selecting from these festival lists: it is exciting to find so many potential festivals for one's film, but the cost of submitting to all of them quickly adds up. Some festivals request film screeners be sent on DVD rather than uploaded to these websites; this means costs for creating and mailing the DVDs. Festival projection format requirements are generally digital files nowadays: MP4s, Apple ProRes, and DCP (Digital Cinema Package). Only the latter format requires technical knowledge to properly produce and may require hiring the (expensive) expertise of a professional film finishing house.

Unlike submitting to most academic conferences, submitting to film festivals is very competitive. Selection committees may consider the credentials of a filmmaker and perhaps their associated production and distribution companies. This is not because film festivals are exclusive in principle, but because not all films submitted can be programmed over the short duration of the festival. Films may also be selected for the degree to which they fit a festival's mission, and for their length. Longer films require more time in a festival's schedule, so acceptance of shorter films can be easier to secure. The production value of a film is considered as well; no matter how terrific the content, festival programmers will not consider a film if it looks or sounds bad.

There are many positive and not-so-positive aspects associated with film-festival submission and participation. Significant time on the film-festival circuit can delay a film's broader release, making it less timely and relevant when it reaches the public through other venues. It takes research and effort to connect with industry professionals, and lesser-ranked festivals may offer limited opportunities for networking. And the submission process can become discouraging when rejection letters pile up. There will be acceptances and non-acceptances—to play the game of festival submissions means being prepared to lose some battles. On the positive end, it is exciting and important for a film to be selected for a film festival and maybe even to receive awards. Festival laurels improve the odds that a film will be selected by other film festivals, picked up for theatrical distribution and/or television broadcast, and garner funding for future projects. Professional connections made at film festivals can lead to future production collaborations and distribution agreements.

Internet distribution

Online distribution may occur in conjunction with, or after, screenings on the festival circuit, or if a filmmaker bypasses film festivals altogether. There are several ways to distribute a film on the web and related digital platforms, and these are constantly evolving. The simplest approach is to make a film available for free via YouTube or Vimeo. After uploading, a filmmaker would be wise to generate web traffic through social media and create publicity through newspaper, television, and radio interviews; blogs, magazine and newspaper articles; and so on. The pros of this option are obvious: it is relatively easy and fast. The cons become evident after some time: limited views and quickly declining interest. Additionally, after a film is made freely available, it is virtually impossible to find a distributor or broadcaster who will be interested in it. Many academics working with video do little beyond making their productions "accessible" by uploading them to the internet. In so doing, they may fail to actualize the potential impact of their research.

If a film has good production value, the first move to increase its online audience impact is to release a trailer on the internet and direct people to a project-dedicated website via social media. The next task is to seek distribution through Video on Demand (VOD) platforms that allow viewers to rent or purchase films for small fees. Among the simplest such platforms is Vimeo On Demand. Their contract allows filmmakers to retain most sales revenue after paying an annual subscription fee to the website. Though an ethnographic filmmaker may never become rich from VOD sales (and arguably that is not the point anyway), having a video protected from fully open public view makes it possible to find theatrical distribution and broadcast licensing deals. It also lends the film value and generates interest, as most viewers feel that paying for something makes it more desirable than something that is free.

VOD platforms like iTunes, Amazon, and Google Play do not allow self-distribution like Vimeo On Demand does. To have a film featured on those platforms, a filmmaker must be represented by a content aggregator, which is essentially a distribution company specializing in doing business with those platforms. Securing a distribution agreement with an aggregator requires some good ole networking, but companies like Distribber are making it easier for the average DIY filmmaker to reach out to large-scale VOD platforms. It should be noted that digital distribution on VOD platforms is now infinitely more sensible than selling DVDs—an onerous task requiring significant investment by a distribution company and therefore something that is beyond the financial and time capacities of most ethnographic filmmakers. Subscription Video on Demand (SVOD) platforms like Netflix operate similarly in terms of doing business only with aggregators, yet much less profitably (there is very little money in Netflix for independent producers). Rather unique among SVODs is Kanopy, a sort of Netflix for universities, specializing in educational and intelligent content.

Theatrical distribution

Ethnographic filmmakers interested in screening their films before live audiences for theatrical release have essentially three options. The first entails securing a distribution deal with a well-established company. The company will recoup their initial costs and then take a percentage of the revenue, while doing all the marketing and accounting work. Sadly, few ethnographic films receive this kind of theatrical distribution. The second option entails filmmakers organizing movie-theater screenings themselves. Most cities and university campuses have one or more independently owned cinemas that specialize in independent and alternative (non-Hollywood) productions. Many theater managers will happily rent their venue for single or multiple screenings of a film. Others may offer to split ticket sale revenues instead of charging a rental fee. The third option for theatrical screenings is through web-based networks like Tugg, a company that has established hundreds of agreements with movie theaters in select countries. According to the agreement, a film will play in any movie theater if a minimum number of tickets are pre-sold by a certain date before the scheduled screening. If the minimum threshold is not met in pre-sales, ticket purchases are refunded. If pre-sales are successful, Tugg, the movie theater, the screening promoter, and the filmmaker (the latter two may be the same) split the revenues in varying percentages.

Television broadcast

Television broadcast, another distribution avenue, ensures large audiences for a film through initial broadcast, re-broadcasts, and availability online through cable company VOD platforms. However, television broadcast deals can be difficult to secure without a distribution company and a product that appeals to wide viewership. Filmmakers without distributors can contact television broadcasters to pitch their completed films, works in progress, or production ideas to sell their films or find project funding.

The most likely television venues for ethnographic films remain, at the time of writing, public broadcasters with an educational mandate and public-access community channels. I recommend consulting broadcasters' requirements before beginning to edit your work, as broadcasters have strict specifications when it comes to content, length, and breaks for advertising. The simplest thing to do is to contact a producer by email and then build a relationship over time.

Educational venues

Community organizations and events, school boards, classrooms, university departments, libraries, and even prisons are some excellent educational venues to pursue for screenings and sales. For short films, you don't have to wait to hold educational screenings after a film has run the festival circuit and received television broadcast. Filmmakers themselves, or a knowledgeable teacher, student, or community member, can host educational screenings at community centers and movie theaters. These screenings can be paired with panel discussions or activities for the public on issues the film deals with.

Lessons from *Life Off Grid*

Life Off Grid is an ethnographic documentary of mine that looks at the lifestyle of people who live off the utility grids, usually in remote locations. The film includes formal sit-down interviews and discussions with participants in their interior and exterior living spaces, images of stunning and domestic landscapes, and a bit of reflection along the way on the part of the travelling ethnographer (i.e. me).

Life Off Grid was directed by Jonathan Taggart and produced and co-written by me. Inspired by the potential of film to reach wider audiences, in 2011 I decided to design a fieldwork study that would simultaneously be published as a book and as a film. This was meant as a relatively unique experiment; most ethnographers after all either write or film, very few set out to do both, and even fewer do it (themselves) with the explicit intent of reaching the broadest possible audience. Though overwhelmed by the challenge, I hoped this experiment would eventually yield useful lessons on how to popularize arts-inspired ethnographic research.

The first step in the process involved selection of a timely topic that was of interest both to me personally and to a large niche audience as well as well suited to a visual treatment. To be honest, I had no idea off-grid living would resonate with as many different people as easily as it did in the end. In 2011, there were no reality TV shows on the subject, news stories about the topic were uncommon, and stereotypes and misunderstandings of off-gridders prevailed. Selecting a subject that would spark the curiosity of just about any home dweller in the world was an essential strategic decision. Off-grid living homes and technologies must be seen and heard in order to be understood and respected, and off-gridders' unique stories are to be spoken by their own voice to be truly appreciated—I thought. To all this, I added an explicitly epic element (yes, not emic or etic, but rather epic) to the research design: a grand journey across the second-largest country in the world, across the seasons and every province and territory, in search of off-gridders. This approach, I thought, would make the film not only a case of essential Canadiana but also a recognizable example of the popular "road story" cinematic trope. After hiring Jonathan Taggart, a graduate student of mine who happened to be an accomplished visual artist, he and I hit the road in search of people seeking a better way of life off the grid, while a second graduate student stayed behind to work as a publicist for the project.

The book based on the fieldwork, *Off the Grid,* was published by Routledge in November 2014. About a year after, the film *Life Off Grid* was first screened to a public audience. As I write these words in November 2017, the (85,000 word) book has sold about 1,500 copies, with the majority of sales in Canada. The book is also available in many university libraries and some public libraries. To my knowledge, it has been adopted in full or in part by about a dozen university courses worldwide. It is available through Routledge's own website, as well as through web retailers such as Amazon, Indigo, and others. It has not been distributed to bookstore chains, and to my knowledge it is only available in two very small local bookstores dedicated to local authors. *Off the Grid* has been reviewed very positively by readers on blogs and personal websites and twice, so far, by academic journals. In sum, it was a successful reception but nothing to write a song about. The film, on the other hand, has fared much better.

The documentary *Life Off Grid* is available as an 85-minute theatrical version and a 52-minute broadcast television version. The theatrical release has screened at a dozen film festivals in six countries and has had approximately three dozen public non-festival screenings in North America and Europe (these are screenings that were organized by various non-profits). During November 2015, the film played five times in one of Vancouver's largest (420 seats) independent movie theaters. Three of those weekend screenings sold out. Later in the same season, it played in every major Canadian city, with most of its screenings in Toronto at the Hot Docs Rogers Cinema.

In late 2015, Fighting Chance Films, an Australian distributor, acquired a partial international distribution license and secured screenings for *Life Off Grid* in over two dozen movie theaters in the United Kingdom, New Zealand, and Australia. Fighting Chance made the theatrical version available through Tugg and, thanks to audiences' interest, several screenings took place over time, drawing record crowds in Melbourne and Sydney. The theatrical version is also available in the United States, Australia, Canada, and New Zealand through iTunes, Google Play, Amazon, and xBox; and worldwide on Vimeo On Demand, where it can be rented or purchased for a few dollars.

After two years on Vimeo On Demand, *Life Off Grid* has been viewed well over 50,000 times by people in 62 countries on five continents, while the free trailer has been seen over 147,000 times worldwide. The TV version has been broadcast in Canada by Knowledge Network, a public channel with a cross-country reach through satellite and a strong audience base in British Columbia, where it is available through basic cable. More TV programming later occurred on the SHAW network in Western Canada, through which the film is also available via its VOD platform. Thus far, in my estimate, *Life Off Grid* has been seen in its theatrical and TV versions combined by nearly half a million viewers.

The reasons why the film reached a larger audience than the book are obvious. The book is more expensive, requires a longer time commitment to consume, and is not as easily available. Furthermore, though it is written very much as a narrative and almost as travelogue, the book still has some academic characteristics, whereas the film is purely a product of popular culture featuring beautiful imagery, a pleasing soundtrack, captivating human characters, and no pedantic explanatory voice-over. The film is easier, lighter, quicker, and more convenient to find and consume.

In my opinion, the success of *Life Off Grid* has been greatly dependent on, indeed inseparable from, the existence of the writing(s) behind it. From the very beginning, thanks to the project's communication-student publicists, the fieldwork project was actively pitched to local news and popular media in every province and territory Jonathan and I visited. In the end, "local" came to mean, bit by bit, the whole country as a systematic and rigorous social scientific project. Writings in well-read regional and national magazines (e.g. *Canadian Geographic*), websites (e.g. *Mother Earth News*), and blog aggregates (e.g. *The Huffington Post, Canada*), accompanied by Jon's photography and early video clips, were used as part of media pitches. In turn, the radio, newspaper, magazine, and television interest generated more attention, coverage, appearances, and invited essays for the research project. The "general public" was thus offered a panoply of media products that reinforced and legitimated each other's message: writing expanded upon the film, and the film brought to life the writing. Audiences of the numerous radio interviews and newspaper articles for local, regional, and national outlets, combined with our own authored magazine and blog posts, easily surpassed the total audience for our film and indeed actively generated interest in it, as many of the viewers of the film had read or heard about the research before they saw the movie. Put in different and more concise words: the success of the film would have been unimaginable without the instrumental role writing played in legitimating it and stimulating interest in it. Going public, the project taught me, is not a matter of choosing one medium over another. It is a matter of using as many media and modes of communication as possible to reach the widest possible audiences and the most interested people amongst them.

Lessons from *Low and Slow*

Life Off Grid was a rather expensive and time-consuming production. These projects have immense value but sometimes, I believe, a great deal can be achieved with limited resources, small amounts of time, and a much smaller team. My ethnography on the world of floatplane pilots showed me just that. *Low and Slow* is a 26-minute ethnographic video documenting the occupation of commercial floatplane pilots, showcasing their skills, passion, local knowledge, and occupational concerns. The video is now freely available online at https://vimeo.com/172912004. I independently produced, directed, and edited the film. In the summer of 2017, it broadcast on the Canadian TV channel Knowledge Network. Later on, in the fall of 2017, it was re-broadcast by the SHAW network in British Columbia several times over a month's period.

My objective in designing the research study behind *Low and Slow* was to shed light on the little-known and poorly understood occupation of floatplane pilots and, in particular, to focus on the intensity of their daily experiences. To recruit participants, I went to the nearest floatplane terminal and approached the two pilots and the floatplane terminal manager. Since I knew them personally from flying with their company over the years, they were immediately receptive to my informal request. Luckily, not only did they grant me time for an interview but were also open to me filming normal day-to-day operations. Moreover, they promptly introduced me to colleagues who work for other companies. The data collection consisted of interviews and ride-alongs. At times, pilots were happy to conduct an interview during their down time between flights and then later on take me along for a ride. When their schedule made it difficult to find time between flights, instead they suggested we conduct the interview in the air while I sat next to them in the cockpit.

After screening the video for a few friends in order to gather feedback, and after making the subsequent final tweaks, I contacted one of the producers of Knowledge Network and submitted my work for her consideration. Knowledge Network is a public channel that produces and broadcasts documentary and educational programming of regional, national, and international interest and, to this effect, regularly considers program submissions from local filmmakers and independent production companies. Knowledge Network broadcasts in British Columbia through cable and across Canada on satellite, averaging 1.5 million viewers monthly.

After the video was accepted for broadcasting, I contacted the editors of the peer-reviewed journal *Mobilities* to inquire about the possibility of a video submission and learned that Routledge, the publisher of that journal, nowadays actively solicits multimedia material and offers to post such content on a dedicated website, assigns it a DOI, and gives it a stable URL. To my knowledge, other journal publishers have begun to offer similar services and now even actively encourage article authors to generate video material (such as video abstracts) to accompany their writings. Indeed, I believe that it no longer makes sense to lament that journal editors are not open to considering alternative and innovative multimedia material. The truly interesting subject to discuss at this point is no longer *whether* scholarly journals might consider publishing multimedia material but rather *how* such material should be gainfully utilized in relation to more conventional modes of academic discourse.

I need to be realistic here. I was extremely lucky in receiving so much attention for *Life Off Grid*. Much of it was unexpected and unplanned, but what was expected and planned was made possible by a combination of fortunate circumstances such as a generous grant and a very popular topic, chosen at the right time. Such luck is not always so easy to come by. The much smaller success of *Low and Slow* has shown me that there is a space for video, and indeed a very significant space, even at a much smaller scale. *Low and Slow* was filmed over 3 months on a $3,000 travel budget. It was edited in about 3 months, mostly by myself (with the collaboration of my friend Jules Molloy, who graciously stepped in any time I needed help). With a simple elevator speech email, it caught the attention of a couple of TV producers, and thus it reached a large public audience. Simultaneously, because I never "locked" access to it, it became part of a journal issue—with its accompanying written methodological piece also ending on the old CV. The project was simple, feasible, and wholly repeatable by anyone who has the patience and dedication to follow my incitation, as relayed throughout Part III of this book.

Filmography

5 Broken Cameras. Directed by Emad Burnat and Guy Davidi. 2011. Alegria Productions.
Girl Model. Directed by David Redmon and Ashley Sabin. 2011. Produced by David Redmon and Ashley Sabin.
La Camioneta. Directed by Mark Kendall. 2012. Ek Balam Producciones.
Life in a Day. Directed by Kevin MacDonald. 2011. Distributed by National Geographic Films and YouTube.
Life Off Grid. Directed by Jonathan Taggart. 2015. Distributed by Fighting Chance Films.
Low and Slow. 2017. Directed by Phillip Vannini.
Sweetgrass. Directed by Ilisa Barbash and Lucien Castaing-Taylor. 2009. Harvard Sensory Ethnography Lab.
The Boxing Girls of Kabul. Directed by Ariel Nasr. 2012. National Film Board of Canada.
Up the Yangtze. Directed by Yung Chang. 2007. Produced by Eye Steel Film and National Film Board of Canada.
Vanishing Point. Directed by Stephen Smith and Julia Szucs. 2012. National Film Board of Canada.
Which Way Home. Directed by Rebecca Cammisa. 2009. Documentress Films.
Whores' Glory. Directed by Michael Glawogger. 2011. Lotus Film.

References

Adams, Mags. 2009. "Hearing the City: Reflections on Soundwalking." *Qualitative Researcher* 10: 6–9.

Adler, Patricia and Peter Adler. 2008. "Of Rhetoric and Representation: The Four Faces of Ethnography." *The Sociological Quarterly* 49: 1–30.

Anderson, Ben and Paul Harrison. 2010. "The Promise of Non-Representational Theories." Pp. 1–34 in *Taking-Place: Non-Representational Theories and Geography*, edited by Ben Anderson and Paul Harrison. Farnham: Ashgate.

Bailey, Carol. 2008. "Public Ethnography." Pp. 265–281 in *The Handbook of Emergent Methods*, edited by Sharlene Nagy Hesse-Biber and Patricia Leavy. Thousand Oaks: SAGE.

Barbash, Ilisa and Lucien Taylor. 1997. *Cross-Cultural Filmmaking: A Handbook for Making Ethnographic Documentary Films and Videos*. Berkeley: University of California Press.

Becker, Howard, Herbert J. Gans, Katherine Newman, and Diane Vaughan. 2004. "On the Value of Ethnography: Sociology and Public Policy: A Dialogue." *The Annals of the American Academy of Political and Social Science* 595: 264–276.

Bernard, Sheila Curran. 2011. *Documentary Storytelling: Creative Nonfiction on Screen*. Burlington: Focal Press.

Borofsky, Robert (n.d.). "Public Anthropology: A Personal Perspective." Available online at: http://www.publicanthropology.org/books-book-series/why-a-public-anthropology/.

Borofsky, Robert. 2000. "Public Anthropology: Where to, What Next?" *Anthropology News* 45: 9–10.

Borofsky, Robert. 2011. *Why a Public Anthropology*. Honolulu: Centre for a Public Anthropology.

Brady, Ivan. 2004. "In Defense of the Sensual: Meaning Construction in Ethnography and Poetics." *Qualitative Inquiry* 10: 622–644.

Brettell, C. (Ed.). 1996. *When They Read What We Write: The Politics of Ethnography*. New York: Praeger.

Burawoy, Michael. 2004. "For Public Sociology." *American Sociological Review* 70: 4–28.

Buscher, Monika, John Urry, and Kevin Witchger (Eds.). 2010. *Mobile Methods*. London: Routledge.

Castree, Noel, Duncan Fuller, Andrew Kent, Audrey Kobayashi, Christopher Merrett, Laura Pulido, and Laura Barraclough. 2008. "Geography, Pedagogy, and Politics." *Progress in Human Geography* 32: 680–718.

Conquergood, Dwight. 1990. "Rethinking Ethnography: Toward a Critical Cultural Politics." *Communication Monographs* 58: 179–194.

Crouch, David. 2010. "Flirting with Space: Thinking Landscape Relationally." *Cultural Geographies* 17: 5–18.
Current Anthropology. 2010. Supplement on Engaged Anthropology. 51: S1
Czarniawska, Barbara. 2004. *Narratives in Social Science Research.* Thousand Oaks: SAGE.
Davis, Gail and Claire Dwyer. 2008. "Qualitative Methods II: Minding the Gap." *Progress in Human Geography* 32: 399–406.
Dear, Michael, Jim Ketchum, Sarah Luria, and Doug Richardson (Eds.). 2011. *GeoHumanities: Art, History, Text, at the Edge of Place.* New York: Routledge.
Denzin, Norman K. 2003. *Performance Ethnography: Critical Pedagogy and the Politics of Culture.* Thousand Oaks: SAGE.
Denzin, Norman K., Yvonna Lincoln, and Linda Tuhiwai-Smith (Eds.). 2008. *Handbook of Critical and Indigenous Methodologies.* Thousand Oaks: SAGE.
Dewsbury, J. D. 2003. "Witnessing Space: Knowledge Without Contemplation." *Environment & Planning A* 35: 1907–1932.
Dewsbury, J. D. 2009. "Performative, Non-Representational, and Affect-Based Research: Seven Injunctions." Pp. 321–333 in *The SAGE Handbook of Qualitative Geography*, edited by D. DeLyser, S. Herbert, S. Aitken, M. Crang, and L. McDowell. London: SAGE.
Dicks, Bella, Bambo Soyinka, and Amanda Coffey. 2006. "Multimodal Ethnography." *Qualitative Research* 6: 77–96.
Edensor, Tim. 2007. "Sensing the Ruin." *Senses and Society* 2: 217–232.
Fassin, Didier (Ed.). 2017. *If Truth Be Told: The Politics of Public Ethnography.* Durham: Duke University Press.
Fraser, Mariam, Sara Kember, and Celia Lury. 2005. "Inventive Life: Approaches to the New Vitalism." *Theory, Culture & Society* 22: 1–14.
Fuller, Duncan. 2008. "Public Geographies: Taking Stock." *Progress in Human Geography* 32: 834–844.
Fuller, Duncan and Kye Askins. 2010. "Public Geographies II: Being Organic." *Progress in Human Geography* 34: 654–667.
Gans, Herbert J. 2010. "Public Ethnography; Ethnography as Public Sociology." *Qualitative Sociology* 33: 97–104.
Geertz, Clifford. 1988. *Works and Lives: The Anthropologist as Author.* Stanford: Stanford University Press.
Gell, Alfred. 1998. *Art and Agency.* Oxford: Oxford University Press.
Grimshaw, Anna. 2011. "The Bellwether Ewe: Recent Developments in Ethnographic Filmmaking and the Aesthetics of Anthropological Inquiry." *Cultural Anthropology* 26: 247–262.
Grimshaw, Anna and Amanda Ravetz. 2009. *Observational Cinema: Anthropology, Film, and the Exploration of Social Life.* Bloomington: Indiana University Press.
Gottlieb, Alma. 1997. "The Perils of Popularizing Anthropology." *Anthropology Today* 13: 1–2.
Greenhough, Beth. 2010. "Vitalist Geographies: Life and the More-than-Human." Pp. 39–54 in *Taking Place*, edited by Ben Anderson and Paul Harrison. Farnham: Ashgate.
Gubrium, Aline and Krista Harper (Eds.). 2014. *Participatory Visual and Digital Methods.* Walnut Creek: Left Coast Press.
Hastrup, Kirsten. 1992. "Anthropological Visions: Some Notes on Visual and Textual Authority. Pp. 8–25 in *Film as Ethnography*, edited by Ian Peter Crawford and David Turton. Manchester: Manchester University Press.

References

Hedican, Edward. 2016. *Public Anthropology: Engaging Social Issues in the Modern World*. Toronto: University of Toronto Press.
Hill, Lisa. 2013. "Archaeologies and Geographies of the Post-Industrial Past." *Cultural Geographies* 20: 379–396.
Howes, David. 2003. *Sensual Relations: Engaging the Senses in Culture and Social Theory*. Ann Arbor: University of Michigan Press.
Ingold, Tim. 2000. *The Perception of the Environment*. London: Routledge.
Ingold, Tim. 2007. *Lines: A Brief History*. London: Routledge.
Ingold, Tim. 2011. *Being Alive*. London: Routledge.
Knowles, Gary and Andra Cole (Eds.). 2008. *Handbook of the Arts in Qualitative Research*. Thousand Oaks: SAGE.
Lamphere, Louise. 2004. "The Convergence of Applied, Practicing, and Public Anthropology in the 21st Century." *Human Organization* 63: 431–443.
Lassiter, Luke Eric. 2005. *The Chicago Guide to Collaborative Ethnography*. Chicago: University of Chicago Press.
Latham, Alan. 2003a. "The Possibilities of Performance." *Environment & Planning A* 35: 1901–1906.
Latham, Alan. 2003b. "Research, Performance, and Doing Human Geography: Some Reflections on the Diary-Photograph, Diary-Interview Method." *Environment & Planning A* 35: 1993–2017.
Laurier, Eric and Chris Philo. 2006. "Possible Geographies: A Passing Encounter in a Café." *Area* 38: 353–363.
Leavy, Patricia (Ed.). 2017. *Handbook of Arts-Based Research*. New York: Guilford Press.
Lippard, Lucy. 1998. *The Lure of the Local*. New York: The New Press.
Lorimer, Hayden. 2005. "Cultural Geography: The Busyness of Being More-than-Representational." *Progress in Human Geography* 29: 83–94.
Lorimer, Hayden. 2012. "Surfaces and Slopes." *Performance Research* 17: 83–86.
Lorimer, Hayden and John Wylie. 2010. "LOOP (A Geography)." *Performance Research* 15: 6–13.
MacDougall, David. 2000. *Transcultural Cinema*. Princeton: Princeton University Press.
MacDougall, David. 2006. *Film, Ethnography, and the Senses: The Corporeal Image*. Princeton: Princeton University Press.
Madison, Soyini. 2011. *Critical Ethnography: Method, Ethics, and Performance*. Thousand Oaks: SAGE.
Manning, Erin. 2015. "Against Method." Pp. 52–71 in *Non-Representational Methodologies*, edited by Phillip Vannini. New York: Routledge.
Marks, Laura. 2000. *The Skin of the Film*. Durham: Duke University Press.
McClancy, Jeremy and Christian McDonaugh. 1996. *Popularizing Anthropology*. New York: Routledge.
Merleau-Ponty, Maurice. 1962. *Phenomenology of Perception*. New York: Routledge.
Morris, Nina. 2011. "Night Walking: Darkness and Sensory Perception in a Night-Time Landscape Installation." *Cultural Geographies* 18: 315–342.
Morse, Janice. 2004. "Alternative Modes of Representation: There Are No Shortcuts." *Qualitative Health Research* 14: 887–888.
Murphy, Alexander, H. J. deBlij, B. L. Turner II, Ruth Wilson Gilmore, and Derek Gregory. 2008. "The Role of Geography in Public Debate." *Progress in Human Geography* 29: 165–193.
Nichols, Bill. 2010. *Introduction to Documentary*. Second Edition. Bloomington: Indiana University Press.

Özerdem, Alpaslan and Richard Bowd (Eds.). 2013. *Participatory Research Methodologies*. Farnham: Ashgate.
Peirce, Charles Sanders. 1958. *Collected Papers of Charles Sanders Peirce*. Boston: Harvard University.
Pelias, Ron. 1999. *Writing Performance: Poeticizing the Researcher's Body*. Carbondale: Southern Illinois University Press.
Plummer, Ken. 1999. "The Ethnographic Society at Century's End: Clarifying the Role of Public Ethnography." *Journal of Contemporary Ethnography* 28: 641–649.
Purcell, Trevor. 2000. "Public Anthropology: An Idea Searching for a Reality." *Transforming Anthropology* 9: 30–33.
Rambo Ronai, Carol. 1995. "Multiple Reflections of Childhood Sex Abuse: An Argument for a Layered Account." *Journal of Contemporary Ethnography* 23: 395–426.
Reville, George. 2004. "Performing French Folk Music." *Cultural Geographies* 11: 199–209.
Richardson-Ngwenya, Pamela. 2004. "Performing a More-Than-Human Material Imagination During Fieldwork." *Cultural Geographies* 21: 293–299.
Rose, Mitch. 2010. "Pilgrims: An Ethnography of Sacredness." *Cultural Geographies* 17: 507–524.
Ruby, Jay. 2000. *Picturing Culture: Explorations of Film and Anthropology*. Chicago: University of Chicago Press.
Saldanha, Arun. 2005. "Trance and Visibility at Dawn: Racial Dynamics in Goa's Rave Scene." *Social and Cultural Geography* 6: 707–721.
Saville, Stephen. 2008. "Playing with Fear: Parkour and the Mobility of Emotion." *Social and Cultural Geography* 9: 891–914.
Schechner, Richard. 2003. *Performance Theory*. New York: Routledge.
Scheper-Hughes, Nancy. 2009. "Making Anthropology Public." *Anthropology Today* 25: 1–4.
Simonsen, Kristin. 2013. "In Quest of a New Humanism: Embodiment, Experience, and Phenomenology as Critical Geography." *Progress in Human Geography* 37: 10–26.
Simpson, Paul. 2008. "Chronic Everyday Life: Rhythmanalysing Street Performance." *Social and Cultural Geography* 9: 807–829.
Sparkes, Andrew. 2009. "Ethnography and the Senses: Challenges and Possibilities." *Qualitative Research in Sport and Exercise* 1: 21–35.
Stewart, Kathleen. 2011. "Atmospheric Attunements." *Environment & Planning D* 29: 445–453.
Stewart, Kathleen. 2014. "Road Registers." *Cultural Geographies* 28: 549–563.
Stoller, Paul. 1984. "Sound in Songhay Cultural Experience." *American Ethnologist* 11: 559–570.
Stoller, Paul. 1989. *The Taste of Ethnographic Things: The Senses in Anthropology*. Philadelphia: University of Pennsylvania Press.
Stoller, Paul. 1992. *The Cinematic Griot: The Ethnography of Jean Rouch*. Chicago: University of Chicago Press.
Stoller, Paul. 1997. *Sensuous Scholarship*. Philadelphia: University of Pennsylvania Press.
Stoller, Paul. 2007. "Ethnography/Memoir/Imagination/Story." *Anthropology and Humanism* 32: 178–191.
Synnott, Anthony. 1993. *The Body Social*. New York: Routledge.
Tedlock, Barbara. 2005. "The Observation and Participation of and the Emergence of Public Ethnography." Pp. 151–171 in *The SAGE Handbook of Qualitative Research*, edited by Norman Denzin and Yvonna Lincoln. Thousand Oaks: SAGE.

References

Thrift, Nigel. 2003. "Performance And…" *Environment & Planning A* 35: 2019–2024.
Thrift, Nigel. 2004. "Summoning Life." Pp. 81–103 in *Envisioning Human Geographies*, edited by Paul Cloke, Peter Crang, and Mike Goodwin. London: Arnold.
Thrift, Nigel. 2008. *Non-Representational Theory*. London: Routledge.
Vaughan, Diane. 2005. "On the Relevance of Ethnography for the Production of Public Sociology and Policy." *British Journal of Sociology* 56: 411–416.
Van Maanen, John. 1984. *Tales of the Field: On Writing Ethnography*. Chicago: University of Chicago Press.
Vannini, Phillip. 2008. "A Queen's Drowning: Material Culture, Drama, and the Performance of a Technological Accident." *Symbolic Interaction* 31: 155–182.
Vannini, Phillip (Ed.). 2012a. *Popularizing Research: Engaging New Media, New Genres, New Audiences*. New York: Peter Lang.
Vannini, Phillip. 2012b. "Bamfield's Unlikely Off-Gridders." *The Tyee*, October 2. Available online at http://thetyee.ca/Life/2012/10/02/Bamfield-Off-Grid/.
Vannini, Phillip. 2012c. "Cutting the Cord." *Canadian Geographic*, June.
Vannini, Phillip. 2012d. "Living Off-the-Grid in BC." *The Tyee*, January 24. Available online at: http://thetyee.ca/Life/2012/01/24/Living-Off-The-Grid-In-BC/.
Vannini, Phillip and Jonathan Taggart. 2012. "Off-Grid World." *Yukon: North of Ordinary*, Fall: 46–50.
Vannini, Phillip. 2015a. "Non-Representational Research Methodologies: An Introduction." Pp. 1–18 in *Non-Representational Methodologies: Re-Envisioning Research*, edited by Phillip Vannini. New York: Routledge.
Vannini, Phillip (Ed.). 2015b. *Non-Representational Methodologies: Re-Envisioning Research*. New York: Routledge.
Vannini, Phillip, Dennis Waskul, and Simon Gottschalk. 2011. *The Senses in Self, Society, and Culture*. New York: Routledge.
Vannini, Phillip and Heather Mosher. 2013. "Public Ethnography: An Introduction to the Special Issue." *Qualitative Research* 13: 391–401.
Vannini, Phillip and Laura Milne. 2014. "Public Ethnography as Public Engagement: Multimodal Pedagogies for Innovative Learning." Pp. 123–141 in *Public Sociology: Pedagogy and Ethics*, edited by Ariane Hanemaayer and Christopher Schneider. Vancouver: UBC Press.
Vannini, Phillip and Jonathan Taggart. n.d. "Phillip Vannini and Jonathan Taggart," *The Huffington Post*. Available online at: http://www.huffingtonpost.ca/phillip-vannini-and-jonathan-taggart/.
Vannini, Phillip and Jonathan Taggart. 2014. *Off-the-Grid: Re-assembling Domestic Life*. New York: Routledge.
Ward, Kevin. 2006. "Geography and Public Policy: Towards Public Geographies." *Progress in Human Geography* 30: 495–503.
Ward, Kevin. 2007. "Geography and Public Policy: A Recent History of 'Policy Relevance'." *Progress in Human Geography* 29: 310–319.
Ward, Kevin. 2008. "Geography and Public Policy: Activist, Participatory, and Policy Geographies." *Progress in Human Geography* 31: 695–705.
Waterston, Alisse and Maria Vesperi (Eds.). 2009. *Anthropology off the Shelf: Anthropologists on Writing*. New York: Wiley-Blackwell.
Wood, Nichola. 2012. "Playing with 'Scottishness': Musical Performance, Non-Representational Thinking, and the 'Doings' of National Identity." *Cultural Geographies* 19: 195–215.
Wylie, John. 2002. "On Ascending Glastonbury Tor." *Geoforum* 33: 441–454.

Wylie, John. 2005. "A Single Day's Walking: Narrating Self and Landscape on the South West Coast Path." *Transactions of the Institute of British Geographers NS* 30: 234–247.

Zompetti, Joseph. 2012. "Persuasive Prestigitation: Exploring the Rhetorical Power of Magical Performances in a Popular Magazine Article." Pp. 114–119 in *Popularizing Research*, edited by Phillip Vannini. New York: Peter Lang.

Index

academic book publishing 46
action footage 130–132
admirative mood 79–80
affect 35, 49, 53
animating lifeworlds 32–33
anonymity 6, 21, 28, 36, 42, 44, 48, 84, 106
anthropology 5, 17, 48, 59
aperture 121–122, 124–125
aperture priority 120
arts-inspired research 4, 6, 15, 21, 24, 22–29, 143, 151
audiences 3–4, 6–7, 14–15, 23, 28–29, 143–145
audio production 99–100, 105–115, 133–134
autoethnography 15, 35, 45, 48, 49, 90

b-roll 110, 130, 134–135
benefits of public ethnography 17–19
blogs 11, 18, 24, 25, 26, 29, 82, 88–89, 96, 105, 141, 144, 145

camera types 100–102, 106
character development 44, 62
citations 43–44
close-up shots 60, 61, 62, 63, 101, 131–132, 137
collaboration 18–21
conditional mood 75–76
constant gain 113–114
corporeality 31, 35, 49
costs 21, 95–104
critical ethnography 15
critical pedagogy 3–4

denouement 87
depth of field 121–122, 124
desiderative mood 81
detail orientation 63–65

documentary film 5, 59–67, 96, 97
drawbacks of public ethnography 21
dubitative mood 77–78

equipment list 97–104
ethnopoetics 50–51
exposure 120–125

F-stop 102, 122, 124–125, 132
film festivals 140–141
filters 103–104, 125
fluidity 80
frame rate 124, 132

geography 5, 32, 48

humor 79–80
hypermedia 8, 82, 89–91
hypothetical mood 77–78

image: composition 126–127; production 118–128
impact 4, 8, 17, 18, 21, 23, 26, 28–29, 41, 42, 141
indentation 45
ineffability 77–78
immediacy 78–79
interview footage 130, 132–134
intimacy 30, 62–63, 74
irrealis mood 74–81
ISO 120, 123–125, 132

journal articles 4, 14, 15, 17, 18, 22, 23, 27, 43, 63, 82, 83, 96, 97
jussive mood 78–79

Lavalier microphones 98, 100, 107–109
Leavy, Patricia 22–29
lenses 99, 101–102
Life Off Grid 8–9, 135, 143–146

logging 136
Low and Slow 145–147

magazines 4, 16, 19, 21, 25, 82–88, 97
manual mode 120
medium shots 61, 131–132, 137
mixing tracks 114
mobility 31, 36–37
monopod 103
multimodality 4, 8, 87–88, 95–98

narrative 4, 6, 30–31, 41, 44, 65–66, 74, 75, 81, 106, 114
newspapers 4, 15, 16, 19, 20, 21, 41, 89, 141, 145
non-representational research and theory 4, 5, 6, 10, 30–38

observational films 59–60
open access 16, 17
op-eds 20, 21, 24, 25, 28

pacing 111, 137–138
paper cut 136
parametric equalizer 115
partiality 75
participatory films 60–67
past tense 78, 87
performance ethnography 15, 19, 21, 34, 96
performativity 31, 32, 34, 41, 52, 74
poetry 26, 50–51
potentiality 76–77
present tense 78, 87
presumptive mood 77–78
proximity 79–80

quotations 32, 45, 53, 75

radio 4, 8–9, 19, 21, 26, 29, 53–54, 105, 111, 114–117, 141, 145
RAW 121

reflexivity 4, 16, 45, 48, 50, 68, 74, 81, 90
ripple delete 113
room tone 109, 111, 113
rule of thirds 126–127

sensuousness/sensuality 4, 6, 31, 32, 35–36, 48–58, 66–67, 74
shotgun microphones 100, 107–109, 110
shutter priority 120
shutter speed 122–123
signposting 42–43, 86
single-band compressor 115
social media 20, 25, 26, 97, 116–117, 134, 139, 141
sociology 5, 17
somatic layered account 48–58
sound editing 111–115
subjunctive mode 51, 80, 87
synchronizing sound 109–110, 133

television 4, 16, 19, 24, 96, 123, 142–143, 144–147
timidity 32
title cards 138
transcribing 111
tripods 102–103

video: distribution 139–147; editing 135–138; production 129–138; shooting 122–125, 129–135
viewfinder 103
visual ethnography 5
vitality 31, 33–34
voice 30
volitive mood 81

white balance 120
wide shots 131–132, 137
wonder 33, 37, 45, 76, 77, 80, 87, 106
writing 4

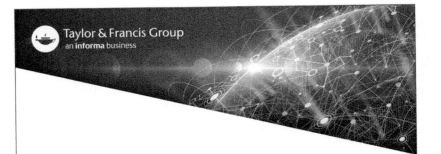